Wasi'chu: The Continuing Indian Wars

Wasi'chu
The Continuing Indian Wars

by Bruce Johansen and Roberto Maestas
with an Introduction
by John Redhouse

Monthly Review Press
New York and London

Library of Congress Cataloging in Publication Data
Johansen, Bruce.
  Wasi'chu.

  Includes bibliographical references and index.
    1. Indians of North America—Government re-
lations—1934-   2. Indians of North America—
Civil rights. 3. United States—Race relations.
I. Maestas, Roberto, joint author. II. Title.
E93.J6   301.45'19'7073   79-10153
ISBN 0-85345-484-1
ISBN 0-85345-507-4 pbk.

Monthly Review Press
62 West 14th Street, New York, N.Y. 10011
47 Red Lion Street, London WC1R 4PF

Manufactured in the United States of America

10 9 8 7 6 5 4 3 2 1

To Richard Oakes, Pedro Bissonette, Anna Mae Aquash, Emma Yazzie, Valerie Bridges, Dale Doney, and John Trudell's wife and three children, who died as the book was going to press.

And to all others who give their time and energy—and sometimes their lives—so that generations unborn may walk together in beauty.

The first people who lived on the northern plains of what today is the United States called themselves "Lakota," meaning "the people," a word which provides the semantic basis for Dakota. The first European people to meet the Lakota called them "Sioux," a contraction of *Nadowessioux*, a now-archaic French-Canadian word meaning "snake," or enemy. The Lakota also used a metaphor to describe the newcomers. It was *Wasi'chu*, which means "takes the fat," or "greedy person." Within the modern Indian movement, *Wasi'chu* has come to mean those corporations and individuals, with their governmental accomplices, which continue to covet Indian lives, land, and resources for private profit. *Wasi'chu* does not describe a race; it describes a state of mind. This book is about resistance to that state of mind and to the economic system which rewards it.

Contents

Acknowledgments

Because much of this material has not been compiled before by any library, we are indebted to many people who gave their time, energy, and money so that this work could be produced. Many people helped, and we want to extend our thanks to a few of them here. Russel Barsh, professor of business, government, and society at the University of Washington, spent many hours giving us constructive criticism on the first three drafts, as did Michael Predmore, professor of romance languages and literature at the same university. Ray Sandoval, John Redhouse, and Bruce Ellison also provided much helpful advice on the manuscript in its various stages of completion. Hank Adams provided especially valuable criticism of the first and second drafts.

Many people provided information or services without charge to us, a fact of crucial importance because our own financial resources are extremely limited. We wish to thank, among others, Ted Bunker, who developed and printed the photographs; Bruce Brown, Mike Taylor, and Kim Steele, who helped with documentation on fishing rights; Russell Simms and the staff of the Three Rivers Indian Center, Dorseyville, Pennsylvania, who provided information on northeastern land claims; John Crazy Bear, who helped us with oral history and geological matters; Mike Ross, Billings, Montana, city planner, who helped with research sources in Montana, as did Jim Boggs and Tom Osborne of the Northern Cheyenne Research Project, Lame Deer, Montana. Joe Ryan, staff person of the National Coalition to Support Indian Treaties, and Tony Cardenas of Northwest Rural Opportunities, Grandview, Washington; Linda and Bryan Edgar, who gave us the best warm showers in Kansas; and Bernie Whitebear of United Indians of All Tribes, who offered invaluable help and advice.

Special thanks also are due Esther Keeswood of Shiprock, New Mexico; Sid, Leroy, and Suzette Mills of Franks Landing, Washington; the Bridges family of Franks Landing; the Loudhawk family of Oglala, South Dakota; the Ridge Bear family of Lame Deer, Montana; Gelvin Stevenson, who criticized the book for Monthly Review; Susan Lowes, our editor; Judy

Ruben, whose enthusiasm for the book rejuvenated us; and Chata, Cubana, Bobby, Angela, and Tina, who sacrificed much during a long project. The members of El Centro de la Raza were also crucial to the book's creation. We could not have written it without the help of all these people.

Bruce Johansen and Roberto Maestas
March 1, 1979

Introduction by John Redhouse

Wasi'chu is the Lakota (Sioux) word for "greedy one who takes the fat." It was used to describe a strange race that not only took what it thought it needed, but also took the rest. It was used to describe the white race.

Wasi'chu is also a human condition based on inhumanity, racism, and exploitation. It is a sickness, a seemingly incurable and contagious disease which begot the ever advancing society of the West. If we do not control it, this disease will surely be the basis for what may be the last of the continuing wars against the Native American people.

Indians have been victims of war and aggression for most of the past five hundred years. The so-called Indian wars were always fought over the issues of land and resources. We have always had something that the *Wasi'chu* wanted. Even after five hundred years of war and genocide, we still have something that they want.

The Spanish conquered the Inca, Aztec, and Mayan civilizations in search of gold and silver. Today, wars are still being conducted for mineral wealth on Indian lands.

After the Indian wars of the 1880s were over, we were left with 150 million acres of land. The Dawes Act of 1887 reduced that to 50 million acres through a forced system of individual allotments. We were then assigned to seemingly worthless and barren lands called reservations. We now own less than 3 percent of what we once had. And now the *Wasi'chu* wants all we have left.

In 1978 Indian people possessed 55 percent of the nation's uranium supply and one-third of the low-sulfur stripable coal reserves. Both coal and uranium are vital to President Carter's national energy policy. In April 1977 President Carter called the achievement of his energy policy the "moral equivalent of war." To many Indian people, that phrase meant that the Indian wars were not yet over and that we must again fight against the U.S. government and multinational corporate interests in order to protect our remaining land and resources.

Many Indian people feel that the Carter administration is one of the worst in modern history. They say that President Carter puts on a democratic face to the rest of the world by advocating

11

human rights for all and treaty rights for Russians and Pana-
manians. And yet as far as the treatment of the Indian people is
concerned, the U.S. government has one of the worst human
rights' records—and certainly one of the worst treaty rights'
records—in the world.

The authorizing legislation creating the Department of
Energy allows the director of the agency to enter into a pact
with the Department of Defense to seize unilaterally and hold
areas of strategic mineral significance if such action is justified
as being in the "national interest." For Indian nations that
have enough energy resources to make a difference in the future
direction of this country, such a stipulation is equivalent to a
threat to call out the cavalry again.

•In recent years the Navajo Nation has rejected a proposed
lease by Western Gasification Company (WESCO) to construct
the nation's first and the world's largest commercial coal-gasification plants on their reservation. The Navajo have also threatened to cancel the leases of Four Corners Power Plant and
Navajo Mine. The power plant is one of the world's worst
industrial polluting sources, while the mine is the largest coal
strip mine in the western hemisphere.

•The Northern Cheyenne and Crow Nations have each taken
legal action to cancel the coal leases on their reservations. The
Northern Cheyenne have to this date halted future construction of the nearby Colstrip Power Plant. The two Indian
nations sit atop one of the world's largest coal deposits.

•The Laguna Pueblo Nation is considering whether to renew
its uranium-mining lease, which includes the largest uranium
strip mine in the world.

Yet for Indian nations to defy the national policies of the
U.S. government and multinational corporate interests is to
defy the two most powerful forces on the face of the earth. To
do so is to invite possible military intervention. For most
Indians, it would not be the first time. During the 1973 Arab
oil embargo the U.S. government made contingency plans to
intervene militarily in order to secure "our" oil in the Mideast
because it was in the "national interest." So if the *Wasi'chu*
government talks about using military intervention to secure
"our" oil in an area halfway around the world, what is it going

to say about securing "our" coal and "our" uranium right here in Indian Country?

The Carter administration maintains a complete silence on any semblance of an Indian policy. Even President Nixon had an Indian policy. This is why Indian people are now saying that Carter's Indian policy is really his energy policy.

Now enter the anti-Indian backlash. Although anti-Indian sentiment has always existed, it has now developed into a full-scale national anti-Indian movement, aimed at stripping us of our legal rights and ultimately of our remaining land and resources. The strength of this movement has been manifested by the introduction of eleven pieces of anti-Indian legislation, several recent U.S. Supreme Court decisions adverse to Indian self-determination, and numerous state anti-Indian bills. The Congressional bills range from those that would abrogate all Indian treaties to those that would limit our water rights and tribal self-government. The state bills propose to disenfranchise Indian people of their right to vote and hold public office. The Supreme Court decisions have further undermined our tribal sovereignty and jurisdiction.

It is said that we are now facing the gravest crisis in our history as Indian people. We are still being faced with the military cavalry. Now we are also being faced with the legislative, judicial, bureaucratic, and corporate cavalries, whose missions are one and the same: to destroy the physical and spiritual basis of our existence and survival as a people. What is left of our lives, land, water, resources, way of life, sovereignty, and future is being threatened. The *Wasi'chu* have already taken everything else. Now they want all we have left. Except for the Final Indian War, the circle is complete.

> Niathuau Ahakanith!
> Niathuau Ahakanith!
>
> The whites are crazy!
> The whites are crazy!
> > Lakota song
> > Ghost Dance
> > Wounded Knee, 1890

1

The Past Is Prologue

Gold is a wonderful thing! Whoever owns it is lord of all he wants. With gold it is even possible to open for souls the way to paradise!
>—Christopher Columbus, letter to Isabella and Ferdinand, 1503[1]

Later, I learned that Pahuska[2] had found there much of the yellow metal that makes the *Wasi'chu* crazy.
>—Black Elk, Lakota holy man, on United States Army expedition to Black Hills, 1874[3]

Hernando de Soto was leading a caravan of several dozen explorers and two hundred horses when he reached the Savannah River, in present-day Georgia, during early 1540. On the opposite side of the river he saw a party of the reddish-brown people an early explorer, Christopher Columbus, had named "Indios," out of the mistaken belief that he had landed in India.

The people across the river were carrying a woman whom De Soto took to be a queen. She invited the Spanish party across the river and, following custom, made presents to them. One of the presents was a three-strand pearl necklace that she had been wearing around her neck. De Soto eyed the woman, but he was more interested in pearls than in friendship. He responded to her hospitality by taking the woman prisoner and forcing the men who had been carrying her to lead him to their camp. A people who gave so freely of their pearls must have more of them, he reasoned.

Once in the camp, De Soto's party ransacked buildings looking for pearls. Finding the graves of the dead, they scattered the bones and took the pearls which lay among them. Before leaving, some of De Soto's men raped several Indian women.

Another group of a people the Europeans thought "savage" had just met the bearers of civilization, the carriers of an economic and political system which rewarded the accumulation of material wealth over and above the lives of people, plants, animals, and of the earth itself. The profit-minded system, which the Lakota later would call *Wasi'chu*, was already on its way to devouring the resources of several continents, and destroying millions of human lives in the process, in a relentless search for land and exploitable natural resources.

Ever since the first landings almost five hundred years ago, the *Wasi'chu* has rationalized this expropriation of land, resources, and minds to avoid compromising a humanitarian, law-abiding self-image. It is said that the white race came to do the natives a favor—to civilize, to assimilate, to bless with the cross. American science fiction—as much a reflection of the past as of the future—is full of stories of conquest across new Atlantics, of colonies and mineral extraction on the moon and Mars. The past is prologue.

17

The major thesis of this book is that the economic, cultural, and political forces which propelled mercantile colonialism across the Atlantic are now in retreat; the *Wasi'chu* of today have found it increasingly necessary to exploit domestic people and resources to sustain their system. As this exploitation intensifies, all outside the *Wasi'chu* classes are learning what it has been like to be "Indian."

The story of the past Indian wars is a well-told one; it has been easy and comfortable to categorize the last century, and prior history, as a time inhabited by strangely unenlightened and greedy souls who plundered two continents. To categorize "the past" as a separate time, unconnected to and not influencing the present, ignores the continuance of cultural, political, and economic beliefs and systems which transcend single human life spans. Our thesis is that the mechanisms which motivated the plundering of the past are still present—sometimes more subtle, sometimes more refined—with similar goals: the theft of life, land, and resources from America's first inhabitants. De Soto may no longer be with us, but the systematic mechanisms which prompted him to ransack that river village for pearls are.

In this examination of the system of the *Wasi'chu*, our concerns include, but also surpass, the need to fashion remedies which will free American Indians from a colonial relationship which was born almost five hundred years ago. We will argue that this system threatens all of us—through the potential for nuclear war and environmental destruction in search of profit—with eventual extermination. In the end, the *Wasi'chu*, if allowed, will consume not only native peoples, but also their own children.

Resistance to this colonial system must be based on knowledge of it—past and present. This chapter will supply some historical context to the colonial system for the substantially contemporary material which follows it, including the justifications of conquest, the makeup of the system of human subjugation based on these justifications, the exploitation of human and natural resources which the system of subjugation is designed to make possible, and the resistance to this exploitation by its targets.

The conflicts which are part of this resistance have been, and continue to be, more than a simplistic war between races of people; the Lakota realized this by recognizing the economic propensities, not the race or culture, of those they called *Wasi'chu*. Throughout the history of what, in a confusion of biology with ideology, has come to be called "white-Indian relations," the "white" side advanced across two continents behind Indian scouts, and more than a few non-Indians have continually and faithfully resisted the aggression of those with whom they shared a common European ancestry. For example, R. N. Sutherlin, editor of the *Rocky Mountain Husbandman*, wrote in the August 19, 1876, edition that Indians "should be treated in a manner which would be credible for our nation, not wheedled and dallied for the sake of private speculation." Six months after the U.S. Army massacre at Wounded Knee, an unnamed poet contributed the following to the *Great Divide*, a white frontier Colorado magazine:

> Huh-ah-huh!
> Mouths are many, deer are few
>   Huh-ah-huh!
>
> Hu! Hu! Hu-ah-huh!
> Where the bison fed and grew
> Fence and furrow follow through
>   Hu-ah-huh!
>
> Far abroad the paleface strew
> And to face the starving Sioux
> If he tarries let him rue
>   Huh-ah-huh!
>
> Let us scenes of blood review!
> Come and hear the valiant Sioux!
> We have done and we can do!
>   Huh-ah-huh!

In 1863 the *North American Review* published a critique of the double-talk used in signing treaties with native nations.

The article pointed out that while the treaties promised Indians sovereignty, this was denied in practice. The treaties were, the article concluded, a legalistic and moralistic cover for the theft of the land.[4]

What have been called the "Indian wars" never were (and are not today) exclusively a matter between conflicting races. They have been (and are) matters of conflicting ideologies. Just as the Lakota did not call the invaders "palefaces," but "the greedy ones," the Cheyenne called them *Veho*—"spiders"—those who surround and choke their prey. The categorization of peoples by their biological characteristics (including skin color) has been emphasized throughout history by the *Wasi'chu* as part of the colonial system of subjugation, but some non-Indians and many Indians have never fallen prey to this fundamental building block of racist thought.

The differences attributed to peoples' intellects on the basis of biological characteristics have had a central place in the ideology, or rationalization, of subjugation. The domination of a people is an act of war that demands first that those people be portrayed in the subjugators' minds as an enemy, a less-than-human adversary. Throughout the history of conquest racial stereotypes have tended to stiffen when the need for Indian land and resources was greatest. Between times, the savages may have been noble, but they still were portrayed as savages. The image of the savage (which became embodied in U.S. Indian policy) has had two sides: the noble savage (Indian as child figure) and the ignoble savage (Indian as warrior, or resister).[5] The stereotypes of Indians created in the European mind have been used to justify conquest around the world,[6] from colonialism in Africa, to the British regime in India, to recent attempts on the part of the United States to "pacify" Vietnam by destroying "gooks." Any imperialistic culture finds it necessary, in defense of its own humanistic self-image, to demean its victims.

Early in the history of American colonization religion began to play a large role in the rationalization of conquest. Despite the fact that the Indians who greeted the first Puritan settlers taught them the survival skills (including a taste for turkey)

which made the first Thanksgiving possible, John Cotton interpreted a smallpox epidemic which reduced native populations in
the area from about ten thousand to just one thousand as an act
of God. God, reasoned Cotton, had cleared the wilderness of its
original inhabitants to make way for His chosen people.[7] Without a germ theory of disease, Cotton's pilgrims had no way of
knowing that "God's will" came ashore with their own breath;
the Indians, never before exposed to smallpox, had a very low
resistance to it.

Such decimation by disease was repeated across the continents of North and South America. The most recent estimates
of pre-Columbian native populations on the two continents
have been revised sharply upward. The present estimate, made
with the help of complex mathematics developed by Henry
Dobyn, is ninety million native inhabitants in North and South
America, of which ten million to twelve million are believed to
have lived within the borders of the present-day United States.[8]
As recently as a decade ago the commonly accepted population
figures were fifteen million for the two continents, including
eight hundred thousand within the United States's present
boundaries. Given the newly revised population figures, it is
clear that the spread of disease, often inadvertent, killed many
more Indians than the invaders' guns. Cotton, however,
seemed not to sense any duplicity in setting out to "save" the
souls of those Indians who had not fallen victim to his God's
need to clear a homeland for the Puritans. They had died as
heathens; they could live, reasoned the seventeenth-century
religious mind, as Christians. In their own minds, the bearers
of the cross—French, Spanish, and English—came not to
usurp two continents, but to spread a saving gospel.

Religion mixed with economic motives. In Spanish America,
Indians mined minerals and farmed—virtual serfs on their own
land—between sessions with prayer books. On the borders of
English America, missionaries spread the "good word," as
military tacticians considered handing out smallpox-laden
blankets.[9] The ability to make a dichotomy between the
"saved" and the unrepentant allowed violence against those
Indians who would not submit without compromising the self-

image of the invaders, in much the same way that U.S. soldiers burned villages in order to "save" the Vietnamese. Thus, the Pequot were massacred in New England in the 1640s, and in 1645 an Indian captive was reportedly skinned alive and dragged through the streets of New Amsterdam (now New York City).[10] Society matrons played kickball with the severed heads of Indian prisoners in the same city. The governor of New Netherlands introduced scalping to North America as a means by which Indian-hunting bounty seekers could collect their payments.[11]

After the United States became a nation, nationalistic sentiments were joined with those of religion to form the intellectual justification for what became known as Manifest Destiny—a belief that expansion of the nation, including subjugation of native peoples, was divinely ordained, that the "superior race" had an obligation to "civilize" those who stood in its path. The ideology of Manifest Destiny accompanied the usurpation of two-thirds of the United States's land mass during the nineteenth century. With expansion taking place so rapidly, there was little room in the conquerers' imagery for the earlier vision of the noble savage; the act of usurpation had to be masked—as much from the victimizers as from the victims—by nationalism, by religion, and by pseudoscience. It was during this time that racism bloomed. In the United States,

> the political rhetoric of 1800 was permeated with optimism for the human race and a belief in racial improvability; that of 1850 with pessimism for "inferior" races and a belief in ineradicable racial weakness.[12]

By the standards of the three hundred years before 1800, settlement during the nineteenth century virtually raced across the continent, following the war with Mexico and the acquisition of the Pacific Northwest, as well as the Louisiana Purchase. During the first half of the nineteenth century milder forms of justification sufficed because the Indians could still be moved "out of the way." The Trail of Tears, on which the Cherokee were forced to march in 1838, for example, was cited by Andrew Jackson as a humanitarian act: the Cherokee (and other Indian nations) would be allowed to follow their own ways in "Indian Territory," now Oklahoma.

After 1850, however, the desire for land on the part of a rapidly increasing non-Indian population demanded a more elaborate justification of seizure, for the continent was to be completely occupied. The railroads not only provided speedier transportation, they also fueled a boom in land speculation which populated the West. Less than a decade before the first transcontinental railroad was completed Charles Darwin published *Origin of Species* (1859), and its biological message—"survival of the fittest"—was quickly applied to the realm of Indian affairs, as well as to the predatory capitalism that characterized the quickly industrializing nation. The "fittest" came to mean those with the technological and military means of suppression. Might made right. Many sciences grew up to justify the policies enacted in the name of social Darwinism—attempts to make palatable to a Christian and law-abiding nation the violent usurpation of most of a continent. One such science was craniology—the measurement of intelligence by skull shape and size. Whites had conveniently large skulls and so, according to the science, were more intelligent than Indians or other non-white races. Belief in such a science became so popular that its opponents took to citing Ralph Waldo Emerson's hat size (a small six and seven-eighths) in refutation.

Out of the maze of religious, nationalistic, and scientific justifications for conquest which around 1850 combined into the doctrine of Manifest Destiny came a virulent form of racism, required to support the seizure of land and resources. The *Democratic Review* of June 1846 editorialized: "Race is the key to what seems obscure in the history of nations. Everywhere, the whiter race has ruled the less white."[13] Notwithstanding the undercurrent of thought which refuted such assumptions, racially based beliefs swept through the scholarly and popular press of the time. A race-theory buildup preceded the war with Mexico. Mexicans, many of whom are part Indian, were subject to the same racism as Indians: "The depiction of Mexicans as a mixed, incapable race emerged before the beginning of the war with Mexico."[14]

In the popular press many characterizations of savage Indians emerged, far outweighing the less racist sentiments. One weekly frontier newspaper described Indians as "a beastly, rapacious, cunning imitation of humanity"; and several years later the same paper advised whites to "receive them [Indians] when they apply for peace and have them grouped together and slaughtered as though they were so many bands of rattlesnakes."[15]

During 1846 U.S. Senator Thomas Hart Benton declared that Anglo-Saxons, with the help of Celts, would advance to the shores of the Pacific and then begin the "even grander" task of colonizing Asia, an early version of Teddy Roosevelt's "big stick" politics a half-century later. These two races, declared Senator Benton, "had alone received the divine command to subdue and replenish the earth." Indians had no right to the land; Anglo-Saxons and Celts did, however, because the "white races" used the land "according to the intentions of the Creator."[16]

In the halls of Congress the desire to control land and resources was often fused with the desire to colonize:

[Congress must] apprise the Indian that he can no longer stand as a breakwater against the constantly swelling tide of civilization... An idle and thriftless race of savages cannot be permitted to stand guard at the treasure vaults of the nation which hold our gold and silver... the prospector and the miner may enter and by enriching himself enrich the nation and bless the world by the results of his toil.[17]

Clergymen, as well, lent their weight to the mission of conquest:

Thus the Finns were replaced by the Aryans in Europe and Asia, the Tartars by the Russians... and the aborigines of America and Australia... are now disappearing before the all-conquering Anglo-Saxons. It would appear as if these inferior tribes are only a precursor of a superior race, voices in the wilderness crying: "Prepare the way of the Lord!"[18]

The linking of the Aryans and the other European colonizers in American history did not go unnoticed in Germany a half-

century later. Adolf Hitler studied American Indian policy and
with twentieth-century technology and absolutist zeal set out
to model his concentration camps in part on the Indian reservations of the late nineteenth century:

> As [John] Toland points out, Hitler's concept of concentration
> camps as well as the "practicability of genocide" owed much to
> his studies of American and English history. Hitler had admired
> the camps [of the British] for the Boers, in South Africa, and for
> the Indians, in the American West; he was full of praise for the ef-
> ficiency of American extermination—by starvation and combat—
> of the savages who could not be tamed by captivity.[19]

During World War II, then, the United States waged a
"great war" against a fascist state whose most odious policies
were those which Hitler had borrowed from American Indian
policy. The ideology of Manifest Destiny translated into German during the twentieth century contributed to the concept of
Lebensraum. As startling as such a thought may be to many
Americans, it is not so odd to many Indians, who as targets of
the doctrine of Manifest Destiny came to know it with a famil-
iarity denied most of those who lived behind the frontier. To
Indians, the "winning of the West" was a defensive battle to
preserve their homelands and cultures against encroachment.
Popular American history glorifies Patrick Henry's words:
"Give me liberty, or give me death," and ignores those of
Sitting Bull: "If we die, we die defending our rights."

The rationalizations of five hundred years' vintage have
served to obscure, for some, the object of the subjugation
system: to procure land and resources and to assimilate or,
failing that, exterminate the original inhabitants of the
Americas.

The rationalizations also mask the clash between two fundamentally different world views. The Judeo-Christian view is
anthropocentric: the human race is charged (as reflected in the
Biblical book Genesis) with dominating the natural world. The
Native American view, on the other hand, meshes humankind
with nature as part of its dominant ways. The European immi-
grants had a well-defined concept of wealth and private prop-

erty, which fueled their ambition for accumulation—a characteristic the Lakota noted in the term *Wasi'chu*; native cultures, with a few exceptions, held no such concept. The European world view most often centered on the individual; the natives' on the communal values of the tribe, clan, or nation. The Europeans (especially as the Industrial Revolution transformed mercantalism into industrial capitalism) devoted much energy to technology, in particular to that of weaponry, which made possible the subjugation of the earth ordained in Genesis; native cultures, for the most part, did not.

European nations sent explorers to the New World in search of gold and other standards of value in their cultures, in part to replenish treasuries depleted by constant warfare in Europe; many native people (such as Black Elk, quoted above) looked with amusement, or dread, at the seemingly supernatural effects that gold seemed to have upon these people. The Spanish came first and were most successful in finding gold. They subjugated the Incas, the Aztecs, and other native nations in search of it. The French also sought gold, as did the English, but neither in their initial colonizations found much of the "yellow metal which drives the *Wasi'chu* crazy." The French did find furs; the English found rich farmland on which a tobacco-export economy was built.

By the end of the eighteenth century the newly independent United States had cleared the Eastern seaboard of most of its original inhabitants. At the turn of the century the most intense wave of westward migration began in earnest. Throughout this drive, land speculation—keyed on the belief in property as a commodity—drove the westward movement.

By the 1820s, speculation was driving the Indian nations of the Southeast from their homelands. Speculators, often backed by Eastern and European banks, bought large tracts of land from the federal government (which had procured it, often forcibly, from native nations). The land was sold in smaller tracts, at considerable profit, to settlers. The Cherokee, Chickasaw, and Choctaw at first relinquished large areas of their ancestral lands in return for sizable reservations. By the 1830s, however, the speculators wanted even the remaining reservation lands and lobbied the federal and state governments for it. This land hunger produced the Jacksonian plans for removal. Indians were given the choice either of taking an allotment and living on it as would any white landowner or of moving en masse to "Indian Territory" in present-day Oklahoma.[20]

Most Cherokee resisted removal. They had built a relatively stable and prosperous life on what remained of their homelands at the junction of Georgia, North Carolina, and Tennessee. They had schools, a written language, and a newspaper, the *Cherokee Phoenix*. Their homes and farms were in many cases more substantial than those of their white neighbors. In 1827 the Cherokee established their own constitutional republic.

Neither the incoming president, Andrew Jackson, nor the state of Georgia liked such premonitions of independence; what irritated many Georgians even more was that a year later gold was discovered on Cherokee land. The Georgia state legislature asserted jurisdiction over the Cherokee Nation, and President Jackson, who had fought Indians as an officer, refused to assert the federal jurisdiction mandated by the treaties. The Cherokee went to court and won. Jackson retorted: "[U.S. Supreme Court Chief Justice] John Marshall has rendered his decision. Now let him enforce it!"[21] The Georgia legislature then passed laws making it a crime for the Cherokee to mine their own gold. The Cherokee government was forbidden by Georgia law to meet except to discuss removal. Whites who had been working on the Cherokee's behalf were not allowed to enter the reservation without a state permit; this law was aimed, in part, at the *Phoenix*, whose printers were white.[22] Several thousand gold seekers invaded the reservation, destroying fields and invading homes, even before the government could complete plans for an orderly removal. As a result the Cherokee were forced during midwinter 1838 to march on foot to Indian Territory. Some fourteen thousand men, women, and children began the Trail of Tears; along the way about four thousand died, some from starvation as government contractors pocketed food-ration money.[23]

The handling of the Cherokee and other southeastern Indian nations became something of a historical model for the *Wasi'chu*. After the frontier crossed the Mississippi at midcentury, one Indian nation after another signed treaties, giving up substantial portions of their homelands for peace, federal protection, and annuities. Often the treaties were violated before the ink on them was dry—annuities were not delivered; settlers encroached upon lands guaranteed "in perpetuity." Then, and only then, did most of the Indian nations go to war.

The Lakota, for example, first met the people they called *Wasi'chu* in Minnesota, not the Dakotas. Shortly after 1800 they signed a series of treaties which "guaranteed" them some thirty million acres of land. During the next fifty years, that land base was steadily eroded, until only a ten-by-fifty-mile tract—320,000 acres—remained. Only then, in 1862, did what was called the "Great Sioux Uprising" begin. Following the deaths of several score settlers, a military force subdued the Lakota, captured many of them, and sentenced 306 to death. President Lincoln, pressured by religious leaders, intervened, but 38 Lakota still were hanged in Mankato, Minnesota. After that event, the Lakota were driven to the Dakotas, where a few years later they were "guaranteed" about half of what is today South Dakota in the Fort Laramie Treaty of 1868.

The erosion of the guaranteed land base was repeated as the railroads crept westward, the companies engaging in land speculation with land grants awarded them by the federal government. What had been a few years earlier regarded as the "Great American Desert" was coveted by farmers newly versed in dry-land agriculture.

In a treaty signed in 1868 the Black Hills, the holy land of the Lakota, had been promised to them in perpetuity. In this case, that lasted exactly six years. In 1874 General George Armstrong Custer led an army expedition into the hills, seeking gold. Within a year after he confirmed the rumors of a new El Dorado, the Black Hills were aswarm with devotees of another religion, the materialism based on the yellow metal.[24]

Across the West during the last half of the nineteenth century such treaty violations were repeated as settlers swarmed in, seeking gold, other minerals, and land, faster than the army could drive Indians from their ancestral lands. The trail of gold discoveries—from the Cherokee land, to California, to the

Black Hills and other points in the West—was paved with
Indian blood, and that of non-Indian trespassers. A major
reason why the deaths of General Custer and 204 of his men
were so celebrated in Indian country in 1876 was that it was
Custer who had violated the sanctity of the Black Hills.

The land and resource hunger of the *Wasi'chu* was not stilled,
even after the last remnants of the free Indian nations were
placed on reservations during the fifteen years following the
Custer battle. When the army's role ended on the northern
plains, the pen replaced the sword as the primary lance of the
Wasi'chu. Again, as in earlier conflicts, the *Wasi'chu* said that
they were doing the Indians a favor.

Indians believed otherwise; delegation after delegation visited Washington, D.C., during the late nineteenth century,
asking to be freed from the paternalistic colonial system which
was being constructed by the Bureau of Indian Affairs. The
government answered by increasing Indians' dependency on
handouts; more than fifty million buffalo, the basis of the
Plains Indians' economy, were slaughtered during the last
years of the nineteenth-century Indian wars.[25] Several Indian
tribes were forced to march to Indian Territory—the destination of the Trail of Tears—well into the last quarter of the nineteenth century; fifty thousand people were relocated there from
the Southeast, thousands more were marched there from the
West.[26] Many resisted the move, including the Northern Cheyenne, whose struggle to return to their homeland in eastern
Montana was described by Mari Sandoz in *Cheyenne Autumn*.
By late in the century, however, the Indians' wish to leave the
barren, malaria-infested Indian Territory was being heeded,
not out of benevolence, but out of *Wasi'chu* self-interest. Oil, a
substance which was of little value a few decades before, was
discovered. It was to be extracted to fuel the emerging auto-
mobile-based transportation system.

As the Jacksonian idea of an Indian Territory was dying,
plans were being made to evade the treaties which had established the reservation system. Often pursued in contradictory
fashion, those policies were meant to eliminate Indian cultures
and finally to eradicate the Indians' land base. The biggest land

grab by the pen started, as has been customary, as an Indian-
policy "reform."

Shortly after 1880 Helen Hunt Jackson's *A Century of Dishonor*, a graphic account of Indians' subjugation during the
first century of U.S. nationhood, was published. A fatal flaw in
A Century of Dishonor was its advocacy of measures for Indian
landholding and assimilative education. Helen Hunt Jackson's
program grew out of the philosophy of Jeffersonian philan-
thropy, which held that the solution to the "Indian problem"
lay in Indians' cultural, political, and economic assimilation
into the system which had made native people strangers on
their own land. The major plank in this program was the
reformation of Indians into yeoman farmers in the Jeffersonian
image.

Jackson's book was drawn on as a humanitarian rationale for
the Dawes (or General Allotment) Act of 1887, which decreed
that Indian land heretofore owned in common by members of a
tribe or nation be parceled out among individuals. Each Indian
family head would receive 160 acres, and each child or other
dependent family member would be given 80 acres. The allotment program was touted as a way to "educate" Indians in the
virtues of private-property ownership. The program was seen
as "help" for the Indians, not as a systematic theft of treaty-
guaranteed land. Popular magazines at the turn of the century
often contained articles describing the plans of the settlers—
voters all—who lined up at the borders of reservations about to
be thrown open for postallotmental settlement.

Indian leaders saw through the "promise" of the allotment
acts almost from the beginning. Delegation after delegation
traveled to Washington, pleading that the program be stopped.
Not only was private-property holding contrary to Indian culture; Indians for the most part had neither the training nor
inclination for sedentary farming. Besides, before mechanical
irrigation was developed, most of the land left to the Indians
was too dry for agriculture; a successful ranch in such country
required much more than 160 acres.

The Indians' appeals were ignored; the social engineers of the
time implemented and justified the dictates of the system.

After reservation land was allotted, vast tracts were left over, and much of this was thrown open for settlement by non-Indians. Under the 1887 Allotment Act, 118 reservations were divided up; 38 million acres were taken outright by the government, and 22 million were declared "surplus" and opened for settlement. An additional 23 million acres were sold between 1887 and 1934 by Indians who were forced to alleviate poverty or pay debts, and 3.7 million were sold by Indians who inherited allotments before 1934, often for the same reasons.[27] In total, the "help" promised by the Allotment Act cost Indians almost two-thirds of the land they had owned in 1887: 90 million of about 150 million acres.[28]

The Allotment Act came to an official end in 1934 with passage of the Indian Reorganization Act. Within less than fifty years many individual Indians had been effectively forced off their treaty-guaranteed lands, often into cities, to become members of the industrial work force. The same process forced other U.S. minority groups to migrate to cities within roughly the same period—blacks to the Northeast and Midwest; Chicanos, suffering the aftermath of the War of 1848 and the violation of the Treaty of Guadalupe Hidalgo, to southwestern cities. By the early 1970s an estimated 250,000 Indians had moved from reservation lands to urban areas.[29] During the 1960s such movement had been encouraged, and subsidized, by the government as part of a relocation program. This form of legislated cultural fragmentation followed unsuccessful—and bitterly protested—plans enacted during the Eisenhower era to "terminate" reservations.

Although the passage of the Indian Reorganization Act in 1934 had stopped some of the allocation policies, the theft of land by the pen continued. Between 1936 and 1976 more than 1.8 million acres of Indian land were taken by governmental action alone. These appropriations were usually paid for, but no amount of money could compensate Indian nations and individuals, whose hopes for an economic base and a cohesive community were damaged.[30] The figure above includes land taken through eminent domain, legislation, and other governmental action but does not include that acquired for rights-of-way for roads, pipelines, powerlines, and other federal and state projects.[31] Included in the 1.8 million acres were 175,000 acres taken for the Garrison Reservoir from the Fort Berthold Reservation, 101,952 acres taken from the Cheyenne River Reservation for the Oahe Reservoir, and 161,520 acres taken from the Wind River Reservation for the Riverton Project.[32]

In short, the 1934 act did little to stop the economic and governmental pressures which had been stripping Indians of their land for centuries. Despite the allocation of millions of dollars for purchase of land formerly taken, by 1950 Indians had gained 7.6 million acres—and lost 8 million.[33] Moreover, by 1950 Indian land policy was beginning to change again, and land losses accelerated. Yet another assimilative panacea was decreed: "termination." Within the next two decades 1.5 million acres were taken out of Indian ownership, and about eleven and a half thousand people were forced off their landholdings.[34] Many of the Indian nations which were "terminated" were beginning to be successful in developing their own economic base. The Menominee of Wisconsin, for example, had set up a tribally operated sawmill when their 3,270 members were forced from a 233,881-acre reservation in 1961; the Klamath were beginning to build economic self-sufficiency on the traditional base of hunting and fishing when their 2,133 members lost a land base of 862,662 acres in 1961.[35]

The relentless economic pressures which forced many Indians to sell their land to alleviate poverty contributed to the erosion of tribal land bases caused by official government policy. Even land the Indians owned was often not used by them—not because they were lazy or ignorant (as the stereotype goes) but because they lacked capital.

Having subjugated Indians in order to usurp a continent and at the same time having clouded this seizure in justifications, the white conquerors in their version of American history have often ignored the fact that intellectual ideas, as well as land and resources, were usurped from Indian cultures during the westward movement. During the last two hundred years Indian concepts have had an important impact on widely divergent social, political, and economic systems: that of the United States and those based on the thought of Karl Marx and Friedrich Engels. It has been ironic—and evidence of a major contradiction—that the Indian cultures which contributed so much to the intellectual underpinnings of the societies they were forced to confront faced eradication by those same cultures; that repression has been so widespread that many Americans today have not been told of the debt they owe to Indian thought. Across the Atlantic, however, the debt has more often been openly acknowledged, especially as it contributed to the ideas of economic egalitarianism formulated by Marx and Engels.

The history of this intellectual debt begins about 1390, the date that Arthur C. Parker estimated as the founding of the Iroquois' Great Law of Peace (also known as the "Great Immutable Law," or *Ne Gayanesha-gowa*).[36] The Great Law, passed down from generation to generation with the aid of wampum belts, was the constitution of a confederacy of Indian nations, which included the Mohawk, Seneca, Cayuga, Oneida, and Onondaga. The Tuscarora joined the confederacy in 1714. Scholars other than Parker assert that the confederacy and the constitution were founded later than 1390; by almost all accounts, however, the Five (later Six) Nations' political and economic systems were intact by the time large numbers of Europeans reached the New World, where they combined the confederation's ideas with their own heritage.[37]

The Great Law and Iroquois custom prescribed a system of political and economic democracy unknown to Europeans of the time, whose political ideas for the most part were still feudal. The governing council of the confederacy consisted of fifty civil chiefs. The basic unit of representation was the extended family, from which the women nominated chiefs. The governing council was divided into three groups: the older brothers (Mohawk and Seneca), younger brothers (Cayuga and Oneida), and firekeepers (Onondaga). In a fashion which would later influence the structure of government set up in the U.S. Constitution, the older and younger brothers (similar to the two houses of Congress) debated motions and reported a decision to the firekeepers (akin to the executive branch), who cast the deciding vote if the two brotherhoods could not agree.[38]

While in session the governing council operated with a temporary executive, a speaker, elected by acclamation. Also sitting in on the meetings were war chiefs, who were expressly elected by members of each tribe to report back to the people on the conduct of their representatives. Intricate checks on the power of the civil chiefs were built into the Great Law; the chiefs themselves were called *hoyar-na-go-war*, "counselor of the people." The civil chiefs, as well as the pine-tree chiefs, were subject to popular recall for abuse of office. Economic customs also acted to prevent abuse:

> Their great men, both sachems [civil chiefs] and captains [pine-tree chiefs], are generally poorer than the common people, for they affect to give away and distribute all the presents or plunder they get in their treaties or war, as so to leave nothing for themselves.[39]

The Great Law instructed leaders that they should not seek redress for popular criticism of their performance in office. At a time when the governments of Europe used laws of seditious libel, as well as the powers of parliamentary privilege, to stifle criticism, the Great Law instructed leaders that "the thickness of their skins shall be seven spans" and that their minds must be "filled with a yearning for the people of the great confederacy. . . not only in the present, but also future generations. . . the unborn or the future nation."[40]

Suffrage within the confederacy was almost universal; no slaves were kept, and women voted. Since a concept of communal ownership prevailed, property requirements were not a qualification for political participation. The Great Law prohibited civil authorities from entering a person's home without permission.

Benjamin Franklin, who in the early 1750s was involved in the administration of Indian affairs, became the conduit for Iroquoian ideas after attending several Iroquois treaty conferences at Carlisle (now in Pennsylvania) around 1750. Alfred Owen Aldridge has written that Indian ideas—especially political and religious concepts—influenced Franklin's intellectual development during that period.[41]

At Albany, New York, in 1754 a conference of colonial representatives was held to address complaints by Indians of harassment by settlers and to consider a plan of union for the colonies. The latter was an idea of Franklin's. He wrote:

> It would be a strange thing if six nations of ignorant savages[42] should be capable of forming a scheme for such a union and be able to execute it in such a manner as that it has subsisted ages and appears insoluble; and yet that a like union should be impracticable for ten or a dozen English colonies . . .[43]

J. E. Chamberlin has commented:

> The Albany Congress has been widely celebrated by some writers on early colonial history, partly because it was there that Benjamin Franklin first espoused . . . a more general plan, which was also drawn up at Albany by Franklin for a confederation of the American colonies; and it was generally held that the model of the Great Iroquois Confederacy was a significant influence on both the Albany Plan and the later Articles of Confederation.[44]

The oral history of the Iroquois holds that Franklin, while at the Albany conference, listened to a recitation of the Great Law of Peace, although neither the official proceedings of the conference[45] nor the writings of Franklin[46] show that he attended such an event. The official proceedings of the Albany Conference do, however, indicate that on several occasions Franklin (and other delegates) were excused from sessions to confer with Indian leaders. The Iroquoian leaders and the colonial delegates were in close proximity for three weeks during the last part of June and the first half of July 1754. The proceedings point to a cordial atmosphere, in which diplomats of two groups of nations met as equals. They also indicate that negotiations with the Indians were completed before the colonial delegates discussed the plan of union.

However the transmission took place, it is certain that the Iroquoian influence is strong in the Albany Plan of Union, the Articles of Confederation, and the United States Constitution, all of which were influenced by Franklin's contributions. Both the Albany Plan of Union and the Articles of Confederation provided for a weak executive, much like that of the Iroquoian council. Moreover, many of the provisions of the Great Law of Peace, although recognized in principle in the Constitution, were not implemented until the nineteenth and twentieth centuries. For example, the obligation of leaders to bear public criticism and scrutiny was a basis of the First Amendment's guarantee of free speech, but that right has been repeatedly frustrated throughout U.S. history by sedition and obscenity laws, executive secrecy, and industry's control, through advertising subsidies, of communications outlets. Even criticism of public officials could not approach Iroquoian standards until the U.S. Supreme Court ruling in *New York Times vs. Sullivan* (1964) stipulated that the skins of government employees must be seven spans in thickness. Suffrage expanded only slowly with the abolition of property qualifications, poll taxes, and racial bars and the grant of the vote to women; even today the political structure inhibits the growth of political parties other than the two established ones, which are supported primarily by money contributed toward campaign advertising. More than half the voters are so frustrated by the structural inhibitions that they routinely abstain. The Iroquoian prohibition against a person's home being invaded was also written into the Constitution; however, as will be described in later chapters, agents of the "law" have routinely violated this protection, especially on Indian nations. The Iroquoian concept of popular recall was written into many state constitutions in the nineteenth century; however, at the federal level impeachment is difficult and cumbersome, as was illustrated by the tenacity with which Richard Nixon held on to office before his resignation. The role of "ombudsman" was practiced by the Iroquois war chiefs long before the twentieth century, when similar offices were established in some parts of the United States, and the concept was attributed to the Scandinavians.

At each turn, the truly democratic propensities which U.S. law borrowed from the Iroquois have been fought and subverted by the dominant economic interests. Nowhere is this subversion so evident as in the policies governing Indian affairs which are *legally* supposed to protect Indian resources and treaty rights but which *actually* have been perverted by *Wasi'chu* economic interests. The result has been an Indian system which imposes on native populations cradle-to-grave control designed to obliterate cultural identity, political independence, and economic control, factors which could impede the exploitation of Indian land, resources, and life for private profit. In the Americas this exploitation has been the backbone of a colonial relationship for almost five hundred years—in direct contradiction to the traditions of the Iroquois as well as most other (but not all) native American cultures.

Across the Atlantic a century after Franklin absorbed the *political* import of Iroquoian ideas, two philosophers who would have a large impact on world history absorbed the *economic* essence of the Great Law of Peace. Marx and Engels avidly read Lewis Henry Morgan's writings on the Iroquois and incorporated Iroquoian ideas into their vision of the future of economic relationships.

Marx read Morgan's *Ancient Society* (1877) between December 1880 and March 1881 and took at least ninety-eight pages of notes as part of his study of the prominent anthropologists of his day, a group to which Morgan—who had spent much of his life studying the Iroquois—belonged.[47] Marx's notes, in a mixture of English and German, adhere closely to the text of *Ancient Society*, with little extraneous comment. What particularly intrigued Marx about the Iroquois was their democratic political organization and its mesh with a communal economic system—which was, in short, economic leveling achieved without coercion.[48]

Marx had planned a book based on the notes he was taking, but although he remained an insatiable reader his ability to synthesize and analyze what he had read declined after 1873, in part because of advancing age and the health problems inflicted by a life of poverty. He went on collecting material but no longer had the ability to organize it.

After Marx's death in 1883 Engels inherited the notes and in 1884 published *Origin of the Family, Private Property and the State*. The book sold well, going through four editions in German by 1891. Engels, who wrote the book as a "fulfillment of a bequest" from Marx, sought to show that Morgan's account "substantiated the view that classless communist societies had existed among primitive peoples" and that these societies had been free of the evils associated with capitalist societies.[49]

Ancient Society and its offspring, including Engels' book, apparently provoked lively debate—and book sales. Many socialists were influenced by Engels' appreciation of Morgan. In 1891 Karl Kautsky translated *Ancient Society* into German. August Bebel used Morgan's theory of the matrilineal gens to forecast the equality of women under socialism. His work went through fifty-one editions and was translated from the German into English by Daniel de Leon. De Leon wrote that Morgan was a "socialist prophet."[50]

De Leon was not alone in his estimate of *Ancient Society*. Engels wrote to Kautsky on February 16, 1884: "There exists a book on the origins of a society as definitive as Darwin's work for biology...I can see from his very detailed extracts that [Marx] wanted to introduce it to the Germans himself."[51] Engels was also convinced that Morgan had confirmed the materialist interpretation of history: "Morgan spontaneously discovered Marx' materialist conception of history, and his conclusions with regard to present-day society are absolutely communist postulates."[52]

In *Origin of the Family* Engels gave his reason for paying so much attention to Morgan: "I have given Morgan's account... in some detail because it gives us the opportunity of studying the organization of a society which, as yet, knows no state."[53]

Engels' tone seemed to indicate that Morgan had seen the future and that it worked:

Everything runs smoothly without soldiers, gendarmes, or police; without nobles, kings, governors, prefects or judges; without prisons, without trials. All quarrels and disputes are settled by the whole body of those concerned...the household is run communistically by a number of families; the land is tribal property, only the small gardens being temporarily assigned to the households—still, not a bit of our extensive and complicated machinery of administration is required...There are no poor and needy. The communistic household and the gens know their responsibility toward the aged, the sick and the disabled in war. All are free and equal—including the women.[54]

In the chapters which follow we will argue that American Indian cultural, political, and economic traditions have much to teach us. First, however, we will examine the subjugation system as it exists today, the resources which the descendants of the *Wasi'chu* have coveted during the last third of the twentieth century, and the attempts which are presently being made by American Indians to free themselves from a new form of colonialism.

I
The Subjugation System

The Making of a Savage:
The FBI's
Creative Writers' School

To establish the nation...it was necessary to consider the Indian as less than human. That is the first precept of genocide...Genocide depends on the debasement of the victim prior to the act...[Genocide] demands a history of pragmatic ignorance without which the nation could not survive.
        —Earl Shorris[1]

Photos by Bruce Johansen.

When General William Westmoreland in the film *Hearts and Minds* characterized the Vietnamese as valuing life less than "we in the West," he was underlining a basic justification for genocidal warfare, one which had been used in varying degrees for almost five hundred years of *Wasi'chu* warfare against the original inhabitants of the Americas. The racism which underlies such assumptions allows the stereotyping of a less-than-human enemy; it allowed *Wasi'chu* policy-makers to see themselves as humane carriers of civilization and democracy as they rained fire and death over Vietnam; it allowed the *Wasi'chu* to see a savage while being a savage.[2]

The myth of the savage has accompanied *Wasi'chu* expansion across the continent and around the world; the "history of pragmatic ignorance" has produced "gooks" of all origins and colors. Indians, the first targets of this virulent strain of racism, have seen the assumptions of inferiority and "savageness" codified into U.S. Indian policies for centuries. The most overt exploitation of the "savage" myth has been used when the *Wasi'chu* have found it necessary to subjugate by physical violence. Indian policy has historically been based on assumptions that Indians were "children" or "wards" in need of "help" —civilization—just as the Indochinese needed "help" in their civil war "to protect democracy" and, as the *Wasi'chu*, who sometimes are honest wolves, add, "our national interests," meaning the maintenance of hegemony over land, resources, and people in a colonial manner.

When Indians began to reject—and to challenge—the *Wasi'chu* self-justification, they also challenged these so-called national interests—the fish, the land, the coal, the oil, the water, and the uranium that the *Wasi'chu* corporate managers coveted. And so the battle was joined. The FBI, the domestic shock troop of subjugation, set out to refurbish the myth of the savage Indian in order to create a self-justification for eradication.

The living room of Rene Howell's home at 20 North Street, Rapid City, South Dakota, is relatively large. The house, however, could hardly begin to hold the two thousand gun-toting savages that an internal FBI memo said were going to meet there June 25, 1976.

The FBI had distributed its memorandum by teletype within its own organization as well as to the Secret Service, the U.S. Marshal's Service, and the Department of the Interior.[3] The memo, attributed to "a source with whom insufficient contact has been made to determine reliability, but who is in a position to furnish reliable information," said that Rene Howell was not only going to host the two thousand American Indian Movement (AIM) "Dog Soldiers"[4] but also their M-16s and carbines, and that at her house orders would be given for dispersal around South Dakota to carry out a program of terrorism during Bicentennial Weekend. The "Dog Soldiers," according to the memo, planned to blow up several buildings, assassinate the state's governor, and snipe at tourists and others from hills overlooking South Dakota's freeways.

Howell, supposed hostess for the "meeting," was rather surprised when she learned about it. A member of Senator James Abourezk's South Dakota staff (the senator's son was also implicated as a "Dog Soldier") brought the memorandum to her on June 23. Abourezk had been a consistent defender of the American Indian Movement, and the memo named his son, Charles, as a "gunrunner" for the supposed "Dog Soldiers."

The day after Howell got a copy of the memo, Rapid City police, disguised as construction crews, began to bulldoze a vacant lot next to her home. They were looking for the "Dog Soldiers" M-16s and carbines, but all they found were a handful of spent shotgun shells and a notebook which had no connection to the purported "Dog Soldier Society."

The text of the memo had some Indian activists wondering whether the FBI had set up a creative-writers' school or was paying informers by the inch:

"Dog Soldiers," who are pro-American Indian Movement (AIM) members who will kill for the advancement of AIM objectives, have been training since the Wounded Knee, South Dakota, incident in 1973. These Dog Soldiers, approximately 2,000 in number, have been training in the Northwest Territory (not further described) [sic] and also an unknown number have been training in the desert of Arizona. These Dog Soldiers allegedly are undergoing guerilla warfare training experiences (not further described) [sic].

The Dog Soldiers are to arrive at the Yankton Sioux Reservation, South Dakota (Wagner, South Dakota), in order to attend the traditional Sioux Sun Dance and International Treaty Conference. The Sun Dance and Conference are to occur on the Yankton Reservation in early June of 1976 and this Sun Dance and Conference are to serve as a cover for the influx of Dog Soldiers. (The Second Biennial International Indian Treaty Conference is scheduled for May 28-June 6, 1976, Yankton Reservation.)

At the conclusion of the activities at the Sioux reservation the Dog Soldiers are to meet on June 25, 1976, or immediately thereafter, at 20 North Street, Rapid City, South Dakota, the residence of Rene Howell. At this meeting final assignments will be given to the Dog Soldiers for targets throughout the state on the fourth of July weekend. Currently the Dog Soldiers from the Northwest Territory are in the state of South Dakota watching the movements of public employes at public buildings. The Dog Soldiers' assignments are to be carried out between July 1 and July 5, 1976.

Alleged targets are as follows:

1. The Charles Mix County Courthouse, Lake Andes, South Dakota, where valves on the heating systems are to be set (including the safety valve) in such a way that the boiler will blow up.

2. State Capitol, Pierre, South Dakota, (no further detail) [sic].

3. Fort Randall Dam, Pickstown, South Dakota, would have turbines blown up, short circuiting power.

4. The Dog Soldiers were "on line" to assassinate the governor of South Dakota.

5. Sniping at tourists on interstate highways in South Dakota.

6. Taking action to Mt. Rushmore.

7. To "burn farmers" and shooting [sic] equipment in the Wagner, South Dakota, area.

8. To assault the state penitentiary in Sioux Falls, South Dakota, to assassinate an inmate.

9. To blow up Bureau of Indian Affairs (BIA) buildings in the Wagner, South Dakota, area.

The Dog Soldiers are allegedly to be armed with M-16s and carbines which are hidden in Porcupine, Rosebud Indian Reservation.[5]

Sam Moves Camp, an acting AIM member [sic], Pine Ridge, South Dakota, allegedly transports the above weapons from Redman Street (number unknown),[6] to the residence of Charlie Abourezk, Porcupine, South Dakota, who is involved with the Dog Soldiers is [sic] the son of a United States senator, James Abourezk, South Dakota. Additionally, Sam Moves Camp allegedly drives a 1968 Oldsmobile, four-door, black-over brown, and resides in La Vista, Nebraska (believed to be a suburb of Omaha, Nebraska).

Source learned that dynamite was stored in the home of Tony (last name obliterated), Greenwood, South Dakota, in September, 1975 and dynamite was also stored at the home of Gregory Francis Zephier, Sr., also known as Greg, Wagner, South Dakota in February, 1975.

Source has heard that Wilburt Provost, also known as Willie, one of Russell Means' "hit men" and that Wallace Little, Jr., also known as (first name obliterated) Little, who is expert with explosives, was once teacher of the Dog Soldiers in Northwest Territory.

Greg Zephier, Wagner, South Dakota, is listed as director of the AIM, South Dakota, according to Janice Stark, clerk of incorporation records, South Dakota secretary of state, as of July 10, 1975.

A second source advised that Russell Means holds no national office in AIM; however, he is member of the AIM Central Committee, the decision-making body of AIM.

Why did the FBI accept, and disseminate, such a work of fiction? The agency may have been trying to sow salt in the political base of Senator Abourezk, a consistent defender of AIM members who have been harassed by law-enforcement agencies. Cooperating with conservative elements in the Bureau of Indian Affairs (BIA), constantly criticized by Abourezk, the FBI may have been working to foment a backlash against "Indian lover" Abourezk in South Dakota. The memo also would serve to terrorize South Dakota citizens into opposing both AIM and Abourezk by picturing them as cooperating in a scheme which was to involve irrational, random violence. The memo gave everyone reason to fear—weren't the "Dog Soldiers" going to snipe at people on the freeways? Citizens of the state had responded to such fear appeals before; William Janklow was elected attorney general after he characterized AIM members as a group of irrational savages and vowed to "put AIM members in jail, if not under it."[7] In 1978, Janklow, his anti-AIM rhetoric a little less homicidal, was elected governor of South Dakota.

The FBI's tactic—also reflected in Janklow's quote—was an old one: remove people's humanity as a pretense for practicing violence against those termed the enemy—debasing the victim before the act. Abourezk asserted that the memo was "part of a smear campaign to discredit [me] because of my longtime criticism of the B.I.A. policies and the F.B.I.'s actions involving Indians in South Dakota."[8] Charlie Abourezk, the senator's son, said that the memo would be used as a basis for an FBI harassment campaign. "Our lives may be in danger," he said, theorizing that the FBI and other law-enforcement agencies might use this and additional false FBI "intelligence reports" as a "hit list."[9] The memo could be used to justify to a fearful non-Indian public increased surveillance of AIM activities.

In her living room in August 1976, Rene Howell said that the FBI was trying to paint AIM and its supporters as terrorists in order to justify the bureau's own terrorist tactics. The FBI's campaign, she said, was aimed at repressing Indians' assertions of their rights to self-determination and control of their own lives, land, and resources. The woman who had been fingered by the FBI as hostess to two thousand gun-toting savages who were to disperse to "kill for the advancement of AIM objectives" slowly sipped a cup of coffee and said:

"According to our sacred pipe, we are never to take a life. We honor the four colors: the red, the white, the yellow, and the black. These are the red people, the white people, the yellow people, and the black people. All human life is sacred. You should treat all people as you would treat your family."

In retrospect, Howell and the rest of her family agreed that the entire episode was "a waste of taxpayers' money."

No one may ever know the extent of such waste, for many of the false memos have never been made public. Another, from the Hartford, Connecticut, police department, was distributed around the country at almost the same time that Howell learned of the "Dog Soldier memo." This one, dated June 18, 1976, outlined a "plot" by AIM, Chicano activist Corky Gonzalez, and one section of the mainly white Students for a Democratic Society to "kill a cop a day in each state." The familiar round of denials followed, and no police were killed. The Hartford memo read:

A spokesman for the Bureau of Indian Affairs stated that they had received information [that] the American Indian Movement had made contact with the Brown Beret, a militant Chicano group in the Denver area with the idea of joining forces at least in instances benefitting both groups. The S.D.S. is also emerging as a militant force and has been in constant contact with A.I.M. and the Brown Beret. Rudolfo (Corky) Gonzalez, leader of the Brown Beret, reportedly has a rocket launcher and rockets either in his possession or available to him along with explosives, hand grenades, and ten to fifteen M-16 rifles with banana clips. The objectives of this group are disturbance and terrorism. They are reported to have plans to kill a cop a day in each state.

Two vehicles have been identified as being set up to accomplish this killing[10] and various ruses have been used to lure law-enforcement officers into an ambush. False reports of family disturbances, drunken drivers and other traffic violations are to be used. When an officer arrives on the scene of a family disturbance or stops a reported vehicle, armed members will cut down the officer when he approaches.

The vehicles are described as a gray van with Colorado license plates AC-2086 and a 1972 Ford Econoline van with Wyoming plates 2915A. Any Department having information please contact the criminal intelligence division at telephone area code 203-566-2610 or executive officer, communications division at telephone 203-566-4240. Toll free 1-800-842-0200 after normal business hours.

It is unknown how many such false reports have been spread in recent years among police agencies. It is known that the volume of intelligence work directed at "militant" Indians has been massive; the FBI collected 316,000 files on the 1973 occupation of Wounded Knee alone.[11]

Despite the FBI-inspired propaganda effort, some non-Indian citizens had begun to reject the stereotypes that the "Dog Soldier memo" attempted to foster. In the trial of two Indians charged with murder in connection with the deaths of two FBI agents on the Oglala Lakota nation in 1975, the FBI's use of fictitious memoranda to stimulate fear among whites may have backfired:

> Last month [July 1976] the Justice Department was unable to quash a subpoena for Mr. [FBI Director Clarence] Kelly's appearance—the first of its kind—at a criminal trial in Iowa where two Indians stood accused of killing two F.B.I. agents in South Dakota.
>
> In the view of the defense lawyers, it was Mr. Kelly's admission on the witness stand that the F.B.I. had issued a nationwide alert of possible violence by Indians over the Bicentennial Weekend without any evidence that such violence would occur that tipped the scales in the defendants' favor.[12]

The two, Darelle Butler and Bob Robideau, were acquitted by an all-white jury in Cedar Rapids. This acquittal, coming so soon after a major FBI play on the "savage" stereotype, indicated that members of the all-white jury may have had some idea of the psychological warfare tactics being used by the shock troops of the *Wasi'chu*. Such a realization by whites—which also occurred when many failed to fall for the "gook" stereotyping of the Vietnamese—is historically important; the ability of the *Wasi'chu* to inspire fear of the "savage" among white Americans has been a key force behind five centuries of expansionism.[13]

Another rather inept attempt to reinforce the "savage" stereotype was directed not within police circles but to the American public, shortly after the two memos discussed above became public. This was a report on AIM by the Internal Security Subcommittee of the Senate Judiciary Committee.[14] The only witness to appear before the committee when it met April 6, 1976, was Douglass Frank Durham, a former FBI-paid operative who had infiltrated the American Indian Movement in 1973. Printed transcripts of the hearing became available in August 1976.

No Indians were asked to testify at the hearing, at which Durham, who had earned about $20,000 from the FBI for his spying, read into the record several falsehoods and several statements which imputed acts of savagery to AIM members, most of them without corroboration.[15] Some of Durham's statements were refuted by his own testimony.

The most spectacular fabrication was a description of events on Easter Sunday, April 22, 1973, in the occupied hamlet of Wounded Knee. On that day, according to Durham, "AIM members hung a man from a cross in full view of marshals and some members of the press. For approximately six hours, the body was pummeled for six hours."[16]

It was a new play on an old theme: the savages taking out their heathenism on all that is Christian. It was also a false tale; no such account was carried in the press.[17] The story was a play on white fears five centuries old.

Durham told the committee that AIM "has possibly moved to the stage of termination of potential or even suspected informants," a phrase which a summary of the committee's hearing related as: "Opponents [of AIM] have been eliminated in the manner of the Mafia."[18] Durham could not cite any evidence of such "terminations." In fact, AIM's handling of Durham himself—even as told by the informer—refutes his contentions. In March 1975, Durham, who was so trusted that he was appointed AIM's head of security during the 1974 Wounded Knee trials in St. Paul, was confronted with evidence that he was an informer. He confessed, and was simply ousted.

At another point in his testimony, Durham asserted that AIM planned to blow up a church in Des Moines, Iowa; the bombing never occurred. He also contended that AIM members planned to kidnap Robert D. Ray, governor of Iowa.[19] At the same hearing Durham said that Dennis Banks, a founding member of AIM met with Governor Ray during August 1973. Durham sat through part of that meeting and described it to the subcommittee as "warm and cordial."[20] Later, during the same day of testimony, Durham flip-flopped again: "I recall, in Des Moines, Iowa, they *attempted* and planned the kidnapping of Iowa Governor Robert Ray, which has to be a little violent."[21]

As had the "Dog Soldier memo," Durham forecast Indian terrorism during the Bicentennial Weekend:

> They [AIM] have the ability to create great havoc and terror within the United States by guerilla activities...such as bombing, murder, kidnapping, you know, this type of activity. A.I.M. has been engaged in just about every one of these activities, including the kidnapping.
>
> I was told while I was in A.I.M. that any patriotic symbol in the United States would be an immediate target for attack [during the Bicentennial]. I was told that Washington, D.C., and Valley Forge were targets, as would be government offices, the Freedom Train, the Wagon Train, and recently information has come to me from another source I have regarding Operation Sail, where diplomats and foreign dignitaries...entering the United States on the east coast...will be a very strong subject of attack...
>
> Some of the information came to me from leaders of A.I.M., directly, such as John Trudell discussed with me directly snipings and indiscriminate shootings of non-Indians and attacks.[22]

In March 1977, the Bicentennial year over and none of Durham's predictions having materialized, John Trudell, national chairman of AIM, stood on a stage in the auditorium in the Student Union Building at the University of Washington, his long black hair cascading down his lanky back. He paced slowly back and forth on the stage, speaking somberly on how rumors of terrorism have been used to justify repression, "They've been doing it for hundreds of years. Each time they want our resources and land, they paint us up as savages."

The FBI's anti-AIM propaganda campaign in 1976 played on non-Indians' stereotypes and fears that had been deeply implanted by hundreds of years of repetition. Indeed, any group—Indian or not—which opposed the *Wasi'chu* way had come under similar attack; the treatment of the Black Panther party[23] and many other progressive groups in the country was documented in the Rockefeller and Church reports on intelligence activities.

The exploitation of the myth of Indian savagery, however, has the longest history. The myth of the savage continues to influence Indian policy. Legally, Indians are regarded as child-like "wards" of the government, in need of assimilation and "civilization." Those who resist the institutional and cultural pressures to conform have been singled out—now, as in the past—for more brutal harassment.

The stain of the savage myth was illustrated in 1974, when Lillian Rosen, a teacher at Public School 183, New York City, decided to teach her pupils that Indians are human beings. She took this extraordinary step after hearing stereotypical slurs from children in her class, who were of white, black, Asian, and Puerto Rican extraction: "The kids don't have the faintest idea that Indians are real people," she said.[24]

One child, reflecting the views of many in the class, said, "Red men spend a lot of time killing people." Asked where they got such impressions, most of the children pointed to television entertainment programs—from "I Love Lucy" to "F Troop." One child cited a cartoon in which an Indian had threatened to make rabbit stew of Bugs Bunny. Another child told Rosen, "If an Indian moved to the city, he'd kill people." The teacher responded that about ten thousand Indians already lived in New York City.

Urban school teachers are not always so sensitive. At times they intensify the stereotypes learned outside the classroom. In one case, Jeanne Baum, a Blackfeet, withdrew her thirteen-year-old daughter, Siba, from Selden Junior High School, Long Island, after a teacher made stereotypical remarks on a book report about Indians. School authorities did not take action to refute the stereotypes, but did to get Siba back into the classroom. In 1976 Family Court Judge Arthur Abrams found Jeanne Baum guilty of "child neglect."[25] Baum asserted that the schools, not she, were guilty of neglect in allowing stereotypical racism to be spread.

The case was appealed, and again a court ordered Siba back to class. Baum refused, moving Siba from reservation to reservation for more than two years. The mother said: "Why are the schools and courts so vigorously defending the teaching of racism? I can answer that. Because racism can be considered a disease to be used as germ warfare against one's own citizens. As such, it is actually a national asset. It provides the rationalization needed to take the lands, lives and livelihoods away from the 'savage' Indians, the 'niggers,' the 'gooks,' the 'spics.' It keeps the poor white person poor and contented with a cheap inflated ego rather than an expensive full stomach. It makes the young people cannon fodder, willing to do the dirty work necessary to keep the power group rich and in control."[26]

Stereotypes form part of the mental superstructure of a subjugation system. They justify inhumane treatment, including violence, against those whose lands and lives are needed by, but not voluntarily offered to, the *Wasi'chu* class. The violence of thought and language of a stereotype is meant to justify the imposition of the subjugation necessary to a class society. For Indian people the subjugation system is disguised as a welfare state, one designed, since the slaughter of the buffalo, to prevent self-assertion—economically, politically, or culturally. The system allows some non-Indians to see Indian people as subhuman and thus to inflict violence upon them. It enforces dependency and condones treating as children people whose ancestors lived and thrived for tens of thousands of years on this land without the "helping hand" of the *Wasi'chu*. The following chapters will survey the subjugation system which underlies the superstructure of stereotypical myth. We begin with the personal violence which the stereotyping breeds.

3
Hearts and Minds

Through the pervasiveness of the bureau's role, the exercise of power and administrative programs by the B.I.A. has come to ensure that every effort by the Indians to achieve self-realization is frustrated and penalized, that the Indian is kept in a state of permanent dependency as his price of survival, and that alienation from his people and past is rewarded and encouraged.

—Edgar Cahn

Pine Ridge Reservation in South Dakota. Photo: Wide World Photos.

While the FBI was concocting fables about Indian savagery during the summer of 1976 the Navajo were being made targets of another kind of savagery, the terror which results from a society's invitation to regard some of its members as less than human in order to justify violence against them.

It was on the evening of July 1, 1976—a week after the "Dog Soldier memo" was released—that the Navajo again met the savages. Esther Keeswood, a Navajo who lives a few miles east of Shiprock, N.M., was returning to her hogan after a day of work at the local chapter house. [2]

She was met by friends and relatives with a startling, but not completely unfamiliar, story: a caravan of seven non-Indian men and women, bound for the Grand Canyon with motor-cycles, a car, and a van, had stopped at the Turquoise Bar, which straddles the reservation's eastern boundary, about five miles from Esther's hogan on Highway 550. The gang had stopped for a few drinks—and to beat up some drunken Indians.

By the time Esther and the other Navajo reached the bar, the motorcycle gang was about finished with the beatings. Esther saw eight or nine middle-aged and elderly Navajo writhing on the dirt-and-gravel parking lot in front of the bar. As she watched, a large young woman emerged from the bar and slugged an elderly Navajo woman, who fell to the ground. The gang then climbed on their bikes and into the car and van, and traveled eastward, toward Shiprock and the highway leading over the Colorado border.

The group of Navajo followed the motorcycle gang because they had learned from experience that tribal police, com-manded by Roland Dart, a white man, often did not stop people who beat up Indians. [3]

In Shiprock, Bureau of Indian Affairs police stopped the motorcycle gang in front of Luther's Market, questioned them, and were preparing to let them leave when about two hundred Navajo converged on the area and told the bikers—and the police—that this punching-bag business had to stop.

A few armed Navajo stood guard over the bikers while the bewildered police looked on. The rest retired to the chapter

59

house for a strategy meeting. An hour later, about 8 P.M., the police again decided to release the bikers; they were told to get out of the state—into Colorado or Utah, a few miles to the north.

The Navajo guards, hoping to avoid bloodshed, relayed word to the gathering in the chapter house. The group of two hundred reassembled and chased the bikers northward. One biker fell, the rest stopped, and the Navajo surrounded them and formed an escort back to Shiprock.

Back in Shiprock "the bikers ran to the police for protection," Esther recalled with sarcasm, noting how ready the group had been to beat up on *defenseless* Navajo. The assembled Navajo told the police that they were demanding that the car and van be searched for drugs and firearms and that charges be brought for the Turquoise Bar beatings. The police complied sheepishly. Two of the bikers were charged with battery and two with simple assault.[4] A group of Navajo followed the police and bikers to Aztec, the county seat, for arraignment, to make sure that another attempt at release was not made along the way.

Among the Navajo of the Shiprock area the Turquoise Bar beatings stirred up bitter memories of several brutal mutilation murders in the Gallup and Farmington areas during 1973 and 1974. During those two years the bodies of ten Navajo—in many cases middle-aged men whose sex organs had been gouged out of their bodies—were discovered. Arrests were made for only three of the killings. Three non-Indian juveniles were arrested for murder near Farmington. They were high-school students, looking for "kicks," raised in a society where stereotypical pressures have pushed Indians into a less-than-human mold. The three boys were sent to a juvenile reformatory in Springer, N.M., for two years. In May 1976, the three—Delray Ballinger, 17, Howard Bender, 17, and Matthew Clark, 16—were paroled to states outside New Mexico.

The three boys had been arrested in connection with the deaths of Herman Dodge Benally, 34, John Earl Harvey, 39, and David Ignacio, 52. Benally and Harvey had had their clothes stripped from their bodies; the clothing was used as a torch to singe the two men's body hair, genitals, and faces. The two men died when their skulls were crushed by heavy rocks. Their mutilated bodies were found April 21, 1974 in an arroyo north of Farmington. Ignacio's body was also found north of Farmington at about the same time, although police indicatd that he had been murdered several weeks before Benally and Harvey. Ignacio died after a large firecracker was exploded in his anus.

Several other mutilation murders remained unsolved. Kee Amerson Jones, 54, and George Dennison, 47, were discovered dead north of Gallup on May 6, 1973. They had been killed with their hands tied behind their backs. The two men's intestines had been ripped out of their bodies and their throats slashed from ear to ear. The body of Gilbert Saunders, 26, was mutilated before it was left near the Gallup city dump in May 1974. A year later a seventy-one-year-old Navajo man died after a broom handle was shoved up his anus, tearing his intestines.

Willie Harrison's body was found in the San Juan River about eight miles west of Farmington on May 10, 1974. Police said that this killing was apparently unrelated to the others. One of Harrison's ears had been cut off and the body burned from the waist down.

On June 9, 1974, three more Indians—Andrew Acquie, 47, Arnold Cellion, 44, and Alfred Yazzie, about 24, were found in a field north of Gallup. Each had been stabbed more than thirty times.

Such killings have had their counterparts wherever members of one cultural group convince themselves—by the false light of racism—that they "value life" more than those to whom they assume themselves superior. The history of racist violence, from the lynchings of blacks in the South to My Lai and other massacres in Vietnam, is the grotesque fruit of the myth of savagery, by which the savage-makers steal from a stereotyped people their humanity and, in so doing, foster savagery themselves. The Navajo had met the savages.

The discovery of the mutilated bodies provoked several days of large and loud, but peaceful, demonstrations by as many as ten thousand Navajo and supporters in Farmington. Many

Chicanos in the area—who had been victimized by similar murders provoked by similar social factors—lent massive support. Thus, these murders led to mobilization to resist the root causes of the climate of death. Formed during the marches, the Coalition for Navajo Liberation (CNL) would become a powerful force against the institutional, cultural, and physical violence directed against the Navajo people.

Fred Johnson, an early leader of the CNL, set the tone for the marches: "We are a peaceful people and very sincere in our grievances. We are marching for our rights."[5] A year and a half later, Johnson himself was killed in a plane crash and explosion, the mysterious circumstances of which led many Navajo to conclude that he had been assassinated.[6]

Throughout the period of the marches Navajo leaders contrasted the peacefulness of their people with the savagery which had been visited upon them. Peter McDonald, the tribal chairman, said, "I am glad, that in our culture such violence would never occur. We Navajos respect our elders and do not even talk harshly to them; much less act violently toward them."[7]

John Redhouse, associate director of the National Indian Youth Council (NIYC) of Albuquerque, N.M., who had attended Farmington High School, the alma mater of the three boys implicated in the mutilation murders, wrote:

> We didn't see the murders as the acts of three crazy kids. We see [them] as part of a whole racist picture. For years, it has been almost a sport, a sort of sick, perverted tradition among Anglo youth of Farmington High School to go into an Indian section of town and physically assault and rob elderly and sometimes intoxicated Navajo men and women...for no apparent reason, other than that they are Indians.[8]

It was toward this "whole racist picture" that the NIYC and the newly formed CNL directed their energies. The roots of the stereotypical image of the Indian which fosters institutional violence, cultural violence, and physical violence lie in the history and evolution of five centuries of U.S. policy toward American Indians.

Beginning with an 1831 opinion rendered by Chief Justice John Marshall of the U.S. Supreme Court, the Indian has been regarded legally as a ward of the United States. "Their [Indians'] relations to the United States resembles that of a ward to his guardian," Chief Justice Marshall wrote. This implicitly paternalistic and racist attitude has been the foundation upon which the system of "wardship"—which treats Indians as immature children—has been built. The Bureau of Indian Affairs (BIA) was created as part of the War Department in 1824 and transferred to the Interior Department in 1849. While the army carried out physical violence against resisting Indians, the BIA set up an institutional system—which still exists today—to carry on cultural war against a proud and formerly independent group of peoples by treating them as children. To this day, nearly every facet of a reservation Indian's life is controlled by federal edict: Indians may not utilize their property—or even withdraw money from their own bank accounts—if the BIA declares them "incompetent" and places them under the "protection" of a guardian. The decisions the BIA makes about Indian lives have virtually no effective appeal.[9]

Some non-Indians have expressed a strange, and rather blind, envy at the BIA's Indian system:

DEAR ABBY: You and "sensitive and sad" can put away your guilt feelings about the American Indians.

I have lived on an Indian reservation for the past twenty-five years, and find no injustice or cruelty, unless it is to the non-Indians who live in states where reservations are located.

All Indians are citizens of the United States, and although they receive all privileges any other citizen enjoys, they do not contribute to any of these privileges!

In 1975, it cost the United States taxpayer $10,000 for each Indian family. At the present expanding rate, it will be $20,000 per family by 1980. Indians get free medical, hospital and dental and optical care from birth to death. They pay no state taxes on homes, cars, land, personal property or income. They may hunt and fish around the year—no bag limit, no license. They can receive free education from Head Start to Ph.D.'s. They are given preference on jobs; some ads read, "Tribal members only need apply." They get wells drilled, sanitary facilities installed on ranches, farms and homes away from municipal facilities—all FREE. The list is endless.

. . . Where else in the world can you get all this free, at tax-payers' expense? So, rejoice: the Indians are doing OK. Wish we had it so good.

— Envious on the Reservation[10]

"Envious on the Reservation," who wishes that "we had it so good," might learn differently if he or she actually traded places with a reservation Indian, whose life is controlled by the cradle-to-grave bureaucracy described in the above letter as a tax-free heaven. The bureaucracy, which dominates Indians' lives on reservations, takes as well as gives: it was established to deprive Indians of their identity, heritage, and culture through a program which enforces idleness, despondency, and dependence. The Indians have paid their taxes for five hundred years.

Edgar Cahn's analysis of the BIA's role in Indian life acknowledges that many Indians resist the agency's abolition because they fear even worse depredations from non-Indians if they are stripped of the limited protection offered by the demeaning "wardship" system.

Through the pervasiveness of the bureau's role, the exercise of power and administrative programs by the B.I.A. has come to ensure that every effort by the Indians to achieve self-realization is frustrated and penalized, that the Indian is kept in a state of permanent dependency as his price of survival and that alienation from his people and past is rewarded and encouraged.[11]

The amount of money the BIA spends to maintain its system of enforced dependency is enormous—nearly $1 billion a year, most of which is consumed by one of the federal government's most inefficient bureaucracies. In 1969 Cahn found that the BIA spent $8,040 per Indian family on the Oglala Lakota Nation at Pine Ridge, although the family median income was only $1,910 a year, less than half of what the federal government itself defined at that time as the "poverty level."[12] Cahn found that the BIA maintains one paid official (a majority of whom are not Indians) for each eighteen "wards."[13]

The structure and practices of the BIA closely parallel those of colonialist administrations in Africa, as described by Amilcar Cabral, an eloquent spokesman for national liberation there.

> The idea of foreign domination . . . would be to choose:
> —Either to liquidate practically all the population of the dominated country, thereby eliminating the possibilities for cultural resistance;
> —or to succeed in imposing itself, without damage to the dominating people, that is, to harmonize economic and political domination of these [colonized] people with their cultural personality.[14]

Cabral believed that cultural activity usually precedes a colonized people's struggle to regain control over political and economic institutions which have been taken from them.[15]

In North America (and to some extent in South America) one can read Cabral's analysis, based primarily on African experience, into the traditional choice provided native peoples by the colonizers: assimilate or starve. To the colonizer, the resurrection of native culture also threatens the hegemony which has been assumed over the political and economic lives of the Indian nations. Thus, the institutions of the conqueror—the government and corporations of the United States—have been maintained to perpetuate the concept of "civilizing the Indians"—assimilation. Only by strip-mining the soul can the colonizer ensure an unchallenged opportunity to strip-mine—or otherwise exploit—Indians' land and resources.

An outstanding feature of day-to-day reservation life is its enforced idleness. Indians' traditional means of economic support—buffalo and fish are examples—have been exterminated or seized. Many of the Indian nations' traditional political functions have been usurped by the BIA and a tribal-government system which is set up to resemble a high-school student government in many respects. Cultural activity, although repressed, survives, despite the fact that until 1934 Indians could be imprisoned for teaching or practicing their religions, languages, or history. In recent years Indian resistance has won the freedom for some degree of cultural expression, although it still exists within a context of institutional constraints, to be described below.

Enforced idleness is a policy of social control—a manifestation of a continuing institutional war against Indian life and culture. Any Indian who asserts sovereignty too forcefully on a reservation can be threatened with the loss of BIA-provided jobs and services.[16] Enforced idleness is a manifestation of the colonialist system which has taken the culture, political power, and economic base from many Indian nations. It also feeds into the colonizer's myth of the savage. Indians—a group of diverse peoples who survived and prospered on this land for tens of thousands of years with no BIA—have been stereotyped as lazy creatures on the dole.

Into the cultural, political, and economic vacuum created by the colonizer's institutional programs has come alcohol, the timeless refuge of colonized peoples. Alcoholism has been an escape for people in limbo—those who have been shorn of their culture, political power, and economic base.

The "drunken Indian" is a creation of the colonizer, who then reinforces the assumption that the Indian is a "child." Stereotype builds on stereotype. Alcohol becomes a means of social control, which is employed baldly and nakedly, despite the well-wishers and liberals who attempt to combat alcoholism without addressing its root causes, which lie in the institutional system of colonization itself. As long as the *Wasi'chu* economic system rewards those who provide dispirited Indians with the means for drinking and as long as the institutional pressures maintain the state of cultural, economic, and political limbo in which many Indians reside, the problem will continue.

The profits to be made from plying Indians with alcohol are immense. Astride the borders of many Western reservations in states where liquor prices are not controlled are bars which charge as much as twice the going rate for beer and hard liquor. The streets of Farmington and Gallup, New Mexico, are lined with bars; there is little incentive in these towns to break down the system which gets Indians into the bars.

Given this context, it was hardly surprising that one of the first targets of Indian activists has been alcohol. Fred Johnson said in the early days of the CNL that one of the group's first tasks would be to "remove the scourge of the white man's alcohol that is destroying the spiritual and physical strength of our people."[17] In June 1974, Johnson filed a lawsuit in federal district court seeking the closure as "public nuisances" of six Farmington-area bars which are patronized almost exclusively by Navajo.[18]

Long after Johnson's death, the bars remained open, filling their cash registers with the money of impoverished Navajo. The economy of Farmington has little use for sober Indians.

The campaign against the bars did not end, however. In 1975 Richard Hughes, a Navajo Legal Services attorney, told the U.S. Civil Rights Commission that

> alcoholism among the Navajos is a pervasive and very profound problem. It is not going to be solved at rehabilitation centers and meetings. I do not know if there is any way to repair the psychological damage to a race that has simply lost its place, to people who have simply lost their identity and know that they are in a society with no place for them . . . The deplorable brutality that is done to Navajo alcoholics who are being fed this poison . . . is an evil that can and should be attacked with all the vigor that anyone can bring to bear.[19]

Following the beatings of the Navajo at the Turquoise Bar, Shiprock-area Navajo collected more than six hundred signatures on petitions urging that the place be closed. The Navajo petitioners accused the bar's owner, Edgar Lake, of doing much more than permitting bikers to beat Navajo on the premises; they said that he failed to make necessary improvements, sold alcohol to habitual drunkards, and locked restrooms, forcing bar patrons to urinate outside. All the charges were confirmed by Lorenzo Garcia, New Mexico's Liquor Control Board hearing officer, in January 1977. He ordered the bar closed for six months and fined Lake $2,500.[20] The CNL and NIYC had won a temporary, and small, victory in their war on alcoholism.

Alcohol is a direct cause of another problem in Indian country: the abnormally large number of Native Americans who are arrested and jailed. The U.S. Civil Rights Commission analyzed arrest records in Farmington between 1969 and 1973 and found that Indians represented between 79 and 84 percent of arrests by city police during each of the five years. Indians make up 8 percent of the city's population, although many more travel from the Navajo reservation to shop, socialize—and drink. Of the Indians arrested during each of the five years, between 85 and 90 percent were detained for reasons related to alcohol.[21] In Sheridan County, Nebraska, near the Oglala Lakota Nation, a total of 1,400 arrests took place in 1974—1,224 of them Indians. One thousand three people were arrested on charges related to alcohol use; 957 of them (95.4 percent) were Indians.[22]

While they are amply represented in court docks and in jail, Indians are rarely present on juries in areas where the majority of their peers are arrested. Although Navajo people represent more than 35 percent of the population in San Juan County, N.M., (which includes a northeastern corner of their reservation) only 12 percent of the grand jurors and less than 10 percent of the petit jurors in the county were Indians during 1973 and 1974.[23] Yet between 1969 and 1973 Indians served 95 percent of the jail time and paid 79 percent of the fines in Farmington's municipal courts.[24]

An especially deadly and tragic law-enforcement problem—traffic accidents—is also related to alcohol use. The two-lane blacktop between Shiprock and Farmington, Highway 550, bears the nickname "slaughter alley." Many Indians die very young—one has not felt the full impact of this on everyday lives until nights are spent in reservation homes, with young Indians recalling the stories of dead friends. Early in the morning the litany of short lives is told, along with the constantly recurring causes—a traffic accident, an alcohol-bred fight, a suicide, a mysterious death after a few days in the reservation hospital. The colonial system which strip-mines the soul also permeates the reservation air with tales of death; the suicide rate among Indians is at least twice the national average.[25]

The colonial system is also one of bondage. A former trading-post employee on the Navajo Nation told the U.S. Commission on Civil Rights in 1975 that non-Indian traders had kept 7,300 Indian families in "virtual bondage" for several years by refusing to extend credit to anyone who would not agree to have mail—including welfare checks—routed first to the traders' stores. John A. Johnson, the employee, said that his bosses padded bills, charged Indians as much as 20 percent a month interest on unpaid loans, and encouraged customers to buy more than they could afford, perpetuating the bondage relationship.[26]

These injustices, however, pale beside some of what takes place inside the Public Health Service hospitals on Indian reservations which "Envious on the Reservation" mentioned. Health care is often so deplorable that Indians who can afford it use private doctors and hospitals. Those who cannot afford private care—and that is the majority—sometimes die prematurely.

A hitchhiker pointed to a large brick building on a small rise west of Pine Ridge Village on the Oglala Lakota Nation. "That's the hospital," he said. "My brother died there. He went to the place with a stomach pain. The doctors told him he had stomach flu and that he ought to go home and rest. He did. A few days later, the pain became worse, much worse. My brother returned to the hospital. He was flown to Denver. But it was too late... his appendix had filled his body with poison. He was not the only one in my family to die there. My uncle died, too. No one knows what happened to him. There have been many others."

In the Southwest Indians who requested health care in Farmington at the San Juan County Hospital were often refused and told to go to the Public Health Service hospital at Shiprock until such discrimination was challenged by Navajo Legal Services in a suit filed in federal court in 1974. The suit contended that Mae Neal, a Navajo woman, had entered the San Juan County Hospital with multiple stab wounds. According to the suit, she was given some treatment but transferred to the reservation hospital before her condition stabilized. She died from complications. By 1977 the San Juan Hospital, under threat of legal action, had agreed to establish a policy whereby "emergency room treatment will be afforded to Indians on the same basis and under the same considerations as such treatment is afforded to and received by other members of the general public." The hospital also agreed to keep an emergency-room log of patients for two years to prove that the promise was sincere.

And what of the Shiprock hospital? Indians have access to free health care there. The Civil Rights Commission described general conditions:

> ... well documented at the Window Rock hearing is that throughout the Navajo's life, from the very hour of birth, the health care delivered under law by the federal government is not only inadequate, it is unsafe.[27]

Many of the reports of ill treatment come not from axe-grinding patients, but from Indian Health Service staff, who find institutional constraints limiting their professional desire to offer life-sustaining care. Dr. Taylor McKenzie, an Indian Health Service (IHS) surgeon, told the Civil Rights Commission that at the six IHS hospitals on the Navajo Nation:

> A number of tragic events have occurred simply because we have not had the nursing personnel to adequately staff the hospital. . . . We have documented about three cases where infants have died there because nobody was there to take care of them.[28]

According to Dr. McKenzie, one healthy newborn baby choked to death in an unattended nursery. An elderly man fell from an unwatched stretcher, where he was being fed intravenously; he died of a broken skull.[29] The report found that "Navajo facilities fail by almost 50 per cent to meet the adequate national standards for health care."[30]

After the Civil Rights Commission's hearings, two nurses who had been assigned to the Shiprock hospital protested conditions and were fired. After employees at Shiprock protested the firings and a team of doctors from the University of New Mexico substantiated their charges, the two women were reinstated—but reassigned to other IHS hospitals.[31]

The two nurses, Valerie Koster and Sandra Kramer, had protested that the grounds outside the hospital were strewn with garbage, which attracted rats and wild dogs. In the nurses' living area toilets were encrusted with slime. They asserted that institutional regulations rewarded employees who spent their time filling out forms instead of caring for patients. There was evidence that doctors and nurses who did care for patients were so harried and short of time that they often made medication errors. [32]

One department of the IHS hospital system which never seems to be short of personnel and funds, however, is that which encourages Indian women to be sterilized, and sometimes performs the operations without their consent. The IHS also seems to have plenty of time and money to conduct medical experiments on nonconsenting Indian patients. "They took away our past with a sword and our land with a pen. Now they're trying to take away our future with a scapel," one Indian woman told Arlene Eisen of *The Guardian*. [33]

A General Accounting Office report, released in December 1976, surveyed sterilization practices in four of the twelve regions with IHS hospitals—Aberdeen, S.D.; Albuquerque, N.M.; Oklahoma City; and Phoenix, Ariz. [34] The study found that 3,406 sterilizations were performed in these four areas between 1973 and 1976; 3,001 of them on women less than forty-four years of age. None of the consent forms offered women before the operations met federal requirements. [35]

An Indian woman told Eisen: "This total disregard for the health and dignity of Native American women is the I.H.S.-H.E.W. version of smallpox-infested blankets, the forced marches and massacres of native peoples...racism continues because it is so deeply entrenched—even 'enlightened' professionals do not see Indian people as human...they still think Indian people are in the way. They still want the land we have left—particularly our mineral resources. There is coal, oil and uranium on our lands." [36]

Many Indian children are not raised by their parents. The BIA may declare a mother "incompetent"—a decision which can only rarely be appealed—and put her children up for adoption. According to the Association on American Indian Affairs

(AAIA), 23 to 35 percent of all Indian children are taken from their parents and placed under some form of foster care—non-Indian homes or institutions.[37]

"The wholesale separation of Indian children from their families is perhaps the most tragic and destructive aspect of American Indian life today," wrote William Byler.[38] Byler found that in Minnesota one of every eight Indian children under eighteen years of age was living in an adoptive home; in 1972 the figure for Indian children at age one was one in four, and per capita Indian children were being adopted away from their families at a rate five times that of other children. In South Dakota the rate was sixteen times, in Washington nineteen times for adoptions and ten times for foster care. In South Dakota 40 percent of all adoptions made through the state Department of Public Welfare between 1967 and 1977 involved Indian children, but Indians comprise only 7 percent of the juvenile population in that state.[39]

Byler also found that about 85 percent of the Indian children taken from their families ended up in non-Indian homes, a figure compiled in sixteen states in 1969. In 1977, 90 percent of the adopted-away Indian children in Minnesota went into non-Indian homes. Such figures, wrote Byler, probably are representative, although this cannot be proved because few states keep adoption records as carefully as does Minnesota.[40]

A North Dakota study cited by Byler said that only 1 percent of children taken from Indian homes were separated because of abuse by parents. It was far more likely that the children were taken on such vague grounds as "permissiveness," "neglect," or "personal deprivation."[41]

Such judgments are often based on ethnocentrism. For example, social workers at times fail to understand the dynamics of the extended family; if an Indian child spends what the social worker deems to be excessive time with relatives, he or she may be removed from parents for reasons of "neglect." Children are sometimes taken as punitive measures against parents. For example, parents of Nevada's Duckwater band of Paiute were threatened with the loss of their children after they removed them from county-run schools and prepared to place them in their own school, which was being opened under an approved federal grant.[42]

Even Indian parents who protect their children may be threatened with removal of them. Yvonne Wanrow, a Colville Indian, was staying with a friend in Spokane, Washington, during August 1972 when William Wesler, 62, who had earlier been convicted of child molestation, threatened her children. Having no recourse, Wanrow shot and killed the man as he advanced on the children. She was convicted of murder in May 1973, sentenced to twenty years in prison, and faced separation from her children. After four years of court fights, Wanrow in 1977 won the right to a new trial.

"The main thrust of federal policy, since the close of the Indian wars, has been the breakup of the extended family and the clan structure [and] to detribalize and assimilate Indian populations," Byler commented.[43] Perhaps no form of assimilation is more personal than adoption of children. It is possible that such practices, in addition to aiding assimilation, also contribute to suicide. A report entitled "Suicide, Homicide and Alcoholism Among American Indians," assembled by the National Institute of Mental Health, drew a profile of Indians who are prone to suicide. According to the report, the suicide-prone Indian "has lived with a number of ineffective or inappropriate parental substitutes because of family disruption. He has spent time in boarding schools and has been moved from one to another."

For the American Indian child whose birth is not prevented by sterilization, who does not succumb to the nation's highest rate of infant mortality, and who is not abducted from its mother, the next rampart of the assimilative colonial system is education. The educational system—whether one operated by the Bureau of Indian Affairs or a public-school system near the child's home reservation—often exacts a high price in terms of personal identity and cultural heritage as it attempts to mold its Indian pupils into a non-Indian belief system.

A small proportion of Indian children now attend "survival schools" operated by traditional Indians, such as the Rough

Rock Demonstration School (Navajo) or similar institutions on the Pine Ridge Reservation, at Franks Landing (Washington), or in western Montana. The majority, however, attend public or BIA-run schools.

About 40 percent of Indian children attend BIA schools, many of them boarding schools hundreds or even thousands of miles away from home; about a quarter of Indian children were, for all intents and purposes, abducted from their homes and parents by this means during the 1970s.[44] Added to the quarter who are adopted outright into non-Indian homes or institutions, a total of about half of Indian children do not live at home during many of their formative years. The remaining half attend public schools.

With the exception of a few sensitive teachers—who fight the institutional sanctions that obliterate Indian self-respect and culture—the schools teach Indians to loathe their own traditions and what remains of their culture. A Congressional subcommittee on Indian education was told in 1968:

> There is not one Indian child who has not come home in shame and tears after one of those sessions in which he is taught that his people are dirty and animal-like, something less than a human being.[45]

Utilizing such denigration, the schools teach Indians submission and self-hate:

> Indian children face unremitting pressure toward submission and cultural anihilation. All who pass through the Indian education system become casualties of education waged as war.[46]

An educational experience which obliterates traditional culture and heritage leaves the child two choices: endure continuing self-hatred, or assume the culture of the conquerer—assimilation or spiritual starvation.

> The B.I.A. education system is not primarily an "education system." It is best understood as a major division of the bureau's own "military-industrial complex" which wages unrelenting war upon Indian survival.[47]

When instruction in Indian culture does creep into the curriculum of the non-Indian schools which hold Indian children, it is usually taught as history—isolated from the political, economic, and spiritual bases on which the remainder of culture rests. It may be fine, under the "enlightened" education of today, for an Indian to be an Indian, as long as the "contamination" of cultural awareness does not broaden to a challenge of the political and economic domination of the colonizer; be an Indian—but hunt your buffalo in the supermarket.

While the operators of public schools on or near reservations acknowledge an Indian's right to learn his or her culture in theory, they deny it in practice. For example, the Quinault Nation of coastal Washington attempted for several years in the 1970s to get instruction in its culture and language in the public school on the reservation. The public school said, fine, find us a teacher. The Quinault proposed a tribal elder with extensive knowledge of the subject matter, but the school board refused to allow the person to teach. The reason: the elder did not have a college degree in education.

Actual schooling is only one facet of childrens' education, of course, and only one front in the cultural war on the heritage of Indian children. Many of the Indian homes on reservations which have electricity also house television sets—where the young may watch "good" cowboys slaughter nasty Indians or Bugs Bunny threatened with the stewpot by a caricatured, "ugh"-grunting Indian.

Wherever the *Wasi'chu* covets the hearts and minds of a colonized people, the emissaries of cultural domination are at work to strip the soul of resistance to the systematic exploitation of land, resources, and the people themselves. Amilcar Cabral, a leading figure in the liberation of Guinea-Bissau, spoke of the same process in Africa:

> As a result of dividing or of deepening the divisions in the society, it happens that a considerable part of the population assimilates the colonizer's mentality [and] considers itself culturally superior to its own people.[48]

One source of stability and power in *Wasi'chu*-dominated cultures—especially in the United States—has been, and remains, the ability to assimilate by offering the trappings of affluence to a minute portion of the colonized peoples, who in turn assume the colonizer's values and turn them against their own people. This mechanism has grown in subtlety as it has been developed, allowing those who assume the colonizer's class interests some freedom to practice their own cultures—in disconnected fragments—as long as the practice is not extensive enough to challenge the *Wasi'chu*'s domination of political and economic power. It is within this context that intertribal conflict has grown within many Indian nations, between native Americans who have assumed the values of the dominant economic class and those who are struggling to maintain traditional culture and to build upon it means of political and economic independence.

On no Indian nation in modern times has this division become more open and violent than on the Oglala Lakota Nation, the Pine Ridge Reservation.

4
The Colonial Police Force

"They're a conquered nation," he [Norman Zigrossi, special FBI agent in charge, Rapid City]says. "And when you are conquered, the people you are conquered by dictate your future. This is a basic philosophy of mine. If I'm part of a conquered nation, I've got to yield to authority...[The FBI must function as] a colonial police force.
                    —David Weir and Lowell Bergman[1]

AIM members being arrested in Custer, South Dakota, in February 1973. Photo: Wide World Photos.

On the Oglala Lakota Nation (Pine Ridge Sioux Indian Reservation), economic conflicts became physical war during the 1970s, as those tribal members who had assimilated the mindset of the *Wasi'chu* acted, through a private police force backed up by the Federal Bureau of Investigation, to repress a growing grass-roots movement which—allied with the American Indian Movement (AIM)—was challenging the *Wasi'chu* hold on land and resources, as well as on the minds of the Lakota.

What resulted was referred to in the popular press as an "intratribal war" or a "law-enforcement problem." The conflict, during which several dozen persons died violently, went far deeper than that. It was the outcome of a century of efforts at subjugation of the Lakota people. The conflict was closely related to the events of the previous hundred years, as well as to the *Wasi'chu*'s continuing quest for the Lakota's remaining land and resources.

The educational system outlined in the previous chapter had inculcated its central values—faith in power, faith in money, belief in a hierarchical and profit-oriented economic system based on individualistic concerns—into those tribal members whose hearts and minds had accepted it. They were, for the most part (but not exclusively) of middle age, people who had grown up at a time when repression of their Indian heritage was greatest. Their opposition came mostly (but again, not exclusively) from an alliance of tribal elders, who had lived closer in time and memory to the era when the Lakota Nation was free of external colonization, and the young, who had grown up during the 1960s and had served as soldiers in Vietnam or had been college students or prison inmates. The opponents of the *Wasi'chu* had managed to escape, to reclaim themselves from the sophisticated subjugation system. In so doing, they came into conflict with Tribal Chairman Dick Wilson.

Wilson was first elected tribal chairman in 1972. Shortly thereafter, traditionals (grass-roots people) organized the Oglala Sioux Constitutional Rights Organization (OSCRO), whose main immediate goal was to win higher rental rates for land leased for ranching. Wilson would not permit the issue to be raised with the Bureau of Indian Affairs (BIA) in the name of

79

the tribe (as the system requires); he responded by outfitting his personal police force, a group so nakedly brutal that it was called (and members even called themselves) the "goon squad," financed by tribal and federal money. When the OSCRO attempted to impeach Wilson, the activities of the goon squad increased. Wilson sat as tribal chairman at his own impeachment hearing and of course denied the traditionals' challenge. The OSCRO appealed to the BIA, which stood by silently. Then the OSCRO asked for support from the American Indian Movement, which included many Lakota. One result of the escalating conflict between the traditionals and Wilson would be the seventy-one day occupation of Wounded Knee in 1973, which was primarily intended to publicly raise the contradictions related to Wilson's policies, which inevitably favored non-Indian ranchers, farmers, and corporations.

During the occupation of Wounded Knee and in subsequent events the FBI steadily became more and more involved in the conflict, siding with the assimilationists. In addition to the traditionals' resentment over alienation of their land and resources (and their resulting impoverishment), a major cause of tension was the FBI's refusal to assume the responsibility vested in the agency by federal law to investigate major crimes on the reservation. The FBI chose instead to act, in agent Zigrossi's words, as a "colonial police force," to repress the challenge to Wilson's—and therefore *Wasi'chu*—power.

Wilson's actions accentuated these class differences. Aside from the money which was siphoned from social needs to pay for police hardware, Wilson padded the tribal payroll with friends and relatives. One of his brothers, for example, was given a $25,000-a-year job heading the tribal planning office[2] on a reservation where the average per capita annual income at the time was less than $1,000 and where more than half the homes had no running water or indoor toilets.[3]

Wilson further irritated the traditionals by taking part in the alcohol-bootlegging trade on the reservation. In so doing, he was plugging into a primary part of the subjugation system, as well as cooperating with the owners of some bars at the reservation's borders. Bootlegging—as well as bar ownership—can be very lucrative; one small bar in White Clay, Nebraska, near the southern border of the reservation, turned a net profit of $200,000 in 1974.[4] "I know the Wilson background," said Al Trimble, who defeated the tribal chairman in his bid for a third term in 1976. "He has lived a whole life exploiting Indian people around here. His dad was a bootlegger. He was a bootlegger himself."[5]

Wilson had thus become part of a class of Indians who—since the first subjugation—have chosen to join forces with the *Wasi'chu* against their own people, in the fashion of a Haitian "Papa Doc" or a Vietnamese General Ky. Appendages of the colonial system, they are rewarded with the sort of relative affluence that the *Wasi'chu* have trained them to covet. Like his contemporary in office, Richard Nixon, Richard Wilson paid homage to larger economic interests; he advised (but did not succeed in convincing) the tribal council to sell the Black Hills; on June 26, 1975, he signed away one-eighth of the reservation to the National Park Service.[6] He also accelerated the transfer of what remains of the Lakota land base from the hands of traditionals to those of non-Indian (or minimally Indian) ranchers and farmers.

The alienation of land is not just a Lakota problem; it is nationwide, as pointed out by the Congressional Joint Economic Committee:

Of 129 reservation areas with populations of at least 200 Indian people and at least 1,000 acres of land, 25 have greater non-Indian than Indian population within their original boundaries, and 38 have lost at least 50 percent of their original reservation areas to non-Indians.[7]

By the middle 1970s 63 percent of Indian-owned agricultural land in the United States was being cultivated by non-Indians.[8] Indian nations' attempts to buy back alienated land only rarely keep pace with the amount impoverished owners are forced to sell. During 1970 alone, 200,000 acres passed out of Indian ownership.[9] In the meantime, the press's concentration on the novelty of land reclamation by Indians stirs a fear of Indian aggression and feeds the backlash movement.

Reduced to a personal level, the loss of land often follows a pattern outlined to the authors in 1976 by an elderly Lakota man: "I lease one allotment [160 acres] with a pump and a fence to a rancher for $400 a year," he said. "The other, with no pump or fence, goes for $320 a year. I'd like to own my own cattle, but one cow costs as much as a year's allotment rental. The BIA says I can't get welfare as long as I own land; I can't even keep up my house and feed myself. I guess I'll have to sell my land and move to the village."

Hundreds of similar cases have carried one-third of the grazing land and 87 percent of the cultivated land on the Oglala Lakota Nation out of Indian ownership since the Allotment Acts of 1887.[10]

Even the figure which lists two-thirds of the grazing land as still in Indian hands is rather deceptive, for about 90 percent of that land is owned, used, or both, by those of less than half Indian blood. A report compiled by Al Trimble while he was BIA superintendent on the reservation (he was 1976-1978 tribal chairman) shows that existing land-leasing systems tend to encourage the transfer of land from full bloods to mixed bloods and finally to non-Indians.

A major mechanism of this long-term transfer, ironically, is an "Indian preference" clause in leasing regulations. An Indian with as little as 1/32 Indian blood may escape competitive bidding by proving that he or she owns cattle. One cow will do. After obtaining the lease for land owned by other tribal members, this middleman may lease the land to non-Indian ranchers at a price higher than that paid to the actual owner, who has no money to buy or raise cattle.

"He [the middleman] parlays the lease into what amounts to ownership of the land," Trimble wrote.[11] According to Trimble's report, Indians with half or more blood quantum actually use only 8.5 percent of the reservation land. Those with more than 1/32 but less than half blood quantum use 59.5 percent; whites use 30 percent.[12]

"Within a short span of time, Oglala land (not jointly owned by the tribe) will be overwhelmingly controlled and owned by Indians who are less than 1/32 Indian blood," Trimble concluded.[13]

Subtle mechanisms such as "Indian preference" clauses have been utilized for decades to reduce the Lakota's opportunities to use—and eventually to own—their treaty land. Wilson's encouragement of such mechanisms sparked challenge from the traditional community, especially since his assumption of office coincided with the traditionals' assertions against the continued alienation of their land, resources, and way of life. Against those who evaded all other means of assimilation the last resort—physical force—was brought to bear.

Between March 1, 1973, and March 1, 1976, at least sixty-one violent deaths occurred in a post-Wounded Knee reign of terror on and near the Oglala Nation's 4,000 square miles of rolling hills, grassland, and rock. All but a few of the deaths were those of AIM activists or supporters, killed primarily by the goon squad. The figure of sixty-one deaths is a conservative one, which counts only those documented by Bureau of Indian Affairs police, the FBI, or the Wounded Knee Legal Defense-Offense Committee (WKLD-OC). Neither the BIA nor the FBI was particularly interested in keeping track of the reign of terror; the WKLD-OC list may be incomplete, largely because the committee's only permanent staff worker on the reservation, Candy Hamilton, struggled against a lack of time and money, as well as official harassment, during those years. She did not even have money to pay for a telephone, an essential tool for legal work on the large reservation; when she attempted to travel, she was often physically blocked by cars and trucks containing members of the goon squad.

Using only the documented political deaths, the yearly murder rate on Pine Ridge Reservation between March 1, 1973, and March 1, 1976, was 170 per 100,000. By comparison, Detroit, the reputed "murder capital of the United States," had a rate of 20.2 per 100,000 in 1974.[14] The U.S. average was 9.7 per 100,000, with the range for large cities as follows: Detroit, 20.2; Chicago, 15.9; New York City, 16.3; Washington, D.C., 13.4; Los Angeles, 12.9; Seattle, 5.6; and Boston, 5.6. An estimated 20,000 persons were murdered in the United States during 1974.[15] In a nation of 200 million persons, a murder rate comparable with that of Pine Ridge between 1973 and 1976 would have left 340,000 persons dead for political reasons in one year;

1.32 million in three. A similar rate for a city of 500,000 would have produced 850 political murders in a year, 2,550 in three. For a metropolis of 5 million, the figures would have been 8,500 in one year and 25,500 in three.

This murder rate of 170 per 100,000 for Pine Ridge *does not* include deaths from causes related to the institutional and cultural genocide of Indians there; it does not include the premature deaths from malnutrition on a reservation where hungry children often play near fat cattle destined for off-reservation supermarkets; it does not include deaths related to malpractice in reservation hospitals; it does not include suicides related to cultural repression and "education" which teaches self-hate; it does not include slow deaths from alcoholism. The murder rate of 170 per 100,000—almost nine times that of Detroit—takes into account only deaths caused by the *physical* repression of Indian resistance.

The political murder rate at Pine Ridge between March 1, 1973, and March 1, 1976, was almost equivalent to that in Chile during the three years after a military coup supported by the United States deposed and killed President Salvador Allende. The *Wasi'chu* were supporting that coup, too—and the reason was resources, mainly copper. Based on Chile's population of 10 million, the estimated fifty thousand persons killed in three years of political repression in Chile at about the same time (1973-1976) roughly paralleled the murder rate at Pine Ridge.

The struggle which resulted in so many violent deaths was also taking place within the realm of tribal politics. When Wilson sought reelection in 1974, Russell Means, an Oglala who had helped found AIM, challenged him. In the primary Wilson trailed Means, 667 votes to 511.[16] Wilson won the final election over Means by fewer than 200 votes in balloting which the U.S. Commission on Civil Rights later found to be permeated with fraud.[17]

Among the findings of the commission were the following:

•Many people who voted were not eligible because they were not enrolled in the tribe. An examination of 793 names on official voting records identified 154 ineligible voters.

• An "undetermined number" of people who voted were not residents of the reservation or did not meet the one-year residency requirement.

• No method was used to check the identity of persons who voted.

• Under Wilson's leadership the tribe did not even maintain an accurate list of enrolled members who qualified to vote.

• Poll-watchers were not used during the balloting.

• No count or record was made of the official ballots distributed during the election; election officials did not even know how many ballots had been printed.

• When Means decided to contest the election, Wilson, the only person with legal authority to call the tribal council into session to consider the contest, refused to do so.

• The Bureau of Indian Affairs refused to oversee the election or to investigate charges of fraud.

• The election was held in a climate of fear and tension. "Wilson was widely reported to have made a statement that he would run all A.I.M. members off the reservation after the election."[18] Two persons connected with the Means campaign lost their jobs, without apparent cause, immediately following the election.[19]

The Civil Rights Commission recommended a new election, which was not held; Wilson answered his detractors by stepping up the terror, examples of which are described in a chronology kept by the Wounded Knee Legal Defense-Offense Committee.

October 17, 1973: Pedro Bissonette shot to death by B.I.A. at a roadblock.

A natural leader, Bissonette had played a leading role in the Oglala Sioux Civil Rights Organization. He had been very important in bringing reservation residents together with the American Indian Movement, which until then had been urban-based. In doing so, he had earned the personal enmity of Wilson and his police force, which—when the opportunity presented itself—resulted in his death.

Fall, 1973: a group of goons shooting M-16s fired at the Little Bear House, striking seven-year-old Mary Ann and causing her to lose her right eye

January 31, 1976: Byron L. DeSersa was murdered by goons during a chase. His car, with five passengers, all unarmed, was chased by six cars of known goons. After the car wrecked, the goons prevented his getting medical attention and DeSersa bled to death.

Following DeSersa's death, federal and tribal authorities showed their usual reluctance to investigate and prosecute the case.[20] Several witnesses did the investigating for them, collecting affidavits from people near the murder scene, which was close to Wanblee on the reservation. One man, Charles D. Winters, was charged in connection with the crime, although several men had surrounded DeSersa while he was bleeding to death.

DeSersa's father, editor of a monthly newspaper in Manderson, on the reservation, demanded justice. DeSersa had often editorialized against Wilson and his policies. In June 1976 DeSersa wrote on the front page of his newspaper:

The DeSersas have waited for many...months for the U.S. attorney and his puppet grand jury to bring Byron DeSersa's killers to justice...There is [sic] only 30 days left to bring justice for the DeSersa killing. After that, then justice will come to the guilty ones...The family will not allow one of its kins to be killed without the forfeit of another. Violence may well occur again.[21]

Many of the traditionals whose families and friends had been victims of the reign of terror found legal channels closed to them. A young Indian stood on a street corner in Pine Ridge Village and told of how his brother had been run down on the side of a reservation road by a purposefully aimed car. "I know who was driving that car," he said. "If the BIA will not prosecute the killer, I will." He offered a shoulder patch with the slogan "Remember Wounded Knee" and said, "I'll have to get that goon, you understand?"

One of the goons' favorite weapons was the automobile. Officially, such deaths could be classified as "traffic accidents."

March 21, 1975: [Two] goons repeatedly ram the car in which the Eagle Hawk and White Hawk families are riding. The car is forced off the road. Edith Eagle Hawk, 37 [and] her four-month old daughter Linda killed. Earl W. Janis and Coomes [a goon] also killed.

Coomes was not the only "goon" to lose his life for revenge:

March 9, 1975: Josh Steele, a known goon, shot dead in his car near his home in Manderson.

The lack of legal redress for traditionals compounded the bloodshed. With the Wilson regime, the BIA police, and the FBI arrayed against them, where could the traditionals turn for redress? The state of South Dakota had no jurisdiction on the reservation. It would hardly have mattered if it had because William Janklow, the state's attorney general, had campaigned for office using the promise that, if elected, he would "put American Indian Movement leaders in jail, if not under it."[22]

Janklow had practiced in the Rosebud Reservation's tribal court until 1974, when he was disbarred; he did not appear to defend himself. Reservation residents reported that they had seen Janklow shooting dogs from his car and driving around the reservation with his pants off in a speeding car.

Dick Wilson not only denied sources of legal redress within the tribal administration to traditionals but also did everything he could to frustrate the efforts of those who *did* represent them—including personally supervising the beatings of legal workers and attorneys. In February 1975 traditionals invited a team of lawyers and legal workers to the reservation. After a day of investigating, the group returned to the small Cessna which had carried them to the reservation to find it riddled with bullet holes. They had to return to Rapid City by automobile, but at a highway exit near the reservation's western boundary, their car was blocked by about a dozen automobiles. Wilson and about thirty other husky men emerged and pointed guns at the legal workers, who had rolled up the windows and locked the doors of their convertible. According to affidavits sworn for a federal grand jury in Rapid City, the goons set upon the convertible and tore open its roof.

Wilson then told the goons: "Stomp 'em!" and the legal workers and attorneys were beaten and told that they would be killed if they returned to the reservation. This account was confirmed by a polygraph test administered to Roger Finzel, a Sioux Falls, S.D., attorney and to Eda Gordon, a legal worker.[23]

During the reign of terror on the Ogala Nation, the FBI studiously avoided its legal responsibility for investigating major crimes in Indian country. "The government uses Wilson in a strategy that began with the Puritans—divide and conquer," said Russell Means.[24] John Trudell, chairman of AIM during many of the events described above, said, "The Green Berets taught the Vietnamese to kill each other. At Pine Ridge, the FBI has been doing the same thing."[25]

There was no shortage of FBI agents on the reservation, however: before Wounded Knee the full-time staff of the Rapid City office had been three agents; after Wounded Knee eleven were assigned there. On the reservation, agents conspicuously walked the streets of Pine Ridge Village, looking appropriately colonial with their short haircuts and shiny black, round-toed shoes. Paramilitary gear, such as tanks and armored personnel carriers, reminders of Wounded Knee, sometimes stood on street corners.

The FBI pleaded lack of manpower when it was asked to investigate murders of Indians by Wilson's goons. Their agents were busy—very busy, it turned out, searching for prosecutable offenses among the 316,000 file classifications gathered during Wounded Knee.[26] All that gumshoe work produced 562 arrests by federal authorities charged against Wounded Knee defendants in the three years after the occupation.[27] The 562 arrests produced only fifteen convictions; five of those came on charges of "interfering with federal officers" while the convicted were trying to get through a federal roadblock on the way to Wounded Knee.

Was a record of fifteen convictions from 562 arrests a usual display of prosecutorial competence on the federal level? Or does it show that the FBI and Justice Department were using a tactic employed during the 1960s against antiwar activists and minority-group leaders which resulted in massive numbers of indictments on conspiracy and other all-purpose charges that tied up activists in court, sapping time, energy, and money from the fight against *Wasi'chu* interests? The government had been able to rely on batteries of tax-paid attorneys and FBI agents to track and prosecute such people so that, whether guilty or innocent, they pay a price.

Russell Means, for example, has been charged with thirty-seven felonies and three misdemeanors since Wounded Knee. The forty charges have come from seven state and five federal indictments. Thirty-nine of the forty charges have resulted in exoneration for him. The prosecutors' judicial batting average—even in the non-Indian courts—has been dismal.

Such legal harassment was a well-documented part of the FBI's Cointelpro, which—if we are to believe the FBI—ended in 1971. The Lakota, who looked down the gun barrel, did not believe that. Trudell called the FBI "the twentieth-century Seventh Cavalry." Norman Zigrossi, special agent in charge of the Rapid City FBI office after June 1975, concurred: he called his agents "a colonial police force."

Trudell said in a speech: "It's the same war [as that a century ago]. Nothing has changed but the faces, and the technology they use. They call it law enforcement—but law enforcement has got nothing to do with it. What they want are our land and resources. For defending ourselves, we are called violent." Trudell saw the Indian struggle as part of a much broader one, a fact recognized by the FBI, which had honed its tactics against many groups and individuals who were black, white, brown, and yellow, as well as red, in skin color. All had opposed *Wasi'chu* attempts to control their hearts, minds, and material resources for economic ends—from striking workers, to the Communist Party, to the Black Panthers and civil-rights activists, to the opponents of war in Southeast Asia, to Chicano leaders, to the Indian resistance.

All had waged a defensive struggle. And as opposition to the FBI's work as a domestic political police force (as well as to that of the Central Intelligence Agency as an international colonial police force) grew in the United States in the 1960s and early 1970s, the "intelligence" agencies turned to a war of semantics to defend themselves. In the early 1970s, as the outline of domestic and international counterintelligence operations emerged from the studies of Congressional committees, the agencies confessed their sins—and said that they had stopped committing them.[28] Yes, confessed the FBI, 238 break-ins had occurred for political purposes between 1942 and 1968;[29] yes, Martin Luther King had his telephones bugged between 1956 and the time of his death; yes, King had been presented in 1964 with tapes of personal phone calls and threatened with exposure of his personal life if he did not kill himself;[30] yes, informers had been deployed in the Black Panthers in an attempt to split the organization and get its members to kill each other;[31] yes, yes, yes, they had sinned. But Cointelpro was over, they said. The CIA developed similar defenses—confessing that 8,500 Americans had had their mail read during a two-year period in the early 1970s and that agents had tried, but failed, to assassinate Cuban Premier Fidel Castro and, frustrated, had tried to spike Castro's food with chemicals that would make his beard fall out.

Along with the grotesquely humorous and futile attempts at disabling individuals and groups that opposed *Wasi'chu* interests, the FBI condoned murder, especially of the Black Panthers. Louis Tackwood, an ex-informer for the Los Angeles Police Department, told the Senate Intelligence Committee that the FBI encouraged police assaults on Panthers, aimed especially at disrupting the party's free-breakfast program, which was gaining wide support and sympathy. "During this period, the police were shooting Panthers left and right, in cars or wherever they could catch them. They were shooting them down as fast as they could find them and the verdict would always be 'justifiable homicide,' " Tackwood testified. Survivors of a 1969 police raid in Chicago, during which Panthers Fred Hampton and Mark Clark were killed, filed a $47.7 million civil suit. Autopsies revealed that Hampton's blood contained an abnormally high level of barbiturates the night he was shot to death; the survivors testified in court that Hampton had been drugged by William O'Neal, an FBI informer who had been Hampton's personal bodyguard. FBI documents entered into testimony revealed that O'Neal was paid $30,000 for his information—including a $300 bonus after Hampton was murdered.[32] As an FBI agent told Sanford Unger, author of *FBI*, "You don't measure success in this area [counterintelligence] in terms of apprehensions, but in terms of neutralization."[33]

The colonial police force's "neutralization" of the Indian resistance began in the Wounded Knee trials. Dennis Banks and Russell Means, two AIM leaders, were charged with three counts of assault[34] on federal officers, one charge each of conspiracy and one each of larceny. Banks and Means, facing five charges each, could have been sentenced to as many as eighty-five years in prison. For several months in 1974, a year after the occupation of Wounded Knee, the defense and prosecution presented their cases in a St. Paul, Minnesota, federal court. On September 16, Judge Fred J. Nichol dismissed all the charges. The judge said that the FBI's agents had lied repeatedly during the trial while under oath, and had often furnished defense attorneys with altered documents. Judge Nichol said that R. D. Hurd, the federal prosecutor, had deliberately deceived the court. "The F.B.I.," said Nichol, "has stooped to a new low."[35]

Seven jurors who had sat through the long trial, as well as three alternates, found the government's tactics so odious that they wrote a letter to Attorney General William Saxbe, advising the government not to appeal the dismissal. Furthermore, wrote the jurors, the charges against ninety other persons scheduled to be brought to trial in connection with the Wounded Knee occupation ought to be dropped.[36] To the chagrin of the judge and jurors, the Justice Department responded by presenting Hurd with an award for "superior performance" during the trial.[37]

Judge Nichol was further angered six months later when he learned that part of what the FBI and Justice Department regarded as "superior performance" during the St. Paul Wounded Knee trial was placing an informer inside the defense camp—not only a clear violation of legal propriety, but also contrary to a sworn affidavit submitted during the trial which stated that the government had not done such a thing.[38]

When Douglass Frank Durham, who had become security director of AIM and who controlled access to Means and Banks during the trial, was confronted by AIM leaders with government documents indicating that he was an informer, he confessed.[39] Testifying before the Senate Internal Security Subcommittee, Durham attempted to rationalize his presence at the trial:

Durham: I advised the F.B.I. that I had been asked to accompany Banks to the trial, and they said they wanted to hold a very thorough briefing for me prior to the beginning of that trial.

Schultz: Did you in fact go to the trial?

Durham: Yes, I did.

Schultz: When did the trial commence?

Durham: Approximately January 8, 1974. I would like to add for the record at this point that I was advised firmly by the F.B.I. not to engage in any activity which would violate any confidences of the defense; to engage in any activities or relate to them any information which had to do with defense tactics, or any legal aspect of the operation of A.I.M. or the defense at that point.

This warning was repeatedly issued, almost monthly, by various agents of the F.B.I. during the time the trial was in session.

Schultz: On the basis of that instruction, did you attempt not to be present at the time the defense counsel and defendants were discussing the case?

Durham: As much as at all possible. If Dennis [Banks] and I were sitting in a room, and an attorney would walk in and start talking, I couldn't jump up and say, "I can't be here. The F.B.I. won't allow it."

Schultz: I understand.

Durham: I tried to ease out as rapidly and subtly as I could. However, I was the person who issued the passes for the defense attorneys to get into their rooms. I was the person who cleared the defense attorneys, to see if they were cleared to go into their own room [*sic*]. I issued the passes for the others to go into the room, and controlled all the security around them. So it was a rather ticklish situation.

I was charged with, for a short period of time, maintaining the [trial] records. I never once glanced at those records, or related any information that I overheard, relating to defense tactics, to the F.B.I.[40]

Whether Durham did or did not funnel defense information to the prosecution at the trial was never clear, but his exposure ended his usefulness to the FBI, which paid him $20,000 during a two-year period.[41] He then went to work for the American Opinion Speakers Bureau, a branch of the John Birch Society, telling already convinced right-wingers that AIM was nothing but a pack of gun-toting savages.

The FBI had first begun its infiltration of the Pine Ridge Reservation in 1974 when Tribal Chairman Dick Wilson, who faced a strong challenge from Russell Means in tribal elections, asked for the agency's help. Agents began to filter onto the reservation, joining the goon squad to harass AIM members and other traditional Lakota. The presence of the FBI heightened tensions for the traditionals, against whom the FBI often sided, with the Wilson administration.

By the end of May 1975 the FBI had sixty agents on or near the reservation. They had been transferred to the Rapid City office on what was officially explained as a "special assignment" to handle an "overload of cases." Most of them were members of SWAT (Special Weapons and Tactics) teams, trained in paramilitary operations. In early June a ten-man SWAT unit was deployed near Pine Ridge Village, where it remained for much of the month. Observers reported that the team spent much of its time practicing assaults on houses. During the same month a thousand national guardsmen were also training in the Black Hills west of Rapid City.

On June 26 Tribal Chairman Wilson signed papers officially transferring one-eighth of the land area of the reservation to the National Park Service, a move long opposed by AIM. The same day two FBI agents, Ronald Coler and Jack Williams, approached a house about fifteen miles west of Pine Ridge Village, officially looking for a fugitive. By early afternoon both of them and one Indian man—Joe Stuntz Killsright—were dead.

Just after midnight on June 27 a bulletin clacked onto newspaper teletypes around the country on the United Press International wire service:

OGLALA, S.D.—(UPI) TWO FBI AGENTS WERE AM-
BUSHED AND KILLED WITH REPEATED BLASTS OF
GUNFIRE THURSDAY IN AN OUTBREAK OF BLOOD-
SHED APPEARING TO STEM FROM THE 1973 OCCUPA-
TION OF WOUNDED KNEE.

THE OFFICE OF SOUTH DAKOTA GOV. RICHARD KNEIP
SAID THE AGENTS, ON THE OGLALA SIOUX RESERVA-
TION TO SERVE A WARRANT, WERE SUCKED INTO AN
AMBUSH, DRAGGED FROM THEIR CARS, AND SHOT UP
TO 15 TO 20 TIMES WITH AUTOMATIC WEAPONS.

THE FBI CONFIRMED THE REPORT. AN AGENT SAID:
"THIS IS A REGULAR COUP DE GRAS [sic] BY THE IN-
DIANS."

The Associated Press followed with its own bulletin at about
1:30 A.M., Central Daylight Time:

OGLALA, S.D. (AP)—TWO FBI AGENTS WERE DRAGGED
OUT OF THEIR CARS WHEN THEY TRIED TO SERVE
WARRANTS ON PEOPLE WHO WERE HOLED UP IN A
HOUSE ON THE PINE RIDGE INDIAN RESERVATION,
GOV. RICHARD KNEIP SAID EARLY TODAY.

Later UPI dispatches said that the agents had been shot
from "surrounding bunkers." The original bulletins did not
mention that an Indian had also been killed.

Most of the news reports—excepting follow-ups by staff
reporters of the *Washington Post* and *New York Times*—wildly
distorted what had actually taken place and never substantially
corrected the first accounts, despite the fact that FBI Director
Clarence Kelly later refuted many of the assertions.[42] Kelly was
in Los Angeles on July 1, where he said that the two agents had
decided June 26 to visit the Jumping Bull Compound, a few
miles east of Oglala Village, to look for a fugitive. They could
not have been "ambushed," since the visit was not planned.[43]
The FBI agents were not carrying warrants, and they were not
shot from bunkers, since the "sophisticated bunkers" were an
abandoned horse shed and a chicken coop at the base of a small
hill below the Jumping Bull house.[44] The agents were not
"dragged out of their cars and executed"; both died well over a

hundred yards from the compound, which contained a number of women and children. The agents were not shot "15 to 20 times"; together they sustained seven wounds, from six or seven bullets.[45]

To compound doubts about the first accounts of the incident, which came from Governor Kneip and State Attorney General William Janklow, the FBI refused to release the tape recording from the agents' car radio of their last words. For several days after the incident reporters were not allowed near the Jumping Bull Compound. Joel Weisman, a reporter for the *Washington Post*, attempted to visit the scene two days after the shootings. An FBI agent at a roadblock told him: "You'd better go away, for your own safety." When Weisman did not move, the agent cocked his gun. Then Weisman left.[46]

After the June 26 shooting about two hundred of the national guardsmen training in the Black Hills were put on standby alert. During the afternoon and evening of that same day several score agents from the FBI, the Bureau of Indian Affairs, and the state of South Dakota[47] converged on the Jumping Bull Compound. They rained machine-gun fire into the compound, and the occupants began to look for a way out. Using the skill at navigating the countryside on which their ancestors had depended for survival, the group threaded its way down the hill, through thick grass and into a stand of trees about a half-mile away. Near the trees the police turned their fire on the men, women, and children who had left the compound; then police advanced up the hill, peppering the house with bullets.

The day after the shoot-out Richard Held, the FBI's number-two man, arrived in South Dakota with a force of 170 heavily armed agents, who began a military-style sweep across the reservation seeking suspects.[48] The agents used M-16s, helicopters, tracking dogs, and armored personnel carriers to conduct a series of raids, during which many Lakota said that the FBI broke into homes without warrants, physically abused innocent bystanders—and found no suspects. The agents were angry and frustrated, according to residents. The FBI's tactics caused a great deal of resentment among many of the traditional Indians, who had watched their friends and relatives killed without a hint of investigative interest by the FBI, which is in charge of investigating violent crimes on the reservation. To them, it was yet another illustration that the government regarded Indian lives as cheap. The U.S. Civil Rights Commission documented these resentments in the weeks following the FBI sweep. Arthur S. Fleming, chairman of the commission, characterized the FBI's search as "a full-scale military-type invasion of the reservation." He wrote to Attorney General Edward Levi that in some cases FBI agents were searching residences on the reservation "without due process of law" and that such tactics had "created a climate of intimidation and terror on the reservation."

The working papers of the Rocky Mountain office of the commission, sent on July 22 to Levi with Fleming's letter, reported that

> in the days immediately following the incidents [of June 26] there were numerous accounts of people being arrested without cause for questioning and of houses being searched without warrants. One of these was the house of Wallace Little, Jr., [49] next door neighbor to the Jumping Bulls. His house and farm was surrounded by 80 to 90 armed men. He protested and asked them to stay off his property. Elliott Daum, an attorney with the [WKLD-OC] committee... informed the agents that they had no right to search without a warrant. They restrained him and prevented him from talking further with Little while two agents searched the house....
>
> Their [FBI] presence has created deep resentment on the part of many reservation residents who feel that such a procedure would not be tolerated in any non-Indian community in the United States. They point out that little has been done to solve the numerous murders on the reservation, but when two white men are killed, "troops" are brought in from all over the country at a cost of hundreds of thousands of dollars.

Trudell in his March 1977 speech at the University of Washington would warn non-Indian Americans not to be smug about their human rights when those of Indians are routinely violated: "Your Constitution, your Bill of Rights, is a contract between the government and yourselves. Our treaties were a 'contract' between the government and the Indian nations. Look at what's being done to us—and you can see what may happen to you."

Despite their tactics—or perhaps because of them—the FBI sweep netted no suspects on the Oglala Lakota Nation. Most of the residents were extremely cool toward the force that had been so loath for so long to investigate the dozens of violent deaths which had occurred on the reservation during previous years. The agents then carried their sweep to the neighboring Rosebud Reservation, where about a hundred of them invaded on September 5 the home of spiritual leader Leonard Crow Dog. The agents arrived in paramilitary gear, with helicopters and armored personnel carriers, during a religious ceremony.

Anna Mae Aquash, who had long been active in AIM, recalled later that a group of agents approached a tipi in which she was sitting and yelled, "FBI! Hands up!" They displayed their badges and automatic weapons in vintage movie-image fashion. Aquash was arrested and charged with possessing a firearm with an obliterated serial number. After her arrest the agents ransacked the house and several vehicles. "They seemed to enjoy smashing things in the house," Aquash later told Candy Hamilton, a Wounded Knee Legal Offense-Defense Committee worker. She said that the agents were apparently looking for weapons on which charges could be based. In their search they even overturned a dog which was lying in a corner concentrating on having puppies. They snickered loudly at an Indian woman who was praying. They kicked sacred pipes across the floor and tore eagle feathers apart. To Anna Mae, it seemed that the agents were so imprisoned in their own culture that they did not know—or care—that they had interrupted a religious ceremony and were defiling objects of great spiritual value. "They had no respect," Aquash told Hamilton.

After she was taken into custody, Aquash was told by FBI agent David Price that "we have been looking all over for you." She was believed to have been a key witness in the killing of the two agents. Although she had been in Cedar Rapids, Iowa, for the trial of a fellow AIM member on the day the two agents

died, the FBI apparently believed that she, through her contacts in AIM, would know who had killed them.[50] For two and a
half months Aquash had traveled around the reservation relatively openly, occasionally hiding with friends when she heard
that FBI agents were nearby. In the middle of July she had
been staying with friends in Oglala Village (half a dozen miles
west of the shoot-out scene) when two agents entered the home.
She hid in the attic, and then decided to leave her sweltering
hiding place. She calmly walked out the door, away from her
would-be captors.

On September 5, however, the FBI finally had a person they
believed to be a well-informed source: Price told Aquash that
the FBI was seeking information on the killers of Coler and
Williams. Aquash said she knew nothing. They pressed her.
Aquash later told Hamilton that Price told her she would be
"dead within a year" if she did not talk, to which, according to
an internal FBI document made public at a subsequent trial she
replied, "You can either shoot me or put me in jail. That's what
you're going to do to me anyway."[51]

The agents continued to press her; direct questioning turned
to ridicule. She was ordered by jail officials to remove her
medicine bundle, which carries items of great personal and
spiritual value. She refused and was taunted as if she were a
child: "Take it off. The bogeyman won't bother you."

The FBI's investigation intensified and expanded nationwide. Five days after the raid on Crow Dog's home, on September 10, eight Indians were traveling in a station wagon through
Southern Kansas along Interstate 35. Members of the group
later reported seeing yellow smoke trailing from the exhaust of
the Ford. Some of the occupants reported hearing what sound-
ed like a ticking sound. They decided to pull onto an embank-
ment.

After emptying the car, three of the eight people returned to
it. One of them, Bob Robideau, followed the ticking to the rear
end of the car. As he peered under the chasis, the car exploded.[52] Metal fragments blinded Robideau; he was taken to a
hospital in Arkansas City, Kansas. As he underwent emergency surgery, he and the seven others were arrested on

charges of possession and interstate transport of weapons with obliterated serial numbers and unregistered explosives. An Alcohol, Tobacco, and Firearms agent even attempted to question Robideau as he was being taken into surgery.

During the next twenty-four hours FBI agents, who had quickly rushed to the scene of the explosion, began to interrogate one of the passengers in the car, fifteen-year-old Mike Anderson. Anderson was questioned for almost twenty-four hours, on and off, without the aid of a lawyer, even after he asked for one. The questioning centered around RESMURS, the FBI code name for the June 26 shoot-out.

During the questioning Anderson was told that he faced a felony charge in Arizona, nine felonies in Kansas, and charges for the murders of the two agents who had died June 26 unless he told the FBI what it wanted to know. Six-foot-four-inch agent Gary Adams towered over Anderson and punctuated his demands by telling the boy he would be beaten in his jail cell unless he cooperated. The FBI thus obtained a prosecution witness for upcoming trials.

Robideau was one of four persons, all active in AIM, indicted November 25, 1975, on charges of killing the two agents at the Jumping Bull Compound June 26. The other three were Dino Butler, Jimmy Eagle, and Leonard Peltier.

A week later Robideau went on trial in the U.S. district court in Witchita, Kansas on the weapons and explosives charges. He had three co-defendants, of whom one, Bernie Nichols, was acquitted. The other two, Keith DeMarrias and Norman Charles, were given probation for three years. Robideau, convicted on nine felony counts, was sentenced to seven ten-year and two five-year sentences, to run concurrently.

Robideau was then transferred to Pennington County Jail in Rapid City, where he joined Butler and Eagle. That left one defendant at large—Peltier—and the FBI believed that it had had at least one look at him.

On November 14, eleven days before the indictments in the deaths of the agents were returned, Oregon state police stopped a van registered to Marlon Brando near Ontario, Oregon, on the Idaho border. Anna Mae Aquash, who had left South Dakota after she had not been informed of an October court appearance there (she was charged with jumping bail), was found in the van, along with Russell Redner, Kenny Loudhawk, and Ka-Mook Banks, wife of Dennis Banks, who also had been traveling in the Ford station wagon which had exploded in Kansas. The FBI stated that two other men had escaped the dragnet which had been quickly thrown up. The two, said the FBI, were Peltier and Dennis Banks. The two men, who police believed to have been Banks and Peltier, drove the van through a rain of gun fire loosed by the several dozen police and FBI agents who had rapidly assembled at the scene. The van was later found empty, half a mile from the scene of the first confrontation.[53]

At the scene the four who had been arrested were told to lay face down on the ground; this was especially unpleasant for KaMook, who was pregnant.

"Are you sure she's pregnant, or does she have an M-16 in there?" KaMook remembered an officer asking. Others poked the four with rifle barrels and ordered: "Turn your head, Indian!" "Don't talk, Indian!"[54]

Aquash was told she would be returned to South Dakota to face the firearms charge still outstanding from the September 5 raid on Crow Dog's Paradise; KaMook Banks that she would be returned to Kansas to face a similar charge stemming from the September 10 station-wagon incident. The van was searched for weapons, which could be used for charges against Redner and Loudhawk.

Finding a buck knife in Redner's belt, police arrested him for "possession of a dangerous weapon with intent to use," a felony. Loudhawk was carrying a folding pocketknife, but he was not charged for it; police charged him with possession of a .44 magnum which had been found under a seat in the van. Again the charge was "possession of a dangerous weapon with intent to use." After being held in an isolation tank at Vale, Oregon, for two days, the two men were arraigned before Nita Bellows, Ontario justice of the peace, who set bail for each of them at $100,000, although neither had prior criminal convictions. Bail was later reduced to $50,000 each in federal court.

On Sunday, the day before the arraignment, the FBI and state police had rehearsed with unusual thoroughness a plan to transfer the prisoners to Portland, Oregon. Each man was placed in a car with three FBI agents; these cars traveled in a caravan of about twenty vehicles. Police positioned themselves thirty miles ahead and thirty miles behind the caravan, moving with it through Boise, Idaho.[55]

In the car, an FBI agent from Rapid City made it very clear to Loudhawk why so much fuss was being made over them: the FBI was looking for suspects in the killings of Coler and Williams the previous June 26. "We could make a deal," said the agent. "Transportation of firearms is a very serious charge."[56] The agent gave Loudhawk a sheet of paper. Loudhawk gave it back to him, silently. They looked at each other. Kenny Loudhawk has a unique talent for rendering someone silent.

He had been told about government promises, about making deals. His great grandfather, who had fought with Crazy Horse, had seen the Treaty of 1868 signed and then broken, as the gold seekers invaded the sacred *Paha Sapa*, the Black Hills. Until January 1973, Loudhawk had had a cousin named Wesley Bad Heart Bull; he was knifed to death by a young white man near Custer, South Dakota. Weeks later the assailant was charged with second-degree manslaughter.[57] To many Indians that charge—a common one when a non-Indian kills an Indian—was worse than no charge at all; it implied that they were subhuman. Local Lakota residents asked the American Indian Movement to arrange a discussion with magistrates in Custer, to attempt to have the charge changed to first-degree murder.

On February 6 the Indians arrived at the Custer County Courthouse fo find a large group of police standing around it in riot gear. The meeting began, anyway. Bad Heart Bull's mother, Sarah, arrived late and requested entry to the courthouse. Police refused. A riot policeman grabbed her and threw her to the ground; a melee followed, and the courthouse caught fire. Sarah was charged with assaulting an officer, convicted, and sentenced to three to five years. The man who killed her son got two months' probation.[58]

Loudhawk thought about those things as he rode to Portland. Redner was thinking of his days in Vietnam, where he was
a paratrooper and where his body was peppered with shrapnel.
He was comparing the *Wasi'chu*'s war against the Vietnamese
with the *Wasi'chu*'s war against the Indian resistance. During
the next two months the two men became well known in Portland. Defense committees were formed, rallies were held, and
day after expensive, taxing day was spent in court. After
months of trial after trial both were freed. A few people said the
"system" had worked—an Indian can get justice in America.
But had justice worked? Redner and Loudhawk may bet you
$50,000 and one buck knife that it had not.

KaMook Banks, returned to prison in Kansas, gave birth to a
baby girl, whom she named Iron Door Woman, to denote the
place in which she was born. Aquash was extradited to South
Dakota—over protests that she would be killed if she was
forced to return. After she arrived, Aquash was again grilled
intensively by the FBI on the whereabouts of Banks and Peltier. Again she said she knew nothing, even after the FBI told
her that if she did not turn informer she would be declared
"incompetent" by the Bureau of Indian Affairs, a declaration
that would probably result in removal of her two children.[59]

When Aquash appeared in court to face the firearms charge,
U.S. District Judge Robert Mehrige freed her on her own recog-
nizance. As she left the state again, government agents—hoping, perhaps, that she would lead them to Banks, Peltier, or
both—trailed her to Rapid City, by car, and to Denver, by jet.
Then they lost her again.

In early December Anna Mae called her family in Nova
Scotia, Canada. Wary of wiretaps, she spoke to her sisters
Mary and Rebecca in Micmac, their native language. Anna Mae
told her sisters that she was going to be killed, that the FBI
was pressing her hard for information on the killings of Coler
and Williams, that she had been allowed to escape but feared
she would be picked up again. She asked Mary to raise her
children if she were killed.[60]

About two weeks later, around Christmas, Aquash wrote a
letter to her sisters, expressing some of the same fears. "My

efforts to raise the consciousness of whites who are so against Indians here in the States was bound to be stopped by the FBI sooner or later. But, no sweat, I'm Indian all the way and always will be. I'm not going to stop fighting until I die, and I hope I am a good example of a human being and my tribe."

On January 24, 1976, Dennis Banks was arrested in El Cerrito, California. Less than two weeks later, on February 6, Peltier was taken into custody by Royal Canadian Mounted Police in southern Alberta, Canada. Both men fought extradition; one of the grounds for the fight was the brutal treatment they expected upon their return to the Dakotas, the "Mississippi of the North." On February 24 their assertions received some forceful—but not at all welcomed—verification.

The shadows were growing along the ridges and buttes of the South Dakota badlands on that day as Roger Amiott, a rancher, inspected the fences around his ranch near Wanblee, in the northeastern section of the Pine Ridge Indian Reservation. An unusually mild wind blew over the badlands. It was about 3 P.M.; the temperature was in the 60s.

As Amiott moved from one fence to another, he noticed a human form at the base of a thirty-foot cliff, about a mile from his house. He was standing a little more than one hundred feet from Highway 44, three miles north of that road's intersection with Highway 73. Amiott moved closer. He saw a woman's body clothed in blue jeans, a jacket, and shoes. The dead woman was wearing several pieces of Indian jewelry.

Amiott returned home, where he called the Bureau of Indian Affairs police in the town of Pine Ridge, an hour's drive to the southwest.

Shortly after 4 P.M. a large group of BIA police and FBI agents converged on the area. One of the FBI agents was David Price. Neither Price nor anyone else recognized the partly decomposed body. They poked around the grass, scribbled notes, and took photographs for almost two hours, and only then was Jim Charging Crow, a veteran ambulance driver, allowed to take the body to Pine Ridge.

Shortly after 7 P.M., the body arrived at Pine Ridge Hospital. Dr. Stephen Shanker noticed that the hair of the dead woman was matted with blood. He turned her head. Blood rubbed onto his hands. Dr. Shanker did not think, he would say later, that she had died of unnatural causes.[61] He was not a pathologist, however, and autopsies were not his job. Someone else would do that.

Dr. W. O. Brown, a pathologist who performed autopsies under contract with the BIA, was called to Pine Ridge from his office in Scottsbluff, Nebraska. He arrived in his private plane the following day. After examining the body, Dr. Brown announced that the woman, still not officially identified, had died of natural causes—exposure to the brutal South Dakota winter.

Dr. Brown had been a vocal critic of the American Indian Movement and a defender of Tribal Chairman Dick Wilson. The official record states that he did not know, when he opened the skull of the dead woman, that she had been an active AIM member, a close confidant of Dennis Banks and other AIM leaders, and a veteran of Wounded Knee.

In the hospital on February 25 Dr. Brown was examining an officially unidentified body. The FBI decided that the only way to identify the woman was to sever her hands and send them to the FBI's crime laboratories in Washington, D.C. Agents on the scene reasoned that the body was too badly decomposed to take fingerprints at Pine Ridge. Ken Sayres, BIA police chief at Pine Ridge, would say later that no one had been called to the morgue to attempt identification of the body before the hands were severed.

A week after the body had been found, the woman—now missing her hands as well as her identity—was buried at Holy Rosary Catholic Cemetery, Pine Ridge.

On March 3 the FBI announced that the woman was Anna Mae Aquash, a Micmac Indian from Nova Scotia. Anna Mae's family was notified of the death March 5, but they did not believe that she had died of natural causes. At thirty-two years of age, she had been in good health and was trained to survive in cold weather. She did not drink alcohol or smoke tobacco. Her friends remembered that she had smuggled food past federal government roadblocks into Wounded Knee during another brutal South Dakota winter, almost three years to the day before her body had been found. A new autopsy was demanded.

At this point there is evidence of confusion within the FBI. On March 9 the FBI requested an order for exhumation of the body from federal district court in Rapid City. The FBI hinted that Aquash might have been killed in a hit-and-run automobile accident. When this story was discounted (body damage was not caused by an accident; she was found a hundred feet from the roadway), rumors that she had been killed by AIM members were spread.

Anna Mae's friends were angered by the rumors and decided to trace them; meanwhile, South Dakota Attorney General Janklow attempted to add to the FBI's assertions that Anna Mae might have been killed as an informer by stating that "some of the best A.I.M. members and leaders are our informants. They would be surprised to learn who our informants are and how many we have."[62] Anna Mae's friends tracked the source of the rumor to an Oglala Village resident, John Stewart, also known as Darryl Blue Lake. Anna Mae's friends suspected *his* loyalty to AIM for which he had been a chauffeur. In summer 1976 Stewart appeared as a government witness in the trial of two Indians charged with murder in the deaths of the two FBI agents killed June 26, 1975.[63]

The FBI had also called Anna Mae an informer in the affidavit filed with the request for exhumation March 9. The information in the affidavit was said to have come from Anna Mae Tanequodle, of Tulsa, Oklahoma, who later denied the FBI's version of her account.[64]

Within two days after the FBI had started the rumor, or fed it, the bureau was denying its own account. On March 11 the FBI office in Rapid City said that Aquash was not an FBI informant. The bureau kept alive the rumor that the Indian resistance may have suspected her, though, by pinning the origin of the rumor on AIM—not on the FBI's own affidavit.[65] In Rapid City Norman Zigrossi, special agent in charge, said that Aquash had never been an FBI informant; in Tulsa on February 19, according to the FBI office there, Tanequodle had told the FBI that Aquash *was* an informant. Tanequodle was identified by the FBI as a "known A.I.M. activist," who had been interviewed in Oklahoma City.[66]

In the midst of the controversy, the body was exhumed. Anna Mae's family retained an independent pathologist, Dr. Gary Peterson, of St. Paul, Minnesota. Dr. Peterson reopened the skull and found a .32-caliber bullet, which he said had been fired from a gun placed at the base of Anna Mae's neck. The bullet had not been hard to find; "It should have been discovered the first time," Peterson said. Asked about the bullet he had not found, Dr. Brown replied, "A little bullet isn't hard to overlook."[67]

Why was Anna Mae executed? And by whom? Many of her relatives and friends concluded that she had been killed "under contract" by the goon squad or by the FBI itself because she refused to cooperate in the search for the killers of the two FBI agents in June 1975. The FBI denied the charges but showed little fervor to solve the murder, especially compared with the nationwide dragnet the bureau had set up for Indian activists following the two agents' deaths.

Her friends remembered Anna Mae by her nickname, "the brave-hearted women." Nogeeshik, to whom she had been married during the occupation of Wounded Knee, remembered her as "spirit-minded and strong-willed. She wanted to make some sort of mark so that her children would not have to grow up the way she had been forced to live." Her sister Rebecca remembered Anna Mae as having had creative abilities in writing, drawing, and music.[68]

In 1960 Anna Mae, then 16, had finished junior high school and was ready to leave the enforced idleness of the Micmac Reserve. She migrated to Boston—as had a number of other young Micmac—and found factory work. During the 1960s she began Indian-rights work as the movement to enforce treaty rights and rediscover Indian heritage grew around the country. She became a teacher and worked as a kindergarten aide with black children in Roxbury. Later she helped form an Indian Center in Boston. By 1972 she was involved in AIM, an involvement which grew into full-time dedication during the 1973 occupation of Wounded Knee. She had a talent for carrying AIM's message of cultural rebirth to older and more conservative Indians who were wary of the group's militant tactics. By 1973 Anna Mae—and the rest of the occupants of Wounded Knee—had come to the notice of the FBI, as well as becoming primary targets of Tribal Chairman Dick Wilson's goon squad. Some AIM members began to carry arms—in self-defense—but they studiously avoided confrontations with the FBI. They knew of South Dakota's dual system of justice and that it was best to work outside it, if possible.

Following the discovery of Anna Mae's decomposed body, the Canadian government and the U.S. Commission on Civil Rights demanded an investigation. The U.S. Justice Department announced that it would look into the case. The murder has not been solved; the "investigation" languished in bureaucratic limbo.

If the authorities were trying to forget Anna Mae, her friends refused to let her spirit pass away. On March 14 a wind much colder than that of February 24 blew near Oglala Village. Anna Mae's body was wrapped in a traditional star quilt, and the women of Oglala mourned for two days and two nights.

Roselyn Jumping Bull remembered Anna Mae as one who had "left her home and her two kids and her good job for us. After she saw how we lived, she said she didn't want those material things, like the job, she had before. She gave herself to us." Anna Mae's two sisters joined the wake. Anna Mae's severed hands were reunited with her body, and her corpse was lowered into the earth in a snowstorm, as a hundred and fifty mourners drummed and chanted. The four colors of the Lakota stood out in the wind from poles around the grave, one at each point of the compass. Medicine men brushed the burial site, which also held the body of Joe Stuntz, with sage and prayed to the four winds.

The north wind blew bitterly cold as Anna Mae's body was lowered into the earth, where it joined the bones of Crazy Horse and Sitting Bull and the three hundred men, women, and children who had died at Wounded Knee in 1890 and the sixty Indians or more who had died in the 1970s Indian resistance.

That day again, as it had so many times in the past, the cold north wind carried the songs of death over the snow-covered grasslands, the rolling hills, and the buttes of the northern plains.

Bruce Ellison, a Rapid City attorney who had represented Aquash before she was killed, said that he, too, had been approached by FBI agents and asked for information about the deaths of Coler and Williams. He refused, but said that during one of the contacts the interviewing FBI agent told him that he "could accept" the theory that another agent or agents in the Rapid City FBI office had carried out the execution of Aquash for "personal reasons," possibly in retaliation for the deaths of the two agents.[69] Officially, however, the murder of Aquash remains unsolved, unpursued, and unprosecuted, like that of Stuntz.

The news of Aquash's death reached Peltier in a Vancouver, British Columbia, prison, where he was being held during extradition hearings. Peltier, who cited the death of Aquash as well as the numerous other unsolved murders of Indians in South Dakota as reasons why he should not be returned there, was under extraordinarily tight security. When not in court, he was held in solitary confinement, under constant guard; in court Peltier was kept in chains. But he had not been convicted of any criminal offense.

H. B. Bjarnson, the director of Oakalla Prison where Peltier was being held, characterized the AIM leader as "very sociable to talk to" but—falling prey to the stereotype of the savage— said he would "never turn his back" to the prisoner.[70] The security precautions were justified on the pretext that AIM was believed to be planning to take hostages at the United Nations Habitat conference, which was to be held in Vancouver during the middle of 1976, to exchange for Peltier's freedom. The plot was one that existed only in the minds of Peltier's jailors.

The AIM hostage "plot" in many ways resembled the fictitious "Dog Soldier memo." Both were used to justify the excesses perpetrated during the pursuit of AIM members and supporters whom the FBI wished to link to the killings of Coler and Williams.

Standing at the extradition hearing in Vancouver on May 13, 1976, Peltier told the court: "This type of selective political persecution against A.I.M. leaders is no different from the abuses of the F.B.I. against the Black Panther Party and the Socialist Workers [documented in the Rockefeller and Church Reports published the year before]. The F.B.I. has abused the court system by harassing and jailing people who resist...an attempt to push us off our reservations...what was once called worthless land [contains] valuable mineral and oil resources."[71]

Not long before, on April 16, Robideau's and Butler's cells in Pennington County Jail, Rapid City, had been searched by sheriff's officers, who said they found hacksaw blades and some partly sawed through bars. The FBI questioned the cellmates of both men and offered them money and help with their charges in exchange for testimony about an escape attempt. Two prisoners, Marvin Bragg (a.k.a. Ricky Walker), facing four rape and three burglary charges, and Carl Buckley, also charged with rape, signed statements implicating Robideau and Butler in an escape attempt. But, for the time being no charges were brought against the pair.[72]

In early May Robideau's and Butler's attorneys won a change of venue from the Eighth Circuit Court of Appeals to Cedar Rapids, Iowa. On his arrival at the Linn County Jail in Cedar Rapids, Robideau was ordered to submit to a fingerprint-ing which his attorney advised him was illegal. He refused to be fingerprinted and asked to call an attorney and the U.S. Marshal's Service. Donald Wharton, a six-foot-five-inch, 225-pound deputy sheriff, responded by kicking Robideau (who is five-foot-ten and weighs 130 pounds) in the groin and forcing him to the floor. As an attorney and another inmate watched, Wharton pounded Robideau's head against the concrete floor, then fingerprinted him forcibly.[73] The Iowa State Ombuds-man's office investigated the beating and found that excessive force had been used. That office recommended that Wharton be suspended pending criminal investigation.[74] The findings were released July 13, three days before an all-white jury found both Butler and Robideau, who had argued self-defense, not guilty of the first-degree murder charges, a recognition by the jury that a state of war existed on the Oglala Nation.

During the trial the government's case fell apart under cross-examination by William Kunstler and his associates on the defense team.[75] One government witness, who contended that Butler had confessed to him in the cell they had shared, said under cross-examination that he would say anything to get out of jail. Another said that he testified against the two Indians after the FBI had promised him a job, money, a new identity, and immunity from the charges pending against him.[76] Within a month and a half after their acquittal, charges were brought against Butler and Robideau for the "escape attempt," for which statements had been obtained during April. The charges were, however, dropped in October, after the two men had been forced to spend a few more months in jail. Butler was then freed; Robideau was held on the conviction obtained in Kansas.

The Cedar Rapids trial was unusual in another way—the defense forced the FBI's acting director, Clarence Kelly, to testify regarding his agency's pursuit of AIM. On July 7 Kunstler asked Kelly whether Cointelpro had been in existence after 1971, when the FBI announced that it had ended:

Kelly: It is not.
Kunstler: Is the program continuing under any name?
Kelly: It is not... I have made repeated inquiries to determine if there be such a possibility and not, certainly, *has anything of this type been revealed to me.*[77]

Kelly characterized AIM as "a movement which has fine goals, has many fine people and has as its general consideration of what needs to be done something worthwhile, and is not tabbed by us as an un-American subversive or otherwise objectionable organization."[78]

At another point in his testimony Kelly said that he had been informed of the distribution of the "Dog Soldier memo," which ascribed a number of fictitious terrorist activities to AIM and that he "knew of no" proof for the allegations.[79]

Kunstler queried Kelly on the truthfulness of FBI assertions that counterintelligence programs had ended in 1971. Kelly had earlier told Congress that FBI burglaries had ended in 1966, only to change that date later to 1975. Kunstler continued:

> My question is, that I assume that when you answered the question in the congressional committee you acted in good faith on the information which had been furnished you both from your central records in Washington [D.C.] and from the memories of people in the bureau. Isn't that correct?
>
> *Kelly*: It is correct.
>
> *Kunstler*: Then you later found out that the [information] which indicated that the activity in question [burglaries] had gone on for some six or seven years, at least, beyond the cutoff date you gave to Congress was contained in the files not in Washington but in New York. Isn't that correct? In a field office in New York... What I am trying to get established, essentially, is that when you testified before Congress, and said that these activities had stopped in 1966, you had testified after doing all you could to obtain the information in Washington... Isn't that correct?
>
> (Objection lodged and sustained)[80]

The point that Kunstler was trying to make was that the head of an agency such as the FBI may not always know what subordinates are doing—and, for purposes of oversight, it is probably advantageous for the head of the FBI to be able to deny knowledge of some field actions.

Out in the field, at the time of the Butler-Robideau trial, U.S. officials were presenting to Canadian counterparts two affidavits, signed by a Lakota woman named Myrtle Poor Bear, which implicated Leonard Peltier in the killings of the two FBI agents. The affidavits stated that Poor Bear had been Peltier's girlfriend, that she had heard him conspire to kill the two agents, and that she had actually seen him kill one of them. Using the two affidavits, Canadian Minister of Justice Ronald Basford concluded that evidence existed to support extradition. His application for political asylum denied, Peltier was returned to the United States on December 18, 1976.

By the time Peltier was returned to the Dakotas, he knew who had killed his friend, Joe Stuntz, on June 25, 1975. Accord-

ing to the *Cedar Rapids Gazette* of June 24, 1976, FBI agent
Gary Adams took the witness stand during the Butler-Robideau trial and "gave credit" to BIA policeman Gerald Hill for
the killing of Stuntz.

In addition, another legal struggle was developing around
the imprisonment of Leonard Crow Dog on charges stemming
from the September 5, 1975, assault on his home by about a
hundred FBI agents. Crow Dog's religious oaths forbid him to
use weapons in an offensive manner. On the day of the raid,
however, the conduct of the small army of FBI agents caused
him to fear for the safety of his relatives and guests. He picked
up a rifle but did not use it. Nevertheless, he was charged with
assault. Two days before the September 5 raid, two other men
had invaded Crow Dog's Paradise and, while Crow Dog slept,
were driven off. On the basis of the September 3 incident the
FBI had obtained a search warrant for the September 5 raid,
which resulted in Crow Dog's trial on charges of assault with a
dangerous weapon. He was convicted after a speedy trial and
sentenced to five years in prison.

Transferred unusually often and rapidly from prison to prison because other inmates regarded him as a hero, Crow Dog
was most often held in solitary. He later recalled being led into
a new prison—he was not sure which one—and watching the
inmates gather at their cell doors chanting, "Crow Dog! Crow
Dog!" In the process of being moved within six months from
prisons in Leavenworth, Kansas, to Lewisburg, Pennsylvania,
to Terre Haute, Indiana, to Rapid City, South Dakota, to
Richmond, Virginia, Crow Dog lost fifty pounds. In Richmond
a prison physician told Crow Dog that his health was failing
because he had a brain tumor. The National Council of Churches, fearing that Crow Dog was being prepared for a lobotomy,
sent two doctors to examine the spiritual leader. Both concluded that he had no brain tumor. Prison authorities later
denied that plans for a lobotomy had been the reason for the
first doctor's diagnosis. The reasons for Crow Dog's failing
health were obvious to the two independent doctors. In Terre
Haute, for example, Crow Dog had been confined to a five-foot
high solitary cell and denied exercise for three weeks.[81] After

hearing of the treatment Crow Dog had received, Amnesty International declared him a prisoner of conscience; he was paroled March 21, 1977, from federal prison in Sandstone, Minnesota, in part because of an intensive campaign on his behalf by the National Council of Churches, which contended that his conviction had been politically motivated.

During the first three months of 1977 the FBI prepared its case against Peltier, the last of the four Indians indicted for the killings of the two agents.[82] At the end of January Angie Long Visitor, a Lakota woman, was seized and taken from her reservation home without a warrant, to be held as a material witness.[83]

Before the trial opened in Fargo, N.D., federal district court in March, the prosecution's case began to fall apart. Discovery proceedings produced a third Poor Bear affidavit, dated February 19, 1976 (before the other two, dated February 23 and March 31), which said that the woman had not been on the scene of the June 25, 1975, gun battle. This information—contained in an affidavit which had not been sent to Canada—contradicted the other two statements attributed to Poor Bear.

More important, Poor Bear herself—a key prosecution witness—recanted. On April 13, out of earshot of the jury, she told the court (having been called by the defense) that she had never seen Peltier before meeting him at the trial, that she had not been allowed to read the three affidavits which bore her name, and that FBI agents David Price and Bill Wood had threatened physical harm to herself and her children if she did not sign them.

During her testimony, Poor Bear was visibly nervous. Responding to a question by defense attorney Elliott Taikeff, she said she was nervous because of her fear of the two FBI agents. Price and Wood "kept telling me about Anna Mae Aquash," Poor Bear said; Aquash's body had been found a few miles from where Poor Bear lived during the same week she was ordered to sign the first two affidavits.

At one point Taikeff asked Poor Bear: "Did Mr. Wood say anything about the subject of getting away with killing people?"

Poor Bear replied, "I think he did."

Taikeff asked, "Do you remember what he said?"

Poor Bear answered, "He said they could get away with killing people because they were agents."[84]

Judge Paul Benson refused to let the jury hear Poor Bear's testimony, ruling it "irrelevant" to the case. The next day the judge changed his mind and ruled the testimony relevant, but still would not let the jury hear it. He ruled this time that Poor Bear's testimony was prejudicial to the government's case and, "if believed," would confuse the jury. Benson had usurped the legal responsibility of the jury as determiner of fact, one of several instances in which the judge acted as an appendage for the prosecution during the trial. Prosecution testimony, which occupied the first five weeks of the case, ranged far afield from what happened on the day of the shootings. The prosecution was allowed to bring up charges against Peltier on which he had not been tried, testimony which ran counter to the federal rules of evidence. The defense's planned two weeks of testimony was shaved to two-and-a half days by Benson, who limited defense testimony to events directly connected with the shootings themselves.

The only evidence which directly linked Peltier to the killings of Coler and Williams (other than that fabricated in Poor Bear's name) came from Frederick Coward, an FBI agent, who said he had recognized Peltier from half a mile away through a seven-power rifle sight. The defense team replicated the sighting and found that the feat was impossible through such a sight at such a distance. In court defense attorneys offered to duplicate their experiment for the jury, so that its members could judge for themselves the veracity of the FBI agent's statement. Judge Benson refused the request.

"Finally," said Bruce Ellison, a member of the defense team, "we brought in someone from a gun shop, who said that any idiot could tell you that it is impossible to recognize someone— even someone you know—from a half-mile away through a seven-power sight."[85]

Three Indian juveniles also testified that they had seen Peltier at the scene. Each of them also testified, under cross-examination, that their testimony had been coerced by the FBI.

Mike Anderson, the boy who had been involved in the station-wagon incident, testified that he had been threatened with beating. Wish Draper said that he had been tied and hand-cuffed to a chair for three hours to elicit his statement. Norman Brown swore that he was told that if he did not cooperate he "would never walk the earth again."[86]

The prosecution—its eyewitness testimony impeached—linked Peltier to the use of an AR-15, a semiautomatic weapon, which was not introduced as evidence because it had been blown apart during the Kansas freeway explosion on September 10, 1975. The prosecution also asserted that Peltier's thumbprint had been found on a bag containing a gun belonging to one of the dead agents. The bag and the gun were found on November 14, 1975, after the two men police described as Peltier and Dennis Banks had escaped the dragnet near Ontario, Oregon.

Throughout the trial, the prosecution colored its circumstantial evidence with invective designed to convince the all-white jury that American Indians, and AIM members in particular, were unreconstructed savages. Prosecutors waved gory autopsy photographs of the dead agents at the jury; they also brought the agents' widows to court. Peltier was characterized as a member of a "blood-crazed bunch" in summary statements.[87]

On April 18 the jury, which had not heard most of the defense's case, returned a verdict: guilty on two counts of first-degree murder. On June 1 Benson sentenced Peltier to two consecutive life terms. Because the extradition agreement with Canada forbade it, Peltier could not be sentenced to death.

The FBI had won a rare victory, with the help of a compliant judge. Many of the agents may have celebrated, for the battle between AIM and the colonial police force had become very bitter and very personal. Agents were rarely seen without side-arms in Rapid City by early 1977. One agent said that those in the Rapid City FBI office even believed that AIM had a "hit list" and was going to assassinate the Rapid City agents, their families, and girlfriends.

As its case against Peltier began to dissolve—an appeal was pending before the Eighth Circuit Court—federal prosecutors visited Milwaukee, Wisconsin, to urge local officials to dig up a five-year-old charge against Peltier there. The charge was attempted murder of two police officers, which had resulted from a November 22, 1972, confrontation in the Texas Restaurant.

According to the complaint, officers Ronald Hlavinka and James Eccel were eating in the restaurant when Peltier confronted them and said, "You aren't laughing now, are you? I'm going to kill you!" The complaint said that Peltier pulled a .32 caliber Beretta semiautomatic pistol from his pants, repeated his threat, and aimed it at the two officers. The state's crime laboratory later found that the gun's firing pin was broken.[88]

The defense contended that the police had been making derogatory remarks about Indians. On the same evening they had beaten Peltier so severely that he could not work for three days afterward. The two officers, contended the defense, were seeking Peltier because he had just returned from an occupation of the Bureau of Indian Affairs in Washington, D.C.

On January 28, 1978, the jury returned a verdict of not guilty after thirteen hours of deliberation. Peltier was returned to the federal government's maximum-security prison in Marion, Illinois, to plan his appeal of the murder conviction.

The appeal had already been heard once—on December 12, 1977—but had to be rescheduled after one of the three-judge panel, William H. Webster, was nominated to head the FBI, posing an evident conflict of interest. The new appeal date was April 12, 1978. On that day security was tight at the Federal Courts and Customs House in St. Louis, Missouri. A few blocks to the east the Gateway Arch—symbolizing the westward expansion that had sparked the first Indian wars—threw a long shadow over the courthouse steps as Federal Protective Service guards checked employees' purses and briefcases. By 8:45 A.M. a modest number of Peltier's supporters had assembled in the courtroom on the fifth floor with members of the defense team. All bowed their heads for a ceremonial prayer.

Outside the courtroom door, at the same time, federal marshals were erecting a portable metal detector—the electronic frisk which had become a standard part of attending the trial or appeal of an AIM member. Steve Robideau (no blood relation to Bob Robideau), a long-time friend of Peltier, ended the prayer. The courtroom was cleared for the other ritual—the march through the federal metal detector.

The defense's appeal centered on two points: first, that Judge Benson had erred in not allowing the jury in Fargo access to Poor Bear's testimony; second, that the AR-15 which the prosecution had tried to link to Peltier could not be identified positively as belonging to him. William Kunstler, who argued the defense case with Michael Tigar, told the court that an October 1975 FBI report supported his assertion that a .223 caliber shell casing found near the dead agents the day of the battle could not be linked to the AR-15 that the prosecution said Peltier had used.[89] Kunstler maintained that there were as many as four AR-15s at the scene of the shoot-out.

After an hour of appeal arguments, the occupants of the courtroom filed down the courthouse steps past a covey of news reporters. Kunstler filled them in on the highlights of the arguments, as did U.S. Attorney Evan Hultman, who had argued for the prosecution.

After speaking to Kunstler, who maintained that "it is the F.B.I. which should be in the dock today, not Leonard Peltier,"[90] one television reporter motioned toward Steve Robideau. He asked Kunstler, "Can we speak to the chief?"

Robideau twisted his long braids and laughed softly. "I'm not chief of anything," he said. "Just a human being interested in human rights."

Peltier was not allowed to attend the appeal hearing. He remained in jail, where he had spent most of the past twenty-six months, waiting, waiting for justice to be done. In September 1978, Peltier's appeal was denied by the Eighth Circuit, which agreed with the defense that Judge Benson might have made some questionable judgments, but also agreed with the prosecution that they were within the judge's authority to make. The case was then submitted to the U.S. Supreme Court, and a delegation which included Robideau visited Europe to seek support for the case. Robideau returned in December with a "letter of support" from Amnesty International.

Two other AIM members—Paul Skyhorse and Richard Mohawk—waited two-and-a-half years for eventual justice as the FBI and Justice Department dragged them through the judicial system on murder charges. Their case had begun before the shoot-out at Oglala and ended, with a verdict of not guilty, a month and a half after Peltier's appeal. It was one of the longest and, by all accounts, one of the most surreal trials in recent American history.

Skyhorse and Mohawk were AIM organizers who had been implicated without a single thread of physical evidence in the October 10, 1974, murder of George Aird, a cab driver in Ventura County, California. On that night Aird was beaten, killed, and robbed of fifty cents at a place called "AIM Camp 13," which had been organized by Douglass Durham about a year before he was exposed as an FBI informant.[91]

Three people were arrested at the scene of the murder. Their bloodied fingerprints were found on Aird's taxicab, and all three had Aird's blood on their clothing. They were charged with murder, robbery, kidnap, and conspiracy.

Ten days after the murder police arrested Skyhorse and Mohawk while they were attending an Indian education conference in Phoenix, Arizona. The two men thought they had been detained as material witnesses because no charges were brought against them immediately after the arrests. They waived extradition and willingly returned to California.

In January 1975 the three original suspects were released, given jobs and other financial support, and solicited for testimony against Skyhorse and Mohawk in exchange for immunity. On their testimony the two men were indicted for the murder of Aird. Durham then went to work, under cover for the FBI, to get other members of AIM to disavow Skyhorse and Mohawk; he wrote a phony letter and pinned it to a post at AIM Camp 13 with a bundle of hair, which was said to be Aird's "scalp." Durham then leaked a story to local news media which asserted that the murder of Aird was the start of an anti-white campaign during the bicentennial year—a foreshadowing in form and content, of the "Dog Soldier memo" of a year later. On another occasion Durham posed as an Indian psychiatrist, who testified at a sanity hearing for Skyhorse that he was irrational and dangerous.

From the beginning of the trial Skyhorse and Mohawk said that their indictments were a politically motivated attempt to discredit AIM.[92] Pretrial proceedings lasted two-and-a-half years; the trial itself thirteen months. It produced seventeen thousand pages of transcript—the longest trial in California history. On May 24, 1978, a jury of four men and eight women returned a verdict of not guilty. Immediately after the acquittal—following the pattern of other trials—other charges were levied; Mohawk was accused of possessing heroin while being held in a Ventura County jail.[93]

Prolonged by a judge whose paycheck was to be stopped by retirement after the trial ended, the ordeal of Skyhorse and Mohawk lasted a full ten months after the prosecution offered a time-served, *nolo contendere* plea bargain, which essentially meant that the two-and-a-half years the men had spent in jail by that time would have satisfied the prosecutor. This offer came after the government's two main witnesses fell apart on the stand. Judge Floyd Dodson refused to accept the plea-bargain agreement after Skyhorse and Mohawk agreed to the prosecutor's offer!

During the next ten months the judge kept getting his paycheck, and California taxpayers kept footing the bill, as the trial droned on until the record led to no conclusion other than not guilty. Ramona Bringas, a former cellmate of two of the first three persons arrested, told the jury that the two women had confessed to the murders after receiving immunity and that they had testified against Skyhorse and Mohawk in exchange for that immunity on instructions of the district attorney.[94] Evidence was introduced indicating that at least six other inmates had heard the two women confess.

At the end of the three-and-a-half-year ordeal Indian activists counted the case a victory: the jailing of innocent persons on such a pretext would undoubtedly help organizing efforts. Ironically, it appears that the FBI's strategy had been to decimate the growing AIM organization in the Los Angeles area, which contains the largest urban-Indian population in the United States.[95]

The use of the courts to keep traditionalist American Indians from asserting treaty and other rights to sovereignty continues as this book is being written; the cases discussed here are only the more prominent of many. What has come to be called the "new Indian wars" do have a rationale. If AIM leaders were not tied up on criminal prosecutions, they would be pressing treaty claims to land which contains rich stores of fossil fuel and mineral wealth. As Peltier wrote from prison,

we may have been happy with the land that was originally re-served for us. But continually over the years, more and more of our land has been stolen from us by the Canadian and American governments. In the late 19th century, land was stolen for eco-nomic reasons...We were left with what was believed to be worthless land. Still, we managed to live and defied [the] wish to exterminate us. Today, what was once called worthless land sud-denly becomes valuable as the technology of white society ad-vances. [That society] would now like to push us off our reserva-tions because beneath the barren land lie valuable mineral re-sources.[96]

During 1977, as Peltier went to trial in Fargo, several multi-national energy companies were prospecting in the Lakota's sacred *Paha Sapa*, as had gold seekers a century before, for the sine qua non of the national security state—uranium. Control of AIM, as well as of the Lakota tribal organization, had become vital to the interests of that state because from the homeland of Crazy Horse and Sitting Bull could come a treaty claim to the Black Hills, which have never been legally ceded.

II

Resources:
The Reason for the System

5

How to Steal a Continent, Continued

Sell land? As we sell air and water. The Great Spirit gave them in common, to all.
—Tecumseh[1]

Some rob you with a gun; some with a fountain pen.
—Woody Guthrie

Black Elk, a Lakota medicine man, was eleven years old in the summer of 1874. His band was camped on Split-toe Creek in the Black Hills of the Lakota Nation, when he remembers the band breaking camp and moving deeper into the hills. Scouts had told the band that many soldiers had invaded the *Paha Sapa* (literally, "hills that are black"), the holy land of the Lakota.[2]

"Afterward, I learned that it was *Pahuska* ["Longhair": Gen. George Armstrong Custer] who had led his soldiers into the Black Hills that summer to see what he could find. He had no right to go in there, because that country [is] ours. Also the *Wasi'chu* had made a treaty with Red Cloud [the 1868 Ft. Laramie Treaty] that said it would be ours as long as grass should grow and water flow. Later I learned too that *Pahuska* had found there much of the yellow metal that makes the *Wasi'chu* crazy.... Later he got rubbed out for doing that," Black Elk recalled.[3]

From the Lakota point of view, General Custer richly deserved what he got at Little Big Horn in 1876. A people who had given so much to the *Wasi'chu* in peace, by treaty, was refusing to part with its treaty-guaranteed holy land, the Black Hills. The Lakota didn't prize the rugged hills for their gold. "Our people knew there was yellow metal in little chunks up there, but they did not bother with it, because it was not good for anything," Black Elk said.[4] They prized the *Paha Sapa* for its natural beauty. It was an excellent place to hunt, to camp, to meditate and receive visions.

Nevertheless, Custer's confirmation that gold lay in the Black Hills started a settlement rush. In 1875 four hundred U.S. Army troops and seventy-five wagons accompanied a geological expedition into the hills; by the time Custer breathed his last, several thousand gold-hungry miners were scouring the Lakota's sacred hills. Throughout the remainder of the 1870s, the U.S. federal government tried to bring the invasion into legal conformity with the treaty through lease or sale of the hills, proposals that, in Black Elk's words, were backed up with the implicit threat that if an agreement were not signed, "the *Wasi'chus* would take that country anyway."[5]

The Lakota did not sign the hills away, and the *Wasi'chu*—the military-industrial complex of the time—fulfilled their threat. They took the hills anyway, prompting the Lakota and Cheyenne to "paint their faces black." One result of those battles has been a remarkably well-remembered U.S. military debacle. Black Elk was surprised at the lack of training the *Wasi'chu* gave their cavalry: "They kept together, and when they came on, you could hardly miss them."[6]

Even as miners were extracting immense wealth from the *Paha Sapa*, as a large tourist industry was building up there, as Mount Rushmore was carved with the likeness of four Great White Fathers—the Lakota refused to sign the hills away, and have continued to do so throughout the century. The United States's offer, through the Indian Claims Commission, still stands; it is $17.5 million, plus interest, a fraction of the value that the *Wasi'chu* monetary system places on the mineral wealth which has been extracted from the hills.

That the treaty claim to the Black Hills ought to be pressed has been one of the ideas advocated by the American Indian Movement. Such a claim, however, would have to be brought in the name of the Oglala Lakota government if the U.S. government were to be legally forced (through its own system) to recognize it.

Such considerations are important for the *Wasi'chu*, in part because of the antiquity of most of the treaties. Treaty-making was ended by Congress in 1871, through a rider of dubious legality which was added to an appropriations bill. The Fort Laramie Treaty, which guaranteed the Black Hills (as well as the rest of what is now the western half of South Dakota) to the Lakota was concluded three years after the Civil War ended, just as the United States was moving from a predominantly agrarian, Jeffersonian economic base into a period of rapid industrialization. At the time the treaty was signed, what had been guaranteed the Lakota was believed to be part of the Great American Desert. The *Wasi'chu* had allowed the Indians what, at the time, was believed to be land of little worth.

General Custer's discovery of gold was only the first indication that the treaty signers had been wrong. Within the next hundred years the Lakota Nation became immensely valuable to *Wasi'chu* interests as technology allowed the development of dry-land farming methods and as rising industrialism created an appetite for natural resources which, at the time the treaty was signed, had little or no value.

In 1868 uranium was not even part of the expert geologist's vocabulary. By the early 1950s, with the proliferation of nuclear weapons and plans for power generation by means of what was then called the "peaceful atom," that ignorance had changed. The Black Hills hold uranium as well as gold; the nuclear fuel was mined in relatively modest quantities in the southern Black Hills for twenty years before the early 1970s, when the demand for armaments and power-plant fuel began to grow rapidly.

A hundred years after General Custer breathed his last in the midst of a gold rush he had started, another geological survey team entered the Black Hills and returned—as had Custer's expedition—with news of mineral wealth. In January 1977 the U.S. Geological Survey announced the discovery of uranium-bearing Precambrian rocks near Nemo, southwest of Rapid City. The news began a rush for claims. During the two months after February 15—deep snow and subzero cold had kept prospectors out of the hills during the preceding month—more than twelve hundred location certificates were filed in the area, most of them by such large corporations as Johns Manville, American Copper and Nickel, and Homestake Mining Company.[7] Homestake had been one of the first and most powerful companies involved in the century-old gold rush; a fortune made in the Black Hills later helped buy William Randolph Hearst a national newspaper chain.

News items in the Rapid City *Journal* charted the new "uranium rush":

A clerk in the Meade County register of deeds office said: "We had approximately 40 locations filed from 1963 through 1976. So far this year [1977] we've had 493"....A count in the same office of Lawrence County, home of the world-famous Homestake Gold Mine...showed 20 locations filed last year, 606 this year.[8]

Some companies had beaten the rush; the Tennessee Valley Authority (TVA), which had licenses to build seventeen nuclear-power plants, already had acquired a processing plant and 65,000 acres of leases in the Black Hills, plus another 35,000 acres just west of the Wyoming border. Union Carbide Corp. also had acquired sizable holdings and—as the claim rush of early 1977 was taking place—had been telling federal and state officials that it was planning to strip-mine for uranium beginning in late 1979 or 1980, depending on the time needed for approval of various permits.[9] The acquisition of these mining properties had taken place as the Federal Bureau of Investigation had become more and more deeply involved in legal prosecutions of the Oglala traditionals and AIM members who were pressing the Pine Ridge tribal officials for assertion of the treaty claim to the Black Hills and surrounding areas.

During the last two weeks of May 1977, as Leonard Peltier awaited sentencing for the alleged murder of two FBI agents, TVA told federal and local officials, ranchers, and businessmen in the southern Black Hills town of Edgemont that it had "mapped extensive mineral reserves and intends to be mining and milling in the area tentatively by 1981."[10] At that meeting the public was told that since 1974, when TVA acquired the properties, six thousand test holes had been drilled and five million to six million pounds of uranium identified. Strip mining was being considered, along with solution mining, a method by which liquid-borne chemicals are injected into the ground (and the water table) to dissolve uranium-bearing ores.

The uranium rush in the Black Hills was only part of an intensified search for the death rock throughout the U.S. West, much of it on Indian lands, which, according to a 1975 Federal Trade Commission report, hold two-thirds of the uranium under the U.S. government's self-defined jurisdiction; this is 16 percent of the country's uranium reserves considered worth recovering at 1975 prices. The increased exploration was taking place against a backdrop of weapons stockpiling and anticipated construction of nuclear power plants, all of which were contributing to an inflationary rise in the price of uranium. In 1958 a pound, in rod form (ready to be installed in a power plant), cost between $25 and $30; it cost between $60 and $65 in 1968, and between $115 and $135 in early 1978.

Uranium, which had not even been known to exist when the Fort Laramie Treaty was signed, had become the new gold of an energy-scarce economy; on top of that, as the essential material for nuclear weapons, it has become the sine qua non of the national security state. To traditional Indians, AIM included, uranium was worse than useless (which had been Black Elk's indictment of gold); it was a harbinger of death and destruction—not only of the beautiful and sacred Black Hills but also of life as it is known on the earth. Gold is mined from relatively small areas; uranium is often strip-mined. Gold is used for works of beauty; uranium is used for works of death, whether purposeful (in weapons) or potential (in nuclear-power plants). A nuclear reactor of average size produces five hundred pounds of plutonium 239 a year. One pound of that, sufficiently dispersed, could produce lung cancer in every person on earth. Several nuclear installations, including that at the federal reservation in Hanford, Washington, have reported radiation leaks during the last decade; the United States has no safe place to put the thirty thousand tons of plutonium waste that the *Wasi'chu* wants to generate from existing and planned nuclear plants during the next forty years.[11]

And so it wasn't pure hyperbole that led traditional Indians of the 1970s to compare Peltier and other jailed AIM leaders with Crazy Horse, who had led their ancestors against the first invasion of the Black Hills during the 1870s. In both cases the object of the *Wasi'chu*'s physical oppression was to remove an obstacle to exploitation of natural resources, seizure of land, and the destruction of the Lakota people, whose culture has been intimately related to that land for untold years. In the middle of 1978 *Akwesasne Notes*, a journal for "native and natural peoples," published in the Mohawk Nation, envisioned this future:

> The actual process won't be as spectacular as the Trail of Tears or the Sand Creek Massacre. There probably won't even be much protest by the liberal groups in the East, because the process will

take place behind a veil of legal subterfuge and under cries for the patriotic need to develop energy and mineral resources. But the results—the long-range results—will be virtually the same. Indian peoples will be displaced, obliterated and slowly choked in the rising dust and smoke of a new kind of gold rush. That, unfortunately, is the prospectus for the future.[12]

Evidence of this prospectus was beginning to emerge in South Dakota in the late 1970s, as the FBI bore down on advocates of Indian treaty rights. Van Linquist, director of South Dakota's water-quality program, warned that leaching of dissolved materials from uranium mining into the water table could make groundwater in some areas unfit for human or animal use;[13] the United States Forest Service listed the areas which have been staked out for uranium mining as underground-water recharge areas for large areas to the south and southwest of the Black Hills.[14]

In the typical fashion of the *Wasi'chu* however, resources were marked for exploitation before consideration was given to the effects of such taking on people and nature. During 1975— the year of the most intense FBI activity on Pine Ridge—the U.S. Geological Survey was compiling an inventory of reservation resources at the request of the Bureau of Indian Affairs. Two years later the air force lent the Environmental Protection Agency two U-2 aircraft for resource inventories in the area, as well as in Montana and Wyoming.[15] At the same time the FBI was conducting intensive aerial mapping of Pine Ridge Reservation settlements, apparently gearing up for new resistance to plans for resource exploitation by Indian people there; the full-time staff at the Rapid City FBI office was raised to twenty-eight agents, compared with eleven three years earlier, before the 1975 gun battle at Oglala.[16]

By June 1978 there were 700,000 acres of state-owned land under lease for exploration of energy resources in South Dakota's six westernmost counties. Among the leasees were several household names, such as Exxon, Union Carbide, TVA, Homestake, and Peter Kiwit & Sons.[17] The figure of 700,000 acres excludes Indian and federal land, as well as that which is privately owned, in the Black Hills-Rapid City area and on Pine Ridge Reservation.

On the reservation itself, the Geological Survey was drawing up the menu for resource exploration and exploitation exactly a century after the invasion of the Black Hills brought about Custer's Last Stand. The report called Pine Ridge "an attractive prospecting area" for oil and gas, noting that several geological formations which produce these two resources in neighboring areas pass through the reservation. The report also said that the sedimentary section (the usual repository of oil and gas) was 3,000 to 4,500 feet thick under the reservation land, which is relatively thin, but that "the numerous potential pay zones [and] the relatively shallow drilling depths" make the land attractive for oil and gas exploitation.[18] Moreover, uranium had been found in water samples from wells and springs on the reservation, and a "wide area" could be explored with a good chance of finding uranium "in sufficient amounts to suggest possible other deposits." In short, the report indicated, the reservation "offers exploration targets for potentially commercial amounts" of uranium.[19] The report was issued in 1976, the year following a decision by Dick Wilson, tribal chairman, to sign away one-eighth of the reservation's land area, which contained locations referred to as potential sites for oil, gas, uranium, and gravel. The deed changed hands in the Interior Department, from the Bureau of Indian Affairs, where Indian land is legally held in "trust," to the National Park Service. The alienation of the area, known as the Sheep Mountain range, came the same day that the two FBI agents and AIM activist Joe Stuntz were killed not far from the reservation village of Oglala—June 25, 1975.

The connection between the repression of AIM by means of the legal system and the corporate desire for the newly valuable resources on which the Lakota had a potential treaty claim was presented by *Akwesasne Notes*:

> It is becoming clearer and clearer why A.I.M. has been targeted, and remains targeted by groups like LEAA [Law Enforcement Assistance Administration] which lists A.I.M. as one of the five most dangerous groups in the United States....It is because of an intensive effort underway by powerful elements in U.S. society to obtain energy, water and mineral resources that are on Indian lands.[20]

Russell Means, most of whose last decade of life has been spent in court defending himself against criminal indictments brought by the federal government and the state of South Dakota, was making similar connections in his speeches to groups on his native nation, where he nearly won the tribal chairmanship in 1974. He was referring to a study of power-industry development on the northern plains issued in 1976 by the Bureau of Reclamation: [21]

> Six hundred thousand non-Indians are going to move in over a 30-year period and take the coal from Wyoming, Montana and the Dakotas, the talconite iron ore and the uranium that is in the gunnery range[22] which Dick Wilson gave away. The natural gas and water ... is going to be taken out of the land over the next 30 years from the Lakota territory. Do you know why they are talking about 30 years? Because there is only enough water in the Missouri River, the Powder River, the Platte and the underground Fort Madison table to remove resources for 30 years. Then the underground water, the coal and the iron will all be gone.... So what is left for us? Filthy air, no water ... we are still going to be living in a desert![23]

And so the *Wasi'chu*, who once avoided the Lakota territory because it was believed to be part of the Great American Desert, now propose to make of a rich and beautiful land an energy cemetery.

South Dakota has been during the last decade the center of the physical repression of Indian assertions of their claims to land and resources. It is not, however, the only part of the country where the *Wasi'chu* are seeking—by one tactic or another—lands once adjudged useless which were marked off for Indian nations and tribes by the 371 treaties negotiated with the United States government. As outlined in chapter 3, physical repression is a last resort of a sophisticated subjugation system; across the country various tactics are being used as part of the general strategy, which is to force all Indians to forsake their lands and cultures and remove themselves from reservation lands. The "final solution" of the "Indian problem" (seen from the Indian perspective, the *Wasi'chu* problem) takes many forms. Only rarely is the battlefield a Wounded Knee; more often it is a government office, a courtroom, or Congress. Most of the rest of this book will be devoted to delineating the continuing attempts to alienate Indians' resources, usually by bureaucratic methods or, as Woodie Guthrie said, by the pen. But, as we shall see, Indian nations are making attempts to regain treaty land and resources stolen long ago.

At the edge of Seattle's black community is one of Lake Washington's most beautiful beaches. It is named after an Indian chief who died because he led his people against repeated violations of a United States government treaty a century ago. Today, few people in Seattle know the name Leschi, except as a beach. The irony is that on these shores in 1856, in an episode of history that the *Wasi'chu* have tried to forget, Chief Leschi was hanged after he had led the Nisqually tribe on a brief but successful war against the United States Army.

After that war the tribe was confined to a 4,700-acre reservation near the southern end of Puget Sound. In 1918 the army came calling again. It wanted to build a base and wanted Nisqually land for it. All but 757 acres were seized by the army and incorporated into Fort Lewis.

In the early 1970s the army wanted to take what was left of the Nisqually land and turn it into a firing range and training ground. In South Dakota General Volney Warner was facing the Indians and Wounded Knee. Major General John Henlon, then commander of Ft. Lewis, suggested in a confidential memorandum that in view of the Wounded Knee "controversy" the land grab be postponed until Indians faded from the media. In 1976 General Warner was commanding Fort Lewis, and he was ready to take the land. The army apparently could not wait to try out the new acres, so they lobbed military shells over Indian homes and buzzed fishermen at work with helicopters and sent tanks and trucks down Nisqually roads. In a memorandum that was supposed to be confidential, the army cautioned against "premature disclosure" of the land grab. The documents also urged caution because the land seized in 1918 had been grabbed by Pierce County and given to the army, and Pierce County could legally take it back.

The army is not short of artillery ranges in the state of Washington. There is one in the Yakima Valley, within earshot of the major settlements on the Yakima Indian Nation. In fact, the army had often fattened its artillery-range inventory at Indian expense; during World War II one-eighth of the Pine Ridge Reservation was condemned for a bombing range. The Lakota are still trying to get the land back.

The Nisqually had greeted the invaders by giving up two million acres of land in 1854 and 1855 under military pressure. In 1918 the army left them 757 acres. Had unfavorable publicity and Indian resistance not stopped the army in 1976, even that might have been snatched.

On July 4, 1976, the bicentennial of the nation which subjugated her people, Yvonne Wanrow decided to get away from the "celebration" by visiting a twenty-five acre tract of land that had been a gift of her mother. She took her children to clear the land, on which she was planning to build a home.

After she arrived, Wanrow was confronted by a farmer and his son.[24] Asked what she was doing there, Wanrow replied that she was going to build a house. "The hell you are," the farmer said. "I've got an iron-clad lease, and it is signed by the BIA." Lease? Wanrow hadn't signed any lease. The land (120 acres) was owned by sixteen Indians, Wanrow included.

"Get off," the farmer said. "I don't want to threaten you or get violent, but I have a lease on this land. You can't live here."

"My mother owned about twenty-five acres of this land, and she did not sign any lease agreement. I own it now, and I haven't signed anything. I looked at the lease at the agency, and only four people from this particular allotment signed it. That is not even a majority, so I don't think your lease is valid," Wanrow replied.

The man said, "Some signed and the superintendent signed for the rest."

After he told her to leave again, Wanrow said, "We will have to wait and see."

"We won't wait and see nothing," the farmer said. "I don't want to be violent, but I will if you don't leave."

"It's the same old story; the white man moves in and begins pushing Indian people around," she replied.

The BIA later admitted the lease was invalid. "For all I know, they could be arranging for another lease without my signature. That is the way they do things," Wanrow said.

Wanrow's experience is an example of modern-day land theft in Indian country. The difficulties she experienced while trying to spend a quiet afternoon on her land illustrate one way in which the BIA has taken advantage of certain problems created by government policy to deny Indians use of their land. When allocation took place, it created an enormous inheritance problem; as land has been passed from generation to generation, ownership has become fragmented. The BIA, purportedly to "simplify" its leasing arrangements, often signs away leasing rights without asking landowners. This is but one abuse of the "guardian-ward" relationship which continues today.

Wary of promises that the government would protect them and their land base, Indians in the 1970s began to take action of their own to regain lost land. At times they went to court or appealed through other administrative channels. When the bureaucracy attempted to paper-shuffle their appeals out of existence, Indians took more direct action to attempt to stop the extralegal drift of their land toward *Wasi'chu* power and money.

Members of the Puyallup Nation were among those who asserted the validity of their treaty rights. By the 1950s urban sprawl from the city of Tacoma, Washington, had swallowed all but thirty acres of the Puyallup Nation. Those acres were reserved for an Indian hospital; which the federal government decided to close in 1954. The land was not given back to the Puyallup, but was declared "surplus" and taken by the state in 1959 for a juvenile-detention facility. The Puyallup appealed through governmental channels for more than a decade before October 1976, when members of the tribe and several dozen supporters walked in and declared the place "Chief Leschi Memorial Hospital." For a week the well-organized group continued the occupation, standing legally on their treaty rights. One week of direct action accomplished what a decade of quiet legal appeals had not—the federal government was forced to admit that the land had been given to the state illegally and to make plans to return it to the Puyallup.

Across the continent, in the northeast during the same period several court suits were asserting Indians' rights to land which had been taken in violation of federal law almost two hundred years ago. The largest of the suits, brought by the Passama-quoddy and Penobscot Nations of Maine, originally asserted rights to almost two-thirds of that state.

In Massachusetts the Wampanoag, who had helped the Pil-grims survive their first winter in the New World and had attended the first Thanksgiving, were seeking 17,000 acres in the town of Mashpee on Cape Cod; another group of Wam-panoag in Gay Head, Martha's Vineyard, were asserting con-trol over 5,000 acres on the island. In Rhode Island the Narra-ganset claimed 3,200 acres in Charlestown; in Connecticut the Schaghticoke wanted return of 1,300 acres in Kent, and the Western Pequot were seeking 1,000 acres in Ledyard. And in New York the Oneidas had filed suit claiming 300,000 acres between Syracuse and Utica.

Most of the suits were based on the Non-Intercourse Act of 1790, which held that land transactions between Indians and non-Indians could not take place without consent of Congress.

The Passamaquoddy suit resulted from the discovery in 1957 by John Stevens, tribal chairman, of old and brittle documents in the home of an elderly woman in northeastern Maine. The documents included a treaty signed in 1794 between the Passa-maquoddy and officials of Massachusetts, which at the time included Maine. The treaty had not been approved by Con-gress. Among the documents were letters from President George Washington thanking the Passamaquoddy for aid against the British during the Revolutionary War.

During the 1950s and 1960s the small reservation left to the Passamaquoddy had been shrinking slowly from the same pres-sures which have reduced many Indian land holdings.[25] U.S. Route 1, had been built through Passamaquoddy land without tribal permission, and scores of non-Indians had simply moved onto the land on either side of the road without asking the tribe or paying for the land. Stevens estimated that at least 6,000 acres had been nibbled away from the small reservation since it was established in 1794.[26] In 1957 Stevens took his old documents to the state attorney general's office in Augusta. An aide said that the official was "too busy" to see him.

For the next nine years Stevens tried to find a local attorney who would represent the tribe in the face of the inevitable hostility that would arise from the non-Indian community. He failed. In 1966 an Eastport attorney, Donald Gellers, agreed to represent the Passamaquoddy, but the next year Gellers was arrested and convicted on state drug charges, a felony at the time. In 1970, after the tribe was forced to fire Gellers because of his conviction, Tom Tureen was hired. Tureen had worked in a BIA boarding school in Pierre, S.D., in 1964 and had become interested in the cradle-to-grave legal control which the federal government exercises over recognized Indian nations. He later remarked, "On the reservation I saw the extent of control the government had over all aspects of tribal life."[27]

Tureen's first legal problem was to establish in court that the Non-Intercourse Act of 1790 did, in fact, apply to the Passamaquoddy. The tribe had been disinherited before the federal Indian system was set up in the nineteenth century, and therefore it was not recognized as a tribe by the federal government. In 1975 federal district court in Maine affirmed Tureen's claim that the federal government's trust responsibility applied to the Passamaquoddy. Later that year, the court ordered the Justice Department to defend the Indians' land claim against the state of Maine.

Tureen and the Passamaquoddy went into court not only against the state but also against some of the United States' largest paper and forest-product companies, which own half the state, including most of the remote, wooded areas to which the Indians had asserted title.

On December 24, 1975, the United States Court of Appeals for the First Circuit in Boston affirmed the district court ruling. The state did not appeal to the U.S. Supreme Court.

By the summer of 1976 the suit was beginning to have widespread effects in Maine, where the statehouse in Augusta had been built in 1832 with money from the sale of Indian land taken in the treaty of 1794. The state's defense was resting on the legal doctrines of "adverse possession" and "laches," which hold that original owners of land cannot assert claims—even if their land was seized illegally—after a long period of time has passed. These doctrines were discounted on June 23, 1976, in Rhode Island Federal District Court, where the Narraganset land claim was being heard. Judge Raymond Pettine held that the state doctrines of laches and adverse possession were "completely futile" because state laws could not supersede federally created treaty rights.

For quite some time the *Wasi'chu* power elite of Maine had been treating the Indians and Tureen with contempt when they tried to arrange an out-of-court settlement; the Passamaquoddy stated over and over that they were not pursuing the matter to cause suffering to non-Indians, but merely to regain enough of their land to enable them to build a viable economic base.[28] The large land owners and their allies in the state government ignored them, going instead to Congress to attempt to have the Non-Intercourse Act abrogated.

Following their string of court victories, the Passamaquoddy and Tureen again indicated their willingness to settle. "Only through the recovery . . . of a land base can we regain the independence and importance which the Non-Intercourse Act was designed to guarantee us, and which we would possess today if the law had not been violated," Indian leaders and Tureen wrote to Maine Governor James B. Longley.[29]

The state government responded as if it were a wagon train attacked by "hostile" Indians. The attorney general supported national legislation which would abrogate the Non-Intercourse Act. Backed into a corner, the state—and the large landowners—had no other alternative.

In Congress the allies of the landowners were preparing to argue that the Congress could ratify the treaty of 1794 ex post facto and meet the terms of the Non-Intercourse Act.[30]

By the end of February 1977 Justice Department attorneys

had determined that the Indians had a valid legal claim to at least five million acres of forest land in northern Maine. At the same time the Passamaquoddy laid aside their title claim to two million acres, most of it held by small landowners on the densely settled Maine coast.[31] The Passamaquoddy and the Justice Department were concentrating on the larger landowners out of the Indians' desire not to cause undue hardship to residents of the state, and out of a legal consideration—filing claims against every landowner would involve a huge amount of legal posturing and paperwork. The Justice Department indicated that unless an out-of-court settlement was reached by June 1, 1977, it would file test lawsuits against "a limited number of large landholders," the same ones who were appealing to Congress to abrogate the legal basis of the claims.[32]

The Indian nations of the Northeast had thus taken a huge step toward recovering part of the land which was taken from them. Like many other Indian nations, they had plans which would allow them to escape from the system of physical, economic, and political colonization that had kept them in bondage and poverty. They were looking toward a future in which the government would no longer tell Indians what was good for them—when Indians would control their own destinies and, with that control, win the freedom to live as they saw fit. The escape from colonization is the basis of self-determination—and economic sovereignty on an adequate land base is one basis of self-determination.

Although the two Maine tribes seemed on the verge of regaining at least part of their treaty lands, the *Wasi'chu* were pressing Congressional proposals to ratify the treaties which justified the Indians' claim—almost two hundred years after the fact. Moreover, in another case a potentially destructive rationale for land theft was developing. The Wampanoag by mid-1978 had lost their claim to 16,000 acres in Mashpee, Massachusetts. United States District Court Judge Walter Skinner upheld a federal jury's March 24, 1978, decision which ruled that the Wampanoag were not legally a tribe when they filed suit in 1976 and therefore were not entitled to pursue their claim under the Non-Intercourse Act. The jury's verdict stated that since the tribe had lost most of its language, religion, traditional government, customs, and traditions, its members no longer were Indians. In other words, if four centuries of assimilation have done their work, its targets have no grounds on which to claim the treaty rights guaranteed their ancestors.

Such a ruling was watched very closely in the West, where many Indian nations—with the advantage of 250 to 300 fewer years of exposure to the *Wasi'chu*—were struggling to maintain the cultural, political, and economic traditions of their ancestors. Convinced that the basis of their community lay in their common land base, the Indian nations of the West had, in large measure, turned against ruinous resource development. This posture laid the groundwork for an intense conflict with some very powerful corporate interests. The object of the conflict, as usual, was land and resources.

6

The Navajo
and National Sacrifice

My sheep are dying. Their noses bleed. The baby goats do not grow up ... This is the biggest, baddest disease ever visited on mankind.
  —Emma Yazzie

As Emma Yazzie approaches her hogan from Shiprock on Highway 550, the sky gradually changes color from the familiar, pastel-turquoise blue of the surrounding countryside to a murky, hazy brown.

Driving the sheep up a hill below her hogan, Emma might have called the muddy sky above her a Chicago sky—if she had ever been to Chicago. But she has never been even as far as Tucson or Phoenix, the industries of which have cloaked her home, her sheep, and herself within a deathly pale of smoke.

Emma Yazzie is near 70; ever since she was two years old, she has lived here, where during the early 1960s four smokestacks near her hogan began to billow the smoke signals of death. The four stacks belonged to the Four Corners Power Plant, the largest single source of electric power—and pollution—in the western United States. Since they were built, consumption of electricity in the United States has doubled, and brethren of the Four Corners plant have begun to appear nearby. Throughout all her years Emma Yazzie's consumption of electricity has been constant: zero.

Chiseled by the wind, her lined face exudes a rugged strength, the march of countless days spent herding sheep in the blazing sun of summer and the blizzards of winter. It is a hard face—weathered as if by sand—and a kind face. A smile etches a valley into it when she talks of the past, of clear skies and fat sheep and goats which gave milk.

Emma wears another face when she describes the power plant. She has words for the plant, melodic Navajo words, which translated mean: "This is the biggest, baddest disease ever visited on mankind."

For thousands of years Emma's forebears woke up to a turquoise sky. Now, she wakes to a brown sky smelling of burning dirty clothes and old tires. Some days the smoke funnels up the hill, over the poisoned lake and the chemical-coated grass, into her hogan. And then she becomes sleepy and ill. A few hundred yards in the back of her home, a giant coal-mining dragline scatters the bones of her ancestors, drawing from the earth the coal which feeds the plant's turbines and generators. In plush boardrooms in distant cities Emma's home is called a "national sacrifice area."

She will not move. Emma says that she will die here and that her bones will be returned to the earth, to join those of her ancestors. She does not say these things in a dramatic tone, to impress visitors. It is the way things are done—the way of the Creation.

"The mother earth is very sacred to the Navajo...we replace what we take...we are born of the earth, and we return to rest," says Emma, slowly and methodically.

But the draglines will not let the dead rest. There is an "energy crisis." Emma's homeland is being turned into billowing smoke and fleeting electricity, and Emma Yazzie does not understand why those people in the cities must use twice as much electricity as they did fourteen years ago. She has been to Shiprock, twenty miles to the southwest, and seen the artificial light, but she does not see much point to it. She is wise and dignified, and the Navajo listen to her. The power plant speaks a language of whistles and groans and mechanical voices, and it does not hear the wisdom of the earth or of the ages.

Emma speaks with her hands as she holds an imaginary lamb. "My sheep are dying. Their noses bleed. The baby goats do not grow up." Emma runs her left hand over the dusty earth, a foot above the surface. "That's as big as they get now."

Emma holds her hands an inch apart. "The wool is this thick now. It comes off in dirty brown balls. Before this disease—this thick." She holds her hands four inches apart.

"And the lambs. I lose half the lambs. The ones which grow up are too skinny to sell. And the goats give no milk."

Before the power plant came, Emma's lambs were fat and her sheep's wool thick. Her goats gave milk. Emma lived relatively well, selling the wool or weaving rugs from it for the trading posts, producing lamb and mutton and selling goat's milk. Now the sheep's thin brown wool barely covers their skin.

Before the year which the men in the plant call 1963, Emma supported herself. Now, she gets eighty dollars a month from the government. The "free enterprise" system of rip-and-run resource exploitation has made her a "welfare Indian." And when the government money runs out, she asks friends and relatives for food. When they are hungry, so is she.

She goes hungry while the affluent bask in electrically heated swimming pools in Phoenix. The coal which provides the electricity which heats the pools comes from the strip mine behind her hogan.

She offers to take visitors into the huge, serpentine mine. "If you go alone, they will turn you back," she says. "They are afraid of me." Driving into the mine, Emma points to spots of brilliant green among the brown scrubland. "These are the reclaimed areas," she says. "Aren't they beautiful? But they won't last. They are drowned in water and fertilizer. And this kind of grass is not even native here. It will not survive." It is public-relations grass, kept for touring government officials and television crews.

At the bottom of the mine, Emma stands, her face to the sun, and points toward the dragline grabbing mouthfuls of earth. The shovel could hold several buses and cars. "That," she says, "is what I am fighting." She is standing at the bottom of the largest coal strip mine in the western hemisphere.

Once the miners staked a road across her pasture for the trucks which rumble out of the mine toward the plant. No one asked her permission. She pulled up the stakes and carried them to the mine manager's office and threw them on his desk, that immaculate desk, and raged: "You power-plant people are watching us starve! You are making money of the coal in Navajo land, and you don't care for anything else! The earth is dying!"

Occasionally Emma joins younger Navajo who protest coal development during lease negotiations in the tribal capital of Window Rock, Arizona. She smiles as she describes the bewildered expression on the face of a riot policeman as she flew at him in her rage.

She is fighting what the men in the power plants call "progress." The developers want to give the Four Corners plant at least three brothers on the Navajo Nation before 1990. In addition, the developers want to build six coal-consuming power plants which will make synthetic natural gas in the Burham area, a few hills south of Emma's hogan. These plants are so dirty that no one can live within thirteen miles of them and so risky and expensive that the banks will not finance them. The developers want billions of dollars from the federal government to build the plants.

Conversation in Emma's hogan does not center on energy policy, however. Nor does it center on the technology of power production or on conservation or on solar, wind, or geothermal power. Emma talks about what she knows and what she sees— the smoke signals of death. The conversational pivot is death, resistance, and survival; dying lambs and poisoned water, and the rape of the sacred earth. The flicks of millions of urban light switches sing Emma Yazzie's death song.

Across a mountain range from Emma Yazzie's hogan the giant coal shovels are digging another strip mine on the Black Mesa, the Mother Mountain of the Navajo Spirit. If the harmony of the Mother Mountain is destroyed, it is said, the *Dine*[1] will die: survival of a people is tied to the survival of the land. Emma Yazzie, by refusing to move from her land, stands for the traditionals, whose Mother Mountain is the Black Mesa.

For the *Wasi'chu*, however, the Black Mesa has become a tabernacle to another religion: that of power, progress, and profits. If the Mother Mountain's harmony is *not* disrupted, the multinational energy companies will have to forgo the sustenance of their religion.

For a long time the economic religion of the *Wasi'chu* regarded this Mother Mountain talk as so much spiritualistic "mumbo jumbo," until non-Indians were forced—by the pollution of their own civilization—to look at the underside of an industrialism that has no regard for people or the earth. Then this "mumbo jumbo" becomes the basis of ecological science built on the premise that humankind's survival depends upon a healthy land. By the rational laws of ecology, it is the rapists of the Mother Mountain who are taking part in a ritual of mumbo jumbo. If Black Elk were alive today, he might call coal "the stiff black dirt that makes the *Wasi'chus* crazy."

The coal which gives the Black Mesa its dark color is like hard dirt in consistency, and until the technology of the *Wasi'chu* could crush the stuff and combine it with water into a dirty porridge and then transport it away in pipelines, the coal companies saw little value in it. At the same time that this technology was being developed, coal strip mining was becoming cheaper for the companies than deep mining in the East. Machines were developed which didn't complain about wages or working conditions, demand pensions, or get black-lung disease. The machines never went on strike. The Western coal rush had begun; the companies were enticed westward not by the exhaustion of coal in the East, but by the manna of their religion, which is profit.

The huge draglines float above the tabletop of the Mesa, giraffe-like, their necks reaching 300 feet into the air; their wheels propelling 2,500-ton bodies. The shovels claw at the earth. The signs around the mine give the name of the company, Peabody.

The coal becomes coal slurry, which, transported to giant smokestack-crowned monoliths in the desert, becomes electricity, which is carried in high-voltage transmission lines across the Navajo Nation to Los Angeles, Phoenix, Tucson, and many other places outside the land of the *Dine.* The spidery, steel superstructures carrying the high-voltage lines stand in stiff order, their cargoes buzzing over Navajo homes, most of which have no electricity.

And across the countless ridges of mountains, across the plateaus and the deserts, in California—where, we are told, everything happens first—the doctors of consumption are at work developing new ways for consumers to use this power which comes out of the breast of the Mother Mountain. The taste and waste makers have been test-marketing an electric toilet seat.

Rusco American Bidet Corporation advertises that for a mere $175 to $195 its electric bidet will substitute for toilet paper a jet of electrically heated water. The company says the bidet is "environmental"—it saves trees.[2] The doctors of consumption do not ask where the electricity comes from.

A majority of Navajo homes are automatically out of the market for the electric toilet seat: they have no running water.

Most Navajo homes are also out of the market for another California dream, the Mobot. This piece of geegaw technology works like this: (1) uproot your lawn; (2) lay down an electric grid; (3) affix Mobot to grid; (4) replant lawn; wait for growth; (5) flick switch; (6) take a nap.

This ultimate in lawn-mowing convenience sold for $700 in 1976, or slightly less than what the average Navajo earned that year.[3] Most Navajo do not have lawns anyway. Besides, they have been using automatic lawn mowers for centuries. The Navajo Mobot does not even leave clippings. They call them sheep.

And so the developers tell the Navajo that there is an energy crisis on—over there, across the mountains. While per capita consumption of electricity was doubling from 1963 to 1975 in the United States, in about half the homes on the Navajo Nation energy consumption was remarkably constant: twice zero is zero. Many of the energy missionaries complain that the Navajo—the common people—just do not get the energy-crisis message. Many of them do not even watch television, where the oil-companies' hired hands preach the message: "We've got more coal than the Arabs have oil! LET'S DIG IT!" Digging it, to many Navajo, is sacrilege and a form of energy colonialism. The coal rush is but a transmutation of the gold rush which drove so many Indians off their lands. The *Wasi'chu* want the resources; the Indians are in the way. Their respect for the earth—and their knowledge of history—and the vestiges of guilt that lie within the *Wasi'chu* for having promised that *this* (and this...and this...) would be the last land grab, all these things are obstacles.

The profit-motivated *Wasi'chu* economy makes any promise that the taking will end impossible. The manna of profits demands growth, what Edward Abbey calls "the ideology of the cancer cell."[4] That ideology puts the doctors of consumption to work, seeking more and more ways for the Alices in this technological Wonderland to consume electric power. The Navajo—their land, their heritage, their lives—are being consumed. Theirs are the lands which the National Academy of Sciences ruefully calls "national sacrifice areas."[5]

The developers have planned at least six coal-fired electricity plants for Navajo Country. In addition, they want the federal government to provide several billions of dollars in guaranteed loans for plants which would convert coal into synthetic natural gas. These plants would feed on Navajo coal. While the coal mining destroys the earth, the power plants would take care of the water and air. Everywhere the missionaries of power development go, they promise to be "good neighbors," but the character of strip mining and power plants makes that promise impossible. Power development is as good a neighbor as an agitated skunk in close quarters, but with a difference: the damage they do will be permanent. The National Academy of Sciences reports that no land has ever been successfully reclaimed after being strip-mined in the arid West; that true reclamation will take centuries.[6] Emma Yazzie's present is being prescribed as the future for many Navajo—all in the "national interest."

The *Wasi'chu* have provided that their "national interest" will also be in the financial interests of some powerful Navajo, a select class which has been inculcated with a reverence for the "yellow metal which drives *Wasi'chu* crazy." Peter McDonald, Navajo tribal chairman, promotes resource development; the rents and royalties paid by the coal-mining companies flow directly into his tribal government. He is a businessman, and he has become very skilled in the *Wasi'chu* way, which means: getting his. The grass-roots people—through whose hogans the dirty smoke flows—call him "MacDollar." He lives in a luxurious ranch house, drives a Lincoln Continental, and draws a $30,000 salary as chairman of an Indian nation where the average per capita income is about $900. In June 1976, while tribal chairman, McDonald also assumed the presidency and controlling interest in Denay Insurance, Inc., a Window Rock-based company. He has spent more than a little time during the past few years flying around the Navajo Nation on energy companies' airplanes, attempting to convince reluctant grass-roots Navajo that energy colonization will be good for them.

Just as the *Wasi'chu*'s implantation of "native elites" has created class tensions between the newly rich oil barons of the Middle East and the homeless, but also Arab, Palestinians, the inculcation of faith in the *Wasi'chu* way has introduced exploitation into the Navajo tribal government structure. The tribal government is made up of a central administration (in Window Rock) and a tribal council, composed of members from 102 "chapters," or local governments. The tribal-government system (which replaced traditional governance for the Navajo and other Indian nations through the 1934 Indian Reorganization Act) has attracted a *Wasi'chu* class of Indians, some of whom have been convicted during the last decade of taking the fat, in Watergate-like situations: Art Arviso, assistant to McDonald, convicted of embezzlement; David Jackson, manager of the Navajo tribal fair, convicted of embezzlement; Larry Wilson, assistant manager of the fair, convicted of embezzlement; Stanley K. Smith, manager of Piñon Credit Union, convicted of embezzlement; Ernie Shorey, license examiner for the state of Arizona, convicted of embezzlement; Pat Chee Miller, director, Navajo Housing Authority, convicted of conspiracy to defraud; Mervin Schaffer, vice president, Jusco Construction Company, convicted of fraud; Regina Henderson, Navajo welfare worker, convicted of embezzlement; Doris McLancer, tribal court clerk, convicted of embezzlement; Laurita Williams, Navajo Election Board clerk, convicted of embezzlement; Ross Roll, tribal employee, convicted of embezzlement.[8]

The usual procedure is for monies from coal and other natural-resource exploitation to flow directly to Window Rock, which presents copious opportunities for embezzlement. Some of the money is returned, through a type of revenue-sharing plan, to the chapter houses. A chapter house controlled in the *Wasi'chu* way may disperse the money by advertising for rug weavers. The chapter house pays the weavers a minimal wage, which comes from the mineral lease rent or royalty, and keeps the rugs for resale at a profit.

McDonald was relatively popular when he was first elected to head the tribal government. Soon afterward, however, he joined the ranks of the native elite in a very decisive way; he lived rather lavishly and promoted energy development—provided the price was right. Opposition to his policies began to grow, especially among the grass-roots Navajo and on the northeastern quarter of the reservation, where much of the proposed energy development would take place.

The Coalition for Navajo Liberation was born in 1974 and continues most active in and near Shiprock; traditionals from

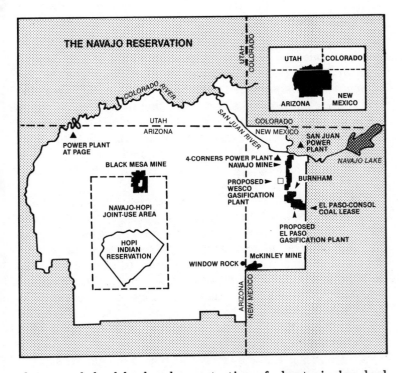

THE NAVAJO RESERVATION

that area helped lead a demonstration of about six hundred people on May 18, 1976, in Window Rock, the tribal capital. The marchers demanded McDonald's resignation. On August 25, 1976, traditionals assembled again in Window Rock during a tribal council meeting. The council was negotiating a coal-strip-mine lease with El Paso Natural Gas and Consolidation Coal, a subsidiary of Continental Oil. Eighteen people were arrested during the demonstration. The majority of the demonstrators were from the area of the reservation where most of the energy development is planned—the Shiprock-Burnham area. Most stand to gain very little from development; most, if it is approved in full measure, will lose at least their land, probably their livelihoods—and perhaps their lives.

At the Burnham chapter house residents voted 228-0 against coal gasification during 1976; in the same year the Shiprock chapter rejected gasification proposals 129-0. The power to negotiate leases and mining plans, however, resides with the tribal council and McDonald. For his "mine it, and make them pay" attitude, the Shiprock chapter voted 255 to 6 to demand that McDonald resign. Opposition to gasification and the coal mining that it requires is so strong in the Burnham area that one tribal council member from the chapter offered to resign under pressure from area residents after he supported El Paso's lease proposal during a debate held in August 1976. Such popular recall has long been an Indian tradition, practiced in the Iroquois confederacy and borrowed, in part, for United States law.

The closer to the grass-roots an energy-development proposal came, the more strongly it was opposed. The tribal council itself has tended to support strip-mining leases while opposing the gasification and power plants which are inevitably proposed to consume the coal. In a letter to Congress written in 1976, forty-one of the tribal council's seventy-six members opposed federal loan guarantees for gasification-plant construction. The same council, however, approved the El Paso coal lease by forty-nine to eleven during August of the same year.

McDonald bragged that the El Paso coal lease was the best of its kind ever negotiated by an Indian nation or tribe. It was the best, in terms of monetary value; the fifty-five cents a ton that was promised the Navajos was almost three times as much as the Crow and Northern Cheyenne had been offered on leases which are now suspended (see chapter 7). It might have been a pretty good lease compared with what the energy companies had offered Indian nations before, but the value of it would diminish with inflation. The lease stipulated that if fifty-five cents a ton was less than 8 percent of the market price of the coal, the Navajo Nation would get 8 percent. Federal law, however, requires that the minimum leasing rate be 12.5 percent.

To the traditionals—especially those near Shiprock and Burnham—a lease was still a lease, however "good" the terms. To them, the leasing was a repeat of history, a trade of land and resources for money, an exchange which has almost always ended in Indian losses. Their opposition to the coal and uranium leases, as well as to the construction of electricity and gasification plants, is more than spiritual; it is a matter of economics and—eventually—of life or death. Energy development would destroy the land and the life upon it—life that seemingly barren land has sustained for hundreds of years or longer.

The Department of Interior, which must approve all plans for energy development on Indian nations after tribal councils negotiate the contracts, held hearings on the El Paso coal lease in March 1977. Cecilia Bitsui, a resident of the Burnham chapter reflected the beliefs of many of her neighbors when she said: "Do we have to wait until the whole land is destroyed before the tribal council says 'enough'? The people in Window Rock are only concerned with money. But no cash payment will replace what my family will lose. My children will not be able to herd sheep in Burnham and learn the ways of the Navajo as I did."

The resistance to energy development runs long and deep. Fred Johnson, one of the founding members and early leaders of the Coalition for Navajo Liberation, told the U.S. Civil Rights Commission in 1974: "Our clean waters are clouded with silt and the wastes of the white man; Mother Earth is being ravaged and squandered. To the Navajo people it seems as if these Europeans hate everything in nature—the grass, the birds, the beasts, the water, the soil, and the air. We refuse to abandon our beautiful land.

"To Navajos, land was something no one could possess, any more than he could possess the air. Land is sacred to the Navajos; it is part of the Almighty's design for life... Mother Earth, because it is the mother of all living. To the whites, this is paganism as well as communistic, and it has to be eradicated.

"All the laws and federal regulations in existence cannot justify the criminal acts of tribal officials who knowingly deceive those who have placed their trust in them...

"To protest is to speak out against, to let it be known that you don't like a certain action... To protest is an act of intellectual commitment. To protest is to hate the inhumanity of another. To resist, we believe, is to stop inhumanity and affirm your own humanity... the Coalition for Navajo Liberation intends to stop the land robberies known as the gasification plants, the T.G. & E. power line, the Black Mesa destruction of land, the Four Corners power plants and the Exxon uranium deal."[9]

Johnson, who was killed in a mysterious crash of a small airplane in early 1976, spoke forcefully about the dangers of strip mining and power generation, which would turn large areas of Navajo land into wastelands unreclaimable for perhaps hundreds of years.

True reclamation involves more than simply filling in the mines and planting grass to cover the scars; it involves restoring the entire ecological community of plants and animals. A National Academy of Sciences (NAS) report states bluntly that this cannot be done in areas with less than 10 inches of rainfall a year; the rainfall over most of the Navajo Nation ranges from six to ten inches a year. The NAS suggests that such areas be spared development or honestly labeled "national sacrifice areas."[10] The amount of money a coal-mining company spends on reclamation is not the crucial factor, asserts the NAS report. Nor are state or federal reclamation laws.[11] Reclamation is simply not possible, at least not until nature heals the wounds itself over several centuries.

Strip mining does more than scar the land. It also disrupts underground water flow and poisons the water itself. Coal seams in the arid West also act as aquifers—they carry water just as some metals conduct electricity. Underground water is important in sparsely populated dry areas, where wells often are the only source of water, and a majority of Navajo rely on well water. Much of the soil in the Southwest (as well as on the northern plains) is high in alkaline salts. Usually the salts are leached out of the surface layers of soil and are concentrated below the topsoil. Strip mining mixes the soil, resulting in salt levels at the surface which kill many native plants. Rain or irrigation water at the surface carries the freed salts into the aquifers, which feed wells and rivers. Every living thing then suffers from salty water. Strip mining also loosens surface soil, which is carried by rainfall and irrigation as silt and mud into rivers and wells.

No amount of corporate goodwill, no number of promises to be a "good neighbor," no amount of money or effort, and no combination of reclamation laws will resolve the fundamental incompatibility of coal strip mining and nature in the arid Southwest. Generation of electricity or natural gas from the coal only compounds the problems, which amount to a sentence of death for the land and a way of life.

Fly ash, produced by burning coal, pollutes the air and water. Even if much of the fly ash is removed from power-plant stacks before reaching the air, it is usually dumped in nearby landfills, where rainfall leaches chemicals into the ground-water.[12] Already the clouds of pollution obscure the turquoise sky around majestic Shiprock, which gives the Navajo town its name; more plants will merely make the pollution denser. Between 100 and 200 pounds of fly ash can be released by the burning of a single ton of coal.[13] The burning of coal also releases sulfur dioxide (SO_2), poisonous to people, plants, and animals. The SO_2 reacts with water vapor in the atmosphere to form sulfuric acid, which returns to the earth as highly acidic rainfall. Coal burning also releases nitrogen oxide, which combines with ozone and carbon in the air to produce smog.

The pollution potential of gasification exceeds that of burning coal. According to research done by the National Indian Youth Council (NIYC),

> there will be at least two... toxic air pollutants (lead and mercury) emitted from those [gasification] plants in such uncontrolled quantities that [they] may inflict permanent damage to all animal, plant and human life in the immediate vicinity of the plants. Expert testimony from a National Aeronautics and Space Administration physicist at recent environmental hearings revealed that all persons living within a 13-mile radius of the plants will have to be evacuated due to the dangerously high levels of lead and mercury... around these plants. In fact, it is predicted that all workers in and around the plants will have to wear protective face masks for health and safety reasons.
>
> Another toxic emission (boron) is greatly feared by the planners of the Navajo Nation Irrigation Project because it could easily wipe out all of the crops grown there.

The dangers to people, plants, and animals—as well as to the earth itself—do not end with the generation of electricity. The transmission lines which ride atop the spidery steel towers across the mountains to consumers carry so much electricity that they create a force field beneath them. Extra-High-Voltage (EHV) transmission lines of the size planned for the Indian coal lands have given several people in Ohio severe shocks. One woman was knocked from her horse by the force field; a man was working in his yard when the force field knocked him unconscious. The power company which owns the line advised the man to wear chains around his ankles to ground the current. Twelve of eighteen persons living near the Ohio EHV lines have reported strong electrical shocks. [14]

The transmission lines may also create their own smog; electricity seeping from the lines combines with elements in the atmosphere to form ozone, a component of smog. [15]

Energy development would require massive amounts of water to be drawn from the arid lands of the Navajo. The consumption of water begins with the mining of the flaky coal of the Black Mesa, where coal slurry is transported through pipelines. Water consumption continues with power generation, especially with coal gasification. One coal-gasification plant requires about 10,000 acre-feet of water a year. [16] About twenty-eight cubic feet of water per second, or 20,270 acre-feet a year, are required to cool the generating equipment of a 1,000 megawatt, coal-fired electricity plant. [17] *All* of the water used in gasification is hydrolyzed into hydrogen and oxygen and lost to the arid southwest. Some of the water used in electricity generation also evaporates; the remainder is returned to its source ten to fifteen degrees Farenheit warmer than it was before entering the plant. [18]

To add insult to injury, the water demands of and pollution generated by proposed (as well as actual) energy-development schemes pose a dual threat to an irrigation project which was included in the Navajo treaty of 1868. The first stages of the 110,000-acre project, near Burnham, began operating in 1976. If completed, the irrigation project will provide employment in the fields or in the food-processing and marketing chain for thirty thousand Navajo. The irrigation project will not destroy the land, poison the air and water, or drive people away from their homes and heritage, as energy development will. However, the pollution and water demands of strip mining and of the gasification and coal-fired electricity plants may kill, or severely damage, the crops.

The irrigation project has long been a dream of the traditional Navajo; its survival is a major reason why energy development is being so bitterly opposed:

> There is much potential in the Navajo Indian Irrigation project for the beginning of a totally Indian-owned and controlled economic base, the possibility of an expanded agricultural project to help alleviate world hunger and the opportunity for Indian people to contribute to [the solution of] the world crisis in a direct and meaningful way, instead of always having to sacrifice their land and resources . . . It is necessary that the Indian people begin to organize and unite toward positively developing and utilizing their own land and resources in alternative ways.[19]

This major confrontation over the differing views of humankind's relationship to nature, a crossroad in the history of the colonization of native peoples, will peak within the late 1970s or early 1980s. Decisions will be made which will promote either the irrigation project or energy development. The water required for the irrigation plant, as well as for the energy development, will have to come from the same shallow, muddy-brown San Juan River, which flows through Shiprock. The two projects are not environmentally compatible, and there is simply not enough water for both.[20]

Another factor in the water-demand equation is the fifty thousand or so people who would be imported to build and operate the complex of strip mines and power plants in and near the Navajo Nation. If these people come, many will likely bring with them the water-squandering habits acquired in less arid climates.

Gerald Wilkinson, director of the National Indian Youth Council, says that those Navajo worried about the harm of uncontrolled strip mining are not totally against resource use. They want, however, for this use to take place in a manner which does not disrupt the earth, human life, traditions, or the irrigation project. Wilkinson suggests that coal should be mined underground, using room-and-pillar techniques, if it is mined at all, and that the coal, once mined, ought to be transported away from the Navajo Nation for power generation. The Navajo Nation should also be a joint partner in any energy project, Wilkinson suggests. Only in this way can Navajo coal be mined without the penalties of energy colonization or the devastation of a "national sacrifice area."

The developers are unlikely to agree to such terms, for they are not coming to the Southwest (and to the West in general) merely to mine coal. They are coming to *strip-mine* coal. If the coal companies want to deep-mine coal, there is plenty in the East and the Midwest, much of it in abandoned deep mines under land the companies have already ruined. At present rates of consumption, there remains enough coal in already opened mines to last the United States seventy-five years.

Converging trends in labor relations and technology, not scarcity of coal, have propelled the coal companies westward. A corporate policy based on bottom-line profit, instead of ecological and human needs, has brought the coal miners to the West, where a million tons of coal a year can be mined with newly developed draglines and only twenty-five men much more cheaply than with a large force of underground miners paid at prevailing union rates.

Nor have the miners of coal come to the West for the low-sulfur coal that will reduce pollution. While it is true that Western coal is lower in sulfur content than Eastern coal when it leaves the ground, it is also lower in heat value. More of it must be burned to produce the same amount of heat as a smaller amount of Eastern coal.[21] In addition, the Western coal acts as an aquifer, and so when removed from the ground it holds much more water than Eastern coal. The water must be removed from the coal; the remaining product is lighter and, therefore, even higher in sulfur content. *By the time it is burned*, Western coal contains no less sulfur per pound than Eastern coal.

In the long run, the energy the coal companies are raping the Navajo Nation, and much of the rest of the West, to produce may not even be necessary. It is probable that if advertising stopped manipulating people toward greater use of energy and conservation were enforced, energy consumption would stabilize or decline. Future coal needs could be met from already opened mines or from careful underground mining in the West. As for natural gas, several experiments are under way which may furnish substantial amounts of ersatz gas generated from methane, a clean-burning gas produced by the decomposition of organic matter. [22]

For example, at Bay St. Louis, Mississippi, the National Aeronautics and Space Administration is harvesting water hyacinths for distillation into methane. The hyacinths are one of nature's fastest growing plants. They thrive on raw sewage and have heretofore been considered a problem because they clog waterways in the South.

Off the southern California coast scientists from the Naval Undersea Center and Cal Tech are designing ocean farms of giant California kelp to be harvested, dried, and converted into methane. [23] Ocean farms measuring 470 miles on each side could have supplied all of the United States's 1976 demand for natural gas, according to Dr. Harold Wilcox, director of the project.

Both of these projects utilize a renewable resource to produce a clean-burning form of energy; they are ecological—in harmony, a Navajo might say, with the Mother Mountain.

There are many other environmentally compatible energy resources which should be more intensively developed and utilized, among them solar power, wind power, and wave and tidal power. There is no energy shortage; there is a shortage of will on the part of many Americans to challenge a powerful, and destructive, resource-consuming industrial bloc which is wedded to fossil fuels—and to the destruction of the earth, which sustains not only the Navajos, but all of us.

This powerful combination of energy companies has been lobbying Congress for more than five years to provide several billion dollars in guaranteed loans for coal-gasification projects. The companies cannot finance the plants through conventional means (mainly stocks and bonds) because the technology is untested and very expensive. In 1976 a bill providing $6 billion in loan guarantees for "synthetic fuels"—80 percent of that for gasification—was narrowly defeated in Congress.

"Because of the large capital investment requirements of the coal-gasification project, it will be difficult if not impossible for our industry to finance these plants by the conventional means of issuing stocks and bonds. Some form of financial federal guarantees will be required," El Paso Natural Gas said two weeks after the 1976 version of the bill (House Resolution 12112) was defeated by a vote of 193-192.[24] The bid for corporate welfare appeared again in 1977 as Senate Bills 429 and 430.

In New Mexico the state's political elite lined up behind the loan guarantees, believing that gasification would bring economic growth—the ideology of the cancer cell—to their state. Governor Jerry Apodaca was there, along with the late Senator Joseph Montoya and Peter McDonald, all hovering close to the bill, like moths around a bright light. At the grass-roots level, the people who would pay the price shouted their collective disapproval.

Bob Duke, the *Albuquerque Journal*'s Washington correspondent, warned, "If Congress [does not approve], New Mexico's coal-gasification projects and Colorado's oil-shale development are virtually certain to be shelved permanently."[25]

NIYC celebrated after the 1976 bill was defeated—but not unreservedly. Its members knew the fight would resume.

> In every sense of the word, we are engaged in a life and death duel. We have no other choice but to carry on with this struggle so that someday our children, their children, and generations yet unborn will in their own time all walk in beauty.[26]

John Redhouse, associate director of NIYC, told the American Indian Policy Review Commission on February 9, 1976:

> This [coal gasification] is only a small part of a larger governmental and corporate conspiracy to steal Indian land and resources. During the past hundred years, the methods may have changed, but the sordid cast of characters and ulterior motives remain the same.

The *Wasi'chu* were following an old script, coming to take land and resources and promising to be good neighbors, telling the Indians they were doing them a favor. The ulterior motive was private aggrandizement. It was an old, old story for the Indians.

Where will we all be 20 or 25 years from now when the coal is all consumed and the companies operating these gasification plants have cleaned up all the resources and moved away? There will be nothing; they will be working elsewhere and we will be sitting on top of a bunch of ashes with nothing to live on . . . [27]

But the story now had ramifications for far more people than just the American Indian population.

The margin has critically narrowed for both Indian and world survival. The Indians are on the edge of and may eventually be drawn into the resource exploitation machine—the mining, production and consumption machine of modern society that transforms and exhausts the earth's resources in response to its own unseeing drives and compulsions. The managers of the machine must plan and guide it to provide the maximum wealth and power for its corporate components. The owners who provide the needed investment put their money where the highest and most secure rewards are offered. The workers have no role except to keep up production. Finally, the machine itself creates the consumption ethic—the pleasure of purchasing and the success motivation geared to material wealth—which, in turn, keeps it going.[28]

During the late 1970s the lines of conflict were drawn between those who wished to preserve in its own way the Navajo Nation as a viable entity and those who believed in taking the rewards of the *Wasi'chu* for their hearts, minds, and land. There were some indications, two years after the Coalition for Navajo Liberation and the McDonald administration faced off with riot police between then in Window Rock, that the message of the *Dine*—the traditional *Dine*—was beginning to be heard more strongly inside the tribal council. As the U.S. House and the Senate passed (after a half-decade of pressure) a multimillion-dollar loan-guarantee program for synthetic fuels (including coal gasification), the Navajo council was moving toward rejecting a WESCO plan for gasification plants near Burnham.

James Abourezk, one of the few consistent defenders in the Senate of Indian treaty rights during this period, said that the loan guarantees were a government subsidy to multinational energy companies, which desired to extend their grip on fossil fuel resources as domestic oil and gas were depleted.[29] "The federal government helped build the nuclear industry," said William Gribeaut, government research manager for the American Gas Association, a pipeline and distributors' trade group. "Now, the synthetic fuels industry needs the same kind of help," he went on in an article that compared the welfare program being concocted for synthetic fuels with the gifts of land made to the railroads a century ago[30]—another corporate land and resource grab which ran the tracks of Manifest Destiny over the backs of several dozen Indian nations.

On February 1, 1978, the Navajo Tribal Council rejected the WESCO proposal, which included four commercial gasification plants. The vote was 48-8. McDonald said WESCO's proposal was not a good business deal: WESCO wanted the tribe to come up with $200 million to invest in the plant. "Gasification has not proved itself," McDonald said.

Nevertheless, WESCO indicated that it would come back to try again. The *Navajo Times* commented, "Many WESCO officials feel, according to a WESCO spokesman, that the upcoming tribal elections may have been the reason the council turned down the proposal and that once the elections are over the council will be more receptive to the idea."[31]

At about the same time the National Indian Youth Council, allied with residents of the Shiprock-Burnham area, refused to approve what McDonald had called the best Indian coal lease ever signed—the one passed in August 1976, which allowed the Navajo Nation fifty-five cents a ton or 8 percent of the market price of the coal. Interior Secretary Cecil Andrus told the Navajo that the minimum coal royalty rate, following amendments to the Federal Coal Leasing Act of 1975, was 12.5 percent—a good indication of where the "best Indian coal lease ever signed" would have stood outside the energy colony.

Like many third-world countries, the Navajo began to show an awareness of their colonization. A tax on sulfur emissions was passed, as was a business tax aimed at the energy companies. The tax, which assesses the gross receipts of a business at 5 percent, exempts traditional livestock and farming enterprises.[32] The targets of the sulfur tax, the owners of two reservation power plants, filed suit during October 1977 in federal court seeking relief. The levy was officially called a "fee," since the contracts the BIA had persuaded the tribe to sign more than a decade ago with the two companies forbade the levying of taxes on them.[33]

During the same period many grass-roots Navajos who had been forced off their land and into employment in power-generating plants or oil refineries went on strike, protesting both their forced draft into the *Wasi'chu* system of work and exploitation on the job. The strikes sparked occupations of some work places, and community residents often joined the workers in them. A Texaco oil refinery in Aneth, Utah, on the northern edge of the reservation, was occupied during April 1978. As the occupants demanded, Texaco agreed to keep its employees from bringing alcoholic beverages onto the reservation, dismiss employees found carrying sidearms on the reservation, reclaim land damaged by oil drilling, compensate Navajo families who suffered losses due to oil drilling (including water wells which had been damaged), preserve Navajo burial sites, and give Navajo people preference in hiring at drilling sites. A few years earlier workers and neighborhood residents had occupied a Fairchild camera plant in Shiprock, N.M., demanding wage raises and an end to sweatshop-like working conditions. The occupants discovered files which indicated the company was planning a move to Taiwan to escape the organization of Navajo workers.

As they fought the *Wasi'chu* plans to force them into the industrial work force through coal mining and power-plant development which would destroy the land and give them little choice, grass-roots Navajos faced another battle over uranium, one which gave them common cause both with other Indian people, such as the Lakota (chapter 5), and non-Indians who opposed nuclear power plants and the spread of atomic weapons.

The spring and summer of 1978 saw tens of thousands of people rallying, from Seabrook, New Hampshire, to the navy's Trident nuclear submarine base near Seattle, against civilian and military uses of uranium. Indians and non-Indians gathered in June 1978 near Grants, N.M., to point to the need to stop the poison at its source.

Uranium had been mined on the Navajo Nation since the early 1950s. About half the recoverable uranium inside the United States lies under New Mexico; half of that is under Indian land. The presence of large uranium deposits was one reason that the first atomic bombs were exploded in New Mexico.

In the thirty years since those first explosions uranium has continued to be mined on the Navajo Nation. It is mined like any other mineral, which means that more than 99 percent of what is taken from the earth is left at or near the mining site as tailings. The mesa-like piles of tailings near Shiprock are more than ugly; they are radioactive. Until the middle 1970s, however, the Atomic Energy Commission assured local residents that the tailings piles—one of which measures a mile long and seventy feet high—were harmless. On windy days the tailings were mixed with dust, blowing into nearby communities, polluting their water and air.

In February 1978, however, the Department of Energy released a Nuclear Waste Management Task Force report which said that the risk of lung cancer for persons living near tailings piles was twice that of the rest of the population.

To make matters worse, the same uranium boom that was prompting prospecting in the Black Hills was causing increasing activity in the Southwest, especially on the Navajo Nation. The price of a pound of uranium oxide had risen from $8 to about $50 during the 1970s; old mines were being reopened, and new ones started.

"It's more than a matter of continued exploitation of our remaining land and resources," said John Redhouse, associate director of the National Indian Youth Council. "It's also an issue of spiritual and physical genocide."[34] Navajo from the Shiprock area were among the first uranium miners; they were not told that they were mining one of the most toxic materials known. Twenty to thirty years after they began mining, an extraordinary number died of lung cancer; Esther Keeswood, a Shiprock resident, said that at least fifty Navajo from the Shiprock area had died within a few years of lung cancer and related diseases. Her assertion was supported by studies by the Public Health Service, which indicate that one of every six uranium miners have died, or will die, prematurely of lung cancer.[35]

"We are not isolated in our struggle against uranium development," Redhouse said. "Many Indian people are now supporting the struggles of the Australian aborigines and the Black indigenous peoples of Namibia [South-West Africa] against similar uranium developments. We have recognized that we are facing the same international beast."[36]

The uranium boom was also ravaging Crownpoint, another Navajo community. More then 700,000 acres of Indian land around Shiprock and Crownpoint were under lease for uranium exploration and development in northwestern New Mexico by late 1978. Some of the most powerful corporations in the world —Atlantic Richfield, Continental Oil, Exxon, Humble Oil, Homestake, Kerr-McGee, Mobil Oil, Pioneer Nuclear, United Nuclear, and others—were in on the mining.[37]

Much of the land in the Crownpoint area is owned so as to allow Navajo only surface rights; the subsurface (including mining) rights are held by the federal government or private companies, such as Santa Fe Railroad. Because of this ownership pattern, many energy companies have started mining without even asking or otherwise informing the occupants who hold surface rights. The exercise of the mining rights tends to destroy the usefulness of the surface, through disturbance of the land, as well as to pollute the water and air.

The expropriation of Navajo resources, under cover of a domestic energy crisis, helped the growing grass-roots resistance in Navajo country to expand into a large popular movement during the 1970s; local residents who did not want their livelihood and traditional culture destroyed by uranium and coal mining, or by coal-fired power- and gasification-plant development, were coming together.

The situation in Crownpoint was symptomatic of the Navajo Nation. When a United States Geological Survey report showed that the water table there would drop a thousand feet as a result of uranium mining, the local residents rose in protest. The report indicated that the water table would only return to its former levels thirty to fifty years after the mines closed.[38] On top of that, much of the water could well be polluted by uranium residues.

"If the water supply is depleted, then this will become a ghost town," said Joe Gmusca, a Navajo attorney. "The only people left here will be the ones who come to work in the mines."[39] The choice that the Navajo were being forced to face in Crownpoint was not a new one: accommodate to the requirements of the *Wasi'chu*, or starve. Those have been the terms of the *Wasi'chu* for a long time; not far from Crownpoint is a mesa upon which, local residents will tell you, many Indians who refused to submit to treaty-making a century ago were driven. There, with the foot soldiers of the *Wasi'chu* circling them, they starved.

The Navajo have not been alone in being confronted with such "choices"; in Montana the Crows and Northern Cheyenne were being readied for national sacrifice, too, because they control some of the West's richest coal reserves. Grass-roots people on these two Indian nations also stood up to the energy companies, telling them that they would decide their own destiny according to the needs of future generations, not the immediate needs of the international supermarket.

7

Montana:
Stopping the Strippers

We all must see ourselves as part of the earth, not as an enemy from the outside who tries to impose his will on it. We who know the meaning of the Pipe also know that, being a part of the earth, we cannot harm any part of her without harming ourselves.

—Lame Deer, Northern Cheyenne

The position of the Northern Cheyenne is clear. In their development proposal, they said, "The Northern Cheyenne [Nation] intends to change Indians' historic role of passive subservience to agencies who are charged with administering of trust responsibility for the benefit of Indian tribes and who in the past have evidenced little more than apathy toward this responsibility."

—James Cannon[1]

Electric power lines on the Navajo reservation in New Mexico. Photo:Wide World Photos.

The *Wasi'chu* had plans for Montana and the rest of the northern plains. Big plans. Few Montanans had heard of the "North Central Power Study" before 1971. That document proposed to make Montana part of an electricity-generating network, also encompassing the Dakotas and Wyoming, which by the year 2000 would make the area the third largest electricity producer in the world, after the rest of the United States and the Soviet Union. In so doing, the project would give the area the landscape of Appalachia and the smog of Los Angeles.

Under such an umbrella of smog the nation's largest single complex of coal-fired electricity and gasification plants would feed the electric toilet seats and Mobots of urban dwellers from Seattle to Chicago—for thirty-five years. Then, according to plan, the easiest and cheapest coal would be gone, and the *Wasi'chu* would move off the pile of ashes their industries had created, their heads swimming in smog, their feet clothed in dust, and look for new places to ruin.

While many Montanans may not have known in 1971 what was being planned for their state, the Interior Department did. And so did the coal companies. Between 1960 and 1970, the decade before the "North Central Power Study" was made public, the coal companies had quietly bought the rights to mine coal on large tracts of western land. Much of it was on Indian reservations. By 1974 the Interior Department had leased 680,000 acres of public lands and approved the leasing of an additional 259,000 acres of Indian lands for coal mining.[2] More than 60 percent of those leases, in the greatest transfer of public and Indian land's mineral rights into the private domain during the twentieth century, were granted during the decade before the "North Central Power Study" was made public.[3] Fifteen billion tons of public coal and an additional five billion tons of Indian coal had been signed away—about thirty-five times the amount of coal produced by the entire United States in 1973.[4] The government had allowed 69 percent of the leases to go into the private domain at "auctions" with only one bidder, and the average bid for permanent mining rights in these leases was less than three dollars an acre.[5]

Obviously, some strip mining was being planned. And, sure enough, when President Nixon announced "Project Independence," his energy self-sufficiency plan, in the early 1970s, it included a growing reliance on coal—especially the thick, rich seams of Western coal, which were so easy and cheap for the companies to strip mine profitably—to reduce reliance on imported oil. The transfer of public and Indian resources to the private domain had now been sanctified as a patriotic act; much of the Mountain West, Montana included, was being marked into "national sacrifice areas." An "energy crisis" had been declared. Pouring out of the television sets in the urban areas came the coal-and-oil-company war cry—we cannot let those Arabs blackmail us; "We have more coal than the Arabs have oil. LET'S DIG IT!"

"Digging it," according to the "North Central Power Study" meant providing fuel for forty-two large coal-fired electricity plants and gasification complexes before the year 2000 in Montana, North Dakota, and Wyoming, atop the Fort Union coal formation, the largest single coal reserve in the world.[6] The Fort Union formation contains about 40 percent of the United States's coal; the United States contains about a third of the world's known coal reserves. The three states of Montana, Wyoming, and North Dakota lie over about one-eighth of the world's total known coal supplies.[7]

"Digging it" involved building the nation's largest power plants; thirteen of the proposed forty-two plants would produce 10,000 megawatts each, or about four times the production of the Four Corners Power Plant on the Navajo Nation.

The forty-two projected power plants would consume 2.6 million acre-feet of water a year, one-and-a-half times the amount used by all of New York City in 1975. An estimated hundred thousand square miles of land would be stripped by the year 2000, an area the size of Italy, tip to toe, or of Pennsylvania and New York combined. This strip mining would take place largely in areas with about ten inches of rain a year, which the National Academy of Sciences had found could not be truly reclaimed for at least a hundred years. The particulate matter—sulfur dioxide, flourine, mercury, and other toxic by-products of the power plants—would give the northern plains pollution rivaling that of Los Angeles.[8] The stable economy of farming and ranching, which supports much of the present population, would be gravely harmed not only by the air pollution but also by the poisoning of underground water supplies, which almost always follows coal strip mining.

Within thirty-five years, according to the plan, the land would be stripped; the draglines would rumble across the devastated land for the last time; the deadly pollution would dissolve over a dead landscape.

If the *Wasi'chu's* energy projections were to be followed by a manipulated urban population, energy demand would triple over 1974 levels by 2000.[9] And the Mobots would be hungry. Perhaps the *Wasi'chu* would turn to the oil-shale mountains of Colorado, majestic mile-high peaks which have the geological misfortune of containing 2 percent kerogen, an oil-like substance. And perhaps the television sets of the year 2000—life-sized, holographic sets, maybe—will announce: "WE'VE GOT MORE OIL THAN THE ARABS HAVE OIL! LET'S DIG IT." And the mountains would crumble, into the gas tanks and onto the bottom lines of the modern American resource-consumption and profit-generation machine. And perhaps the tax-free advertisements would urge motorists to "PUT A MOUNTAIN IN YOUR TANK."

In Lame Deer, Montana, when officials and other leaders of the Northern Cheyenne Nation received the "North Central Power Study," they saw why the brief-case-toting young men had come to them as early as 1966 with promises of money and jobs in exchange for coal. Between 1969 and 1971 the Cheyenne auctioned off leases to 243,000 acres of their 440,000-acre reservation to Peabody, American Metals Climax (AMAX), Chevron, and other corporations. The Bureau of Indian Affairs advised the tribal council to lease; tribal members were told that the jobs and money would be good for them.

In July 1972 Consolidation Coal (owned by Continental Oil) requested 70,000 acres for strip mining and for four gasification plants on Cheyenne land. The tribe began to demur; some members had seen the "North Central Power Study" and had

realized what was being planned—a trade of land for money—
the final termination. On March 5, 1973, the tribal council
voted eleven to zero to direct the BIA to cancel all existing
permits and leases for coal mining. The tribe hired a Seattle law
firm, which drew up a list of violations of federal leasing regulations by the Interior Department—a massive indictment of the
abrogation of trust responsibility, a historic problem for as long
as the BIA has been contained within the Interior Department.

To the Northern Cheyenne, it was an old, old story: the
conflict between the development orientation of the Interior
Department and the trusteeship of Indian land and resources
charged to the BIA was being resolved in favor of resource-
hungry corporations. When the first coal-company geologists
began tossing the bones of their ancestors around Lame Deer,
the Cheyenne were facing another side of resource development,
which the public-relations-minded briefcase toters had not told
them about. The strip mining of the land and construction of
power plants would violate the spiritual sanctity of the earth.
In addition, mining and power-plant pollution would destroy
the small economic base left the Cheyenne by a century of land
hunger, and it would make impossible the development of an
independent economic base once mining had begun. Again the
Wasi'chu had come bearing promises, riding inside the Trojan
horse of betrayal.

The Cheyenne charged that the Interior Department had
failed to perform technical preleasing examinations, to include
legally required environmental-protection clauses in the leases,
and to complete environmental-impact statements. They also
charged that the BIA had violated its trust responsibility by
not telling them of the drawbacks, as well as the benefits, of
mining and energy development and had advised the tribal
council to accept a price for the coal on "unconscionably low
economic terms."[10] On top of the thirty-six alleged violations of
Interior Department regulations, the Cheyenne objected to
Consolidation Coal's plans to bring at least ten thousand non-
Indians onto the reservation, who would inundate the twenty-
five hundred Indians there.

On June 4, 1974, Secretary of the Interior Rogers Morton voided one lease of 12,946 acres to Peabody and suspended the others on the Northern Cheyenne reservation because they were larger than federal leasing rules allowed.

The Crow, whose reservation of 1.4 million acres borders that of the Cheyenne to the west, followed a similar course afterward. Following BIA advice, the Crow had negotiated leases totaling about 125,000 acres with Shell, Peabody, Gulf, and AMAX between 1968 and 1973. A few days before leaving office in January 1977, Secretary of the Interior Thomas Kleppe bowed to the Crow's legal case against his department and suspended the leases.

The companies, unaccustomed to Interior's accepting its trust responsibility over their desires, howled in protest. Shell, which had had a 30,000-acre lease on Crow land and had spent about $1 million exploring its potential, questioned Kleppe's authority and said suit would be filed to reinstate the lease. Shell accused Kleppe of making a decision "which affects the contract rights of private companies without giving us a chance to be heard."[11]

Cancellation of the Shell lease was important to many traditional Crow over and above the environmental and spiritual considerations. Shell, in obtaining the lease, had used tactics which betrayed a corporate image of Indians as incompetent children. At one point Shell sent a form letter to each family on the reservation promising a $200 cash payment if tribal members voted to approve the lease. Robert Howe of the Crow Minerals Committee said that this tactic—sending letters promising cash to impoverished people—was a bribe and "a classic example of . . . trying to exploit our economic condition."[12] Eloise Pease, a member of the Crow Reservation Minerals Committee, reflected the temptation that such a bribe could be when she stated that "I don't think people realize that there are little children here who awake with nothing in the house to eat but a little bacon-grease gravy."[13] On another occasion Shell showed a fifteen-minute company film promoting the benefits of strip mining at the Crow Tribal Fair and attempted to entice Indians to watch it by offering them trinkets.[14]

The Crow Tribal Council refuted assertions that it was merely trying to get more money than the 17.5 cents a ton of coal mined promised in the original Shell lease by voting down—four times—a Shell offer to renegotiate the contract at 40 cents a ton.[15]

By 1976 the Northern Cheyenne had initiated another legal front against the coal companies, again followed by the Crow. The Northern Cheyenne won a "Class I" designation of the air over their nation from the Environmental Protection Agency (EPA). Such a designation disallows "significant deterioration" of air quality and could prevent construction of two coal-fired power plants at Colstrip, fifteen miles north of Lame Deer. Two power plants and a strip mine already are operating at Colstrip—the only coal-fired plants yet built under the plans of the "North Central Power Study." The Cheyenne, noting the effects of strip mining on groundwater purity and supplies, have also asked the Interior Department to ban mining within fifty miles of their lands.[16]

During the fall of 1976 thirty-six Northern Cheyenne toured the energy developments on the Navajo Nation and returned home more opposed to such projects than ever. Michael Bear Comes Out, one of the thirty-six, said that about a quarter of the group had supported strip mining before the trip. "Now," he said, "I think you have 36 Cheyenne who will take up guns to keep mining off the reservation."[17]

The Cheyenne had played a decisive leading role in a popular revolt in Montana, which had effectively stalled energy colonization in that state by 1973. Five strip mines and two coal-fired power plants were operating at that time; no new development took place within the four following years. Four diverse groups —ranchers, environmentalists, Crow, and Cheyenne—fused to stall the strip miners. The powerful coalition forced the state government to shed the development perspective that *Wasi'chu* interests had tried to foist on the residents in a way which has not occurred in New Mexico, where the political elite avidly supports energy development against the protests of grass-roots Navajo. In turning back the forces of energy colonization, Montanans in large part also rejected the mental colonization which grips the elite of New Mexico.

Montana's state government acknowledged soon after the "North Central Power Study" was made public that the proposed development would drain the state's main water source, the Yellowstone River, dry in a drought year. In 1973 the state legislature passed a water moratorium, which halted grants of water permits—and stopped new energy development. In a way, large numbers of state residents had adopted Indian values with regard to the environment.

By the late 1970s there had formed in Montana a remarkable union of the descendents of George Armstrong Custer and the Cheyenne, who had obliterated Custer's Seventh Cavalry a century earlier in southeast Montana. Ranchers, farmers, and environmentalists had joined forces against what they saw as a new invader—the multinational companies and power utilities which were using the BIA and Interior Department to colonize Montana for its coal. Similar alliances were in embryonic form in South Dakota (around the uranium mining in the Black Hills) and in Washington (around the fishing rights and nuclear power), but nowhere had they achieved the power—and the unity—of the Montanans. Montana is a state with a small population (less than a million residents), where only the most rudimentary local elites have formed. It also is a state where the farmers and the ranchers stood to lose from the same proposals which the Indians were fighting. Such was not generally true in other states.

Montanans also have an acute sense of their own history— one of economic boom and bust as each frontier has passed through the state. Mike Ross, a Billings city planner and former director of the Crow Coal Authority, reflected on this "exploitation consciousness": "First, the trappers trapped the rivers dry, then the miners took the minerals, then the farmers plowed the prairies dry, and the topsoil blew away." The shells of past booms and busts haunt many parts of Montana; in the western part of the state, along the continental divide, Butte is gradually being consumed by one of the world's largest open-pit copper mines. In the northeastern part of the state, said Ross, "You can go to places in Fort Peck where there are old shanties with clothes still in the closet. The tables are set for dinner. People got up and walked—just walked—when the topsoil blew away [in the 1930s]." About three hundred thousand people left Montana during the 1930s, when careless farming combined with drought produced an environmental disaster which intensified the economic depression sweeping the United States at the time. Such experiences have welded an Indian-like respect for the earth into the souls of many eastern Montana ranchers and farmers, which combines with a distrust of a boom-and-bust economy to produce resistance to strip mining and power plants.

The combination of the Indians, ranchers, farmers, and environmentalists has been strong enough to wring some significant legal changes out of a state legislature that once was held in a hammerlock by a minerals trust which included the Anaconda Company, owners of the Butte mine. At the turn of the century the minerals trust forced the calling of a special session of the state legislature by laying off three-quarters of the state's industrial work force. As recently as 1959 Anaconda owned seven of the state's fourteen daily newspapers.

And so many Montanans, having experienced some degree of colonization in the past, do not wish to invite the companies back for coal this time. As Ross said, "The attitude now is if they want the coal, they're going to have to pay for it. Otherwise, we ought to leave it in the ground until it turns to diamonds. Then we'll really have a bargain."

"Paying for it" has come to mean, for the coal companies, giving the state a 30 percent tax on all coal mined, one of the nation's highest coal-severance taxes. It has also come to mean that new power plants must run a risk of having to close down during a dry year, for after the water moratorium ended the state rewrote its water-allocation laws to place the power plants in a priority low enough that they would not get the necessary water in a drought year.

The Northern Cheyenne, in many ways in the lead in the opposition to energy colonization, in June 1978 won a major victory which could keep the second pair of Colstrip power plants from being built. The Environmental Protection Agency denied a permit for the two plants because they would degrade the Class I air-quality status of the reservation. If the plants were built, the EPA stated, the sulfur dioxide from their stacks would pollute the Northern Cheyenne's air to a degree not allowed for a Class I area. The combination of the five power companies from Montana and the Pacific Northwest which want to build the plants appealed the EPA ruling to the Ninth Circuit Court of Appeals in San Francisco. As the Cheyenne fought the power companies, two more Montana Indian nations, the Fort Peck and Flathead, requested Class I air-quality status from the EPA.

Such victories—the Northern Cheyenne were the first governmental body in the United States to win a conflict arising from a Class I designation—have not come cheaply. Between 1970 and 1975 the Cheyenne spent an average of $465,000 a year on legal fees and other costs associated with court battles—an average of $150 a year per tribally enrolled reservation resident. The tribe had hired its own attorneys, environmental scientists, and lease negotiators (the Crow had done the same), withdrawing in natural resource matters from the "protection" of the BIA. In so doing, in the words of Tribal Chairman Allen Rowland, they were acting to "ensure the protection and preservation of ourselves as a tribe and [to ensure that] we as a whole will determine our own course."[18] The viewpoint which had taken hold during the decade of the 1970s was best summed up by Russel Barsh, a former attorney for the Crows, now a professor of business, government, and society at the University of Washington: "Exploitation is at the end of all Indian policy."[19] More Indians—and more Montanans—were echoing the century-old words of the Blackfeet chief Curlyhead: "Our land is more valuable than your money. It will last forever. It will not even perish by the flames of the fire. As long as the sun shines and the waters flow, this land will be here to give life to men and animals. Therefore, we cannot sell this land."[20]

The *Wasi'chu* have not, however, gone away; every legal victory is challenged in court; the companies put their immense financial resources to work to back candidates for tribal office who would try to quiet the resistance to resource exploitation. Promises of immediate monetary payments are dangled in front of Indians living on reservations where per capita incomes are less than $1,500 a year, and unemployment ranges up to more than 50 percent during some seasons. The battles, and the legal costs, seem never to end. It is a strange system, say some Cheyenne, which gives you paper rights, and then forces you to spend years in court and hundreds of thousands of dollars to have those rights recognized.

Sammy Ridge Bear, a twenty-three-year-old Cheyenne, often visits a small lake in the wooded hills near Lame Deer. The lake is dying, rimmed by a crust of slime and automobile tires. According to the U.S. Supreme Court, the tribe has rights to the water that flows into this dying lake.[21] Non-Indians have been siphoning off the water. Here lies another expensive legal battle.

Sammy (his nickname is Stoney) feels deeply about the lake's dying. He looks at the slimy surface and remembers the fish he took from it years ago, how the lakes hosted swimmers, and housed spirits. Stoney sings and composes songs of Indian heritage and present-day struggles, songs in which every word has meaning. He fights a century-old system of subjugation which steals from an Indian people their economic and political base and attempts to "educate" them out of their culture. The system aims at strip mining the Cheyenne soul, as well as strip mining the land.

Down the dusty streets of Lame Deer a car filled with out-of-state tourists passes the trading post. It has New Jersey plates. The driver says that the group decided to detour from the freeway "to see some *real* Indians." He remarks that reservation life seems easy, "The government gives them everything." It is a distorted view from the other side of a mental frontier, from envoys of a culture which has taken so much from the Cheyenne, and is poised to take more.

Along the sides of the dusty streets elderly people sit on bare mattresses outside hot, tiny, boxlike houses. There are no

libraries or movie houses on the reservation to disturb the
enforced idleness which breeds despair, loss of purpose and of
identity, and alcoholism. People deprived of purpose drink and
establish status by fighting—and calling it all "a good time."
Death visits Cheyenne homes often, and many times it is related to alcohol—booze-bred fights or traffic accidents. Stoney
lists a number of friends—ages twenty, twenty-one, twenty-
two—all dead.

Stoney turns his wrists upward and shows the slit scars.
Before he understood the system that was working on him, he
took part in it, drinking and fighting and stealing, and then
one cold morning waking hung over, outside the realm of escape, fearing that the past was forever gone and the future
would be no better, that he and his children—if he lives to have
them—would remain strangers in their own land.

Stoney turns his wrists over. He has not tried to kill himself
for several years.

Stoney has been invited into the death trap many times
during his twenty-four years. Understanding the contours of
the trap, he will not walk into it again; he says, too, that his
people will also survive. Fewer Cheyenne will walk into the
early death invited by the *Wasi'chu*'s enforced idleness, cultural repression, and alcohol; fewer will call genocide "a good
time": "The man has no reason to want us to live. There is coal
on our land, and we are in the way."

In the hills a few miles from Lame Deer Stoney takes his
visitors to a small plot of land surrounded by a fence he built.
Inside the fence a few dozen buffalo graze, symbols of rebirth.
It will be a long way back; the Cheyenne are leading many
Montanans along a difficult trail.

8

The Usual and Accustomed Places

ARTICLE III. The right of taking fish at all usual and accustomed places is further secured to said Indians in common with all citizens of the territory...

　　　　　—Medicine Creek Treaty, 1854

A Quinault fisherman. Photo courtesy of Kim Steele and the Quinault Indian Nation.

When the Romans colonized Gaul about the time of the birth of Christ, they found a fish-eating people. Soon the demand for the fish they named *salmo*, "the climber," rose in Roman markets. The waters were overfished; stocks were depleted, until in the ensuing centuries the salmon became extinct in many European rivers.[1] The taste for salmon traveled with the European colonists to the New World; in 1654 Jesuit fathers Le Moyne and Le Mercier, riding the cutting edge of conquest on a diplomatic mission to the Onondaga for the French government, noticed that there were so many fish in Lake Ontario that they could be speared or clubbed with paddles. The last salmon to be caught in that body of water was taken during 1896.[2] Wherever the *Wasi'chu* implanted a civilization that emphasized predatory profit without regard for the needs of nature, the salmon died; by the turn of the century, the descendants of the fishermen who had feasted on salmon in Europe before cattle and sheep were domesticated were looking for the fish in the many streams of the Pacific Northwest.[3] In that area, it was said, one could walk across the backs of the salmon from one stream bank to another when the whites first set eyes on the area during the last century; it is estimated that fifty thousand Indians took eighteen million pounds of salmon a year from the Columbia River watershed before "civilization" began to deplete the runs.[4]

To the Northwest Indian nations the salmon was as central to economic life as the buffalo was on the plains; 80 to 90 percent of the Puyallup diet, for example, was of the pink-fleshed fish.[5] The salmon was more than food; it was the center of a way of life. A cultural festival accompanied the first salmon caught in the yearly run. The fish was barbecued over an open fire and bits of its flesh parceled out to all. The bones were saved intact, to be carried by a torch-bearing, singing, dancing, and chanting procession back to the river, where they were placed into the water, the head pointed upstream, symbolic of the spawning fish, so the run would return a thousandfold.[6]

The ceremonies showed an extraordinary respect for the salmon and a desire to maintain the runs for future generations. With techniques honed by centuries of practice, without the careless industrialism that dammed, polluted, and overfished rivers, Indian fishermen sustained an average annual run of 18 million pounds, which is close to the present catch for the entire state of Washington.

White people began to settle in what is now Washington in large numbers during the 1850s; their primary vocation was cutting timber and growing food for the swelling population of California, where the yellow metal that makes the *Wasi'chu* crazy had been discovered during 1849. The first settlers were predominantly interested in acquiring land, not fish. So when the Indians agreed to give up large amounts of land in exchange for the treaty right to fish at their "usual and accustomed places," the federal government signed. Like the gold of the Black Hills, the salmon of the Northwest did not become valuable in the eyes of the *Wasi'chu* until after the treaties were signed.

Washington became a territory of the United States on March 2, 1853, with no consent from the Indians who held title to most of the land. Isaac Stevens was appointed governor and superintendent of Indian affairs for the territory. As governor, Stevens wished to build the economic base of the territory; this required the attraction of a proposed transcontinental railroad, which, in turn, required peace with the Indians.[7] Stevens worked with remarkable speed; in 1854 and 1855 alone, he negotiated four treaties with six thousand Indian people west of the Cascades. During the same years, he wrested from the Indians most of the present-day states of Montana and Idaho, as well as eastern Washington.

In all the treaties Stevens drove an extremely tough bargain, but the Indians would not relent on one point: the continued right to fish. Stevens said: "It was also thought necessary to allow them to fish at all accustomed places, since this would not in any manner interfere with the rights of citizens[8] and was necessary for the Indians to obtain a subsistence."[9] He said these words after emerging from the signing of the Medicine Creek Treaty on December 26, 1854. The treaty, signed on a small island between the salt marshes not far from the present-day state capital, Olympia, guaranteed the Indians the right to fish at their usual and accustomed places "in common with" citizens of the territory. By signing the treaty, the Indians ceded to the United States 2,240,000 acres of land, an immense sacrifice for the right to fish. [10] Stevens thought he had gotten quite a bargain, because the whites of the time had come to Washington Territory to supply California gold boomtowns with lumber and food, not to fish.

In the seventy years after the signing of Medicine Creek and other treaties in western Washington, the non-Indian population increased considerably. As the salmon were exterminated along much of the American and European Atlantic shoreline, fishermen began to move to the Northwest. By the turn of the century Washington was ignorning the treaties and arresting Indian fishermen who were taking salmon in accordance with them. State police arrested Indians for fishing as early as 1913. [11] By 1929 the state had decided to deny the Quinault their fishing rights and to lease these rights to Bakers Bay, a private company, for $36,000. [12] At the same time that non-Indian fishermen were increasing their catch, the encroachment of civilization was decimating the runs. Around 1914 sixteen million fish were caught; by the 1920s annual catches had declined to an average of six million. In the late 1930s, following construction of several large hydroelectric dams on the Columbia and its tributaries, the annual catch had fallen as low as three million. Salmon are migratory fish; they spawn at the headwaters of rivers and streams, travel downstream as smolts or fry to the open ocean, and then—three, four, or five years after they have hatched—return to their birthplaces to spawn again. Dams severely cut into this migratory cycle; the damage has only been partly remedied by construction of fish ladders and artificial hatcheries. Salmon are also extremely sensitive to changes in water temperature, oxygen content, and turbidity, so sensitive that logging and industrial development have destroyed many of their breeding grounds. In recent years the annual catch has averaged four to six million.

By 1960 the number of non-Indian fishermen—many of whom had migrated from Scandinavia—was rising rapidly, competing for a diminishing fish supply. Between 1947 and

1976 the number of commercial gill-netters rose from 428 to 1,659.[13] Between 1965 and 1974 the number of commercial fishing licenses issued by the state more than doubled, feeding money into a state bureaucracy which grew into an antitreaty police force.[14]

The huge increase in the number of fishermen, and the decrease in runs, was compounded by changes in the nature of the fishery. Indian fishermen traditionally took their catch from the mouths of rivers, using nets and small boats. Non-Indian fishermen, on the other hand, used much more costly open-water fishing gear, including sonar, to get the fish before they returned to the streams to spawn. The cost and energy effectiveness of the Indian fishery has led University of Washington professor Russel Barsh to conclude that open-water fishing should be banned.[15] A root of the problem, wrote Barsh, is that the fish are regarded as a common good in a capitalistic economy—they belong to whoever catches them. The common-good nature of the resource has caused too many fishermen to spend too much energy chasing immature fish across the ocean with expensive gear, to get at them before anyone else does. Instead of addressing this problem, Barsh wrote, state regulatory agencies have used the Indians as a scapegoat: Indians were being accused of "overfishing" in the late 1950s, when they took less than 1 percent of the total state harvest.[16]

By the early 1960s state fisheries police were conducting wholesale arrests of Indians, confiscating their boats and nets. Indian nations took their treaty-rights case to state courts and found them solidly in support of non-Indian commercial interests. In 1962 the Washington State Supreme Court ruled against a Swinomish Indian who had asserted fishing rights under the 1855 Treaty of Point Elliott. The court held that the state had the right to subject Indians to "reasonable and necessary regulations" for conservation.[17] It was a rather hypocritical ruling, considering that the Indians had not built the dams, logged the forests, or constructed the pulp mills which—without regard for the biological needs of the fish—had helped to reduce the runs by three-quarters in fifty years. The ruling, however, was not out of character for a state supreme court which had held in 1916 that at no time did our ancestors in getting title to this continent ever regard the Aborigines as other than mere occupants, and incompetent occupants of the soil ... Neither Rome nor sagacious Britain ever dealt more liberally with their subject races than we with these savage tribes whom it was generally tempting and always easy to destroy and whom we have so often permitted to squander vast areas of fertile land before our eyes.[18]

Denied justice in the state courts, the tribes pursued their claim at the federal level. During the 1960s and early 1970s, they militantly protected their rights. A nucleus of fishing-rights activists from Franks Landing, only a few miles from where the Medicine Creek Treaty had been signed, stood on the law which gave them the right to fish as long as the rivers run.[19] Day by day the rivers ran, the Indians fished, and the paper battle continued in the courts. Vigilante sports fishermen joined state fisheries police in harassing the Indians, slashing and stealing their boats and nets, and, at times, shooting at them. The elders and women stood with the younger men. Maisel and Al Bridges, mother and father, fished beside their daughters, Suzette Mills, Valerie and Allison Bridges. All stood alongside the young men, Hank Adams, Sid Mills, and others. Supporters from Seattle joined the Indians in their confrontation with the police, the vigilantes, and the cold rain. Chicanos from El Centro de la Raza took an active part in these early battles, as did the National Indian Youth Council of Albuquerque, N.M.[20] Marlon Brando, Dick Gregory, and Jane Fonda stopped by to hoist nets, and spread the aura of national publicity, making the Northwest conflict over fish the first widely publicized treaty-rights defense of modern times, although many other struggles were going on—particularly in the North and West, where subjugation was little more than a century in the past.

By 1965 the United States Supreme Court had ruled that Indians had a right to fish at their "usual and accustomed places" but that the state had the right, through its courts, to regulate Indian fishing. The ruling, and a few federal rulings after it, had little practical effect as long as the state, whose fishery managers were adamantly opposed to any Indian fishing at all, held enforcement power. The fish-ins and harrassment continued until February 12, 1974, when United States District Court Judge George Boldt ruled that Indians were entitled to an opportunity to catch as many as half the fish returning to off-reservation sites which had been the "usual and accustomed places" when the treaties were signed.

Boldt had put three years into the case; he used two hundred pages to interpret one sentence of the treaty in an opinion, which, legal scholars say, "is the most carefully researched, thoroughly analyzed ever handed down in an Indian fishing-rights case."[21] The nucleus of Boldt's decision had to do with nineteenth century dictionaries' definitions of "in common with." Boldt said the word meant shared equally. During the next three years the Ninth Circuit Court of Appeals upheld Boldt's ruling, and the U.S. Supreme Court twice let it stand by refusing to hear it.

State officials, and the fishermen whose interests they represented, were furious at Boldt. Rumors were circulated about the seventy-five-year old jurist. It was said that he had taken bribes of free fish and had an Indian mistress, neither of which was true. He was hung in effigy by angry non-Indian fishermen, who on other occasions formed "convoys" with their boats and rammed coast-guard vessels which had been dispatched to enforce the court's orders. At least one coastguardsman was shot. State Senator August Mardesich, himself a commercial fisherman, proposed that the state withhold social services from Indians who failed to comply with the state-fishing laws Boldt had declared unconstitutional.[22] Even while the commercial interests raged, the Indians were catching nothing close to the 50 percent allowed by the Boldt ruling; in 1974 they caught between 7 and 8 percent, in 1975 between 11 and 12 percent, in 1976 between 13 and 25 percent, and in 1977, 17 percent, depending on who did the counting, the Indians or the state.[23]

Among state officials during the middle and late 1970s a backlash to Indian rights formed, which would become the nucleus for a nationwide non-Indian campaign to abrogate the treaties (see chapter 9). Washington State Attorney General Slade Gorton called Indians "supercitizens" with "special rights," and proposed that constitutional equilibrium be re-established not by open state violation of the treaties (Boldt had outlawed that), but by purchasing the Indians' fishing rights. The tribes, which had been listening to offers of *Wasi'chu* money for Indian resources for a century, flatly refused his offer. To them, the selling of fishing rights would have been tantamount to termination.

One thing that the state advocates of treaty abrogation were anticipating was another court case, popularly tagged "Phase II" of the cases which began with Boldt's 1974 ruling. In this part of the case Indians are asking for a voice in matters such as antipollution and zoning regulations, as well as building permits, which affect the size and health of salmon runs which pass through their "usual and accustomed places." The economic stakes of Phase II greatly overshadow those of the first fishing ruling. Among those who would need to consider Indian viewpoints under such a ruling would be land developers, including power companies and other industries which desire plant sites near rivers and streams. As if to foreshadow the case, the tribes of the Skagit Valley (north of Seattle) in June 1978 asked to intervene in federal hearings on two nuclear power plants which Puget Sound Power and Light wants to build. The tribes were concerned about the salmon runs in the Skagit River and the threat that could be posed by the nuclear plants, which would use river water for cooling and then discharge it back into the river several degrees warmer than when it was taken out. Salmon are very sensitive to water temperature. The position of the Skagit Valley tribes was in some ways similar to that of the Northern Cheyenne in pursuing their Class I designation under the Clean Air Act (chapter 7). The basic rationale is that Indian nations should have a voice in developments which might degrade the environment of their reservations or the livelihood of tribal members.

As the treaty Indian tribes moved to implement Judge Boldt's ruling, the state's resistance stiffened again; Boldt himself assumed the state's management power over the fishery piece by piece. On April 25, 1978, however, Judge Boldt withdrew from the second phase of the case but said he would continue to oversee the first phase as much as his health allowed after the major surgery he had just undergone. The day

after he withdrew from the second phase of the case the Ninth
Circuit Court of Appeals in San Francisco upheld Boldt's assumption of the state's fishery management, including allocation of salmon between Indians and non-Indians.

As the legal maneuvering continued, non-Indian fishermen
disobeyed the Boldt ruling in force; several dozen were cited
during 1977 and 1978. United States Magistrate Robert Coop-
er, who had taken Judge Boldt's place on the bench while the
judge recuperated, said that there had been increasing difficulty since 1974 in enforcing the treaty rights of the Indian
nations and that irreparable harm would be done to treaty
fishermen if the lack of enforcement were to continue.[24] The
non-Indian fishermen replied that the Boldt ruling was unconstitutional, although no federal court had agreed with them.

Judge Boldt totally withdrew from the case on February 7,
1979. The day after, he said he was shocked by the violent
tactics non-Indian fishermen had used to resist his ruling. "It
came as a shock to me to discover that the vast majority of
Washington residents, at least those who fish, don't give a
damn about Indian rights," he stated. The judge said he had
great confidence in the Supreme Court, which had agreed to
hear an appeal brought by the state of Washington on February
28, 1979. Among treaty Indians, however, talk was heard that
the Supreme Court—the "Nixon Court," which had already
eroded the rights of many Americans, Indians included—was
readying a "Bakke decision" for native Americans.

The evolving state-federal court conflict over Washington
treaty fishing rights shared some legal ground with the Cherokee cases which had led to the Trail of Tears (chapter 1). In
both cases state agencies and courts were being used by non-Indian special interest groups to wrest control of a resource guaranteed by treaty—the Cherokee's gold, the Northwest tribes'
fish. In both cases federal courts generally interpreted the
treaties as favoring the Indians. And in both cases the federal
executive bowed in with a plan to circumvent the treaties.

President Jimmy Carter's parallel to Andrew Jackson, another Southern semipopulist Democrat, came veiled in the
skilled public relations of the twentieth century, as Jackson's

had been shrouded in the rationalizations of the nineteenth. The vehicle for twentieth century treaty abrogation was a Federal Fisheries Task Force.

After more than a year of investigation the Federal Task Force issued a settlement proposal, to be forwarded to Congress, which, according to the plan, would legislate a solution to the "fish war" which would supersede the Boldt decision. A new Congressional act could also be used in court as evidence that a new agreement had been reached between the federal government and the tribes. It could not be called a treaty (Congress had ended treaty-making in 1871) but could be used to supersede the agreements of 1854 and 1855, upon which the Boldt rulings had been based.

The federal task force's proposal recommended that management of state waters be returned to the state Department of Fisheries—the agency that had evaded treaty rights for years before Judge Boldt himself assumed control of the fishery. A tribal commission would be formed, under the proposal, to manage smaller zones. Steelhead trout management would be returned to the state Department of Game, which for decades before the Boldt ruling had attempted to reserve this agile fish for non-Indian sports activity. Most western Washington tribes would be forced to give up their steelhead catch. The plan proposed to allow treaty fishermen to catch up to 40 percent of the catch, instead of the Boldt formula 50 percent. As a concession, the plan proposed a reduction in the size of the non-Indian fishing fleet and the spending of $15.4 million to increase the size and efficiency of the Indian fleet.

A keystone of the proposal was an "enhancement program," involving $121.6 million budgeted to construct new artificial hatcheries to build the salmon runs back to 1914 levels, or approximately the level which would allow fifteen million fish to be caught each year. Under the plan, the majority of the new hatcheries would be managed by the state.

This was the plan as it would be proposed to Congress, where representatives addled by non-Indian majorities would have a chance to build it (as Congress built the General Allotment Act of 1887) into a device by which to abrogate the treaties.

By the time the final proposal was issued in mid-1978, some Indian tribes questioned the assumption that more hatcheries would automatically produce more harvestable fish; the fundamentally *Wasi'chu* assumption of a technological fix, without full knowledge of natural mechanisms, could fail, they said. Fisheries biologists for the Quinault Indian Nation provided statistics which indicated that if the state really wanted to double the hatchery-bred runs, it could by applying better feeding and breeding standards to existing hatcheries.

At the University of Washington (UW), for example, where highly refined feeding and nurturing methods are used, 160,000 salmon were released during 1972; of those, 2,461 returned to the hatchery, or 1.5 percent. An estimated 1 to 2 percent were caught before returning, giving an estimated survival rate of 2.5 to 3.5 percent. Comparable survival rates for the university hatchery fish released during 1973 were between 3 and 4 percent. For fish released during 1974 the rate was between 5 and 6 percent.

State hatcheries, by comparison, had return rates one-fifth to one-tenth or less that of the UW plant. During 1972, for example, 533,177 tagged fish were released from hatcheries operated by the state at Green River, Minter Creek, and Puyallup (all the streams empty into Puget Sound). The return rate—1,329 were caught or returned—was 0.25 percent. The following year 639,491 tagged fish were released from three state hatcheries, which, like UW's, are located on Puget Sound rivers and streams. The return rate was 0.18 percent. During 1974 the state's return rate for 202,729 fish released from the Green River Hatchery was 0.67 percent.

The differences in survival rates indicate that if scientific breeding and feeding were to be applied to state hatcheries, the surviving runs could be doubled, or more, while spending a fraction of what is proposed for new hatcheries.

The spread of hatcheries also raises other biological questions which tribal fisheries biologists have begun to explore, such as: Do carelessly raised hatchery fish spread disease among the natural runs? Do the large numbers of hatchery-bred fry and smolts which eventually die crowd hardier fish from natural runs out of feeding areas, decreasing the overall return rate? These questions will have to be answered on the scientific level. On the political level the Fisheries Task Force seems to be one step in repressing the exercise of the treaty rights state agencies had ignored—and had harassed the treaty Indians for practicing—until Indian militance forced a clarification of the issue from Judge Boldt's court. The state offensive was one part of a nationwide backlash which emerged against treaty rights during the middle and late 1970s, a movement fueled by economic interests, shrouded by *Wasi'chu* politics and legalities which brought the conditions of the third world home.

III

The Wasi'chu's Last Stand

9

The Third World at Home

The gasification controversy on the Navajo reservation and the stripmining monstrosity on the Northern Cheyenne point out the Interior Department's perversion of responsibility to Indian people. ... In truth the Interior Department serves oil, mineral, land-trust, transportation, fisheries, shipping, forestry and other energy interests at the expense of Indian lives.
—Trial of Self-Determination Proposal[1]

For nearly all tribes, the period 1848-1871 ... represents the beginning of a long "colonial" period. America's "rise to world power" entailed the reduction of Native Americans to the status of a captive population, euphemistically termed "wards."
—Tentative Final Report[2]

The Longest Walk, Washington, D.C., July 15, 1978. Photographs by JEB.

A gentle, but steady October rain was falling against the windows of the Seattle Indian Center on a fall day in 1972. The gray sky which produced the rain contrasted sharply with the artificial sunshine of the television cameras inside the building. The rain's patter was muted by the cameras' whirring. The electronic attention was focused on a press conference given by Hank Adams and Sid Mills, long-time Northwest fishing-rights activists, and on Russell Means, a founder of the American Indian Movement (AIM).

The press conference had two purposes: first, to express grief over the death of Richard Oakes, a Mohawk, who had been a leader of the Indian occupation at Alcatraz three years earlier; second, to demand that the federal government fulfill its treaty obligations to protect Indian people from a rising tide of vigilante retribution—one act of which had claimed Oakes's life—which had followed early assertions of treaty rights. The demand would be carried to Washington, D.C., by a Trail of Broken Treaties that would cross the country to address some of the concerns Oakes had expressed before his life had been cut short.

Oakes had died prematurely—he was 30—fighting the same historical battles which had taken the lives of uncounted numbers of his ancestors during the previous five hundred years. Adams, Mills, and Means, who had come together to mourn Oakes's death and to plan how to carry out his wishes, were living proof that the land-and-resource wars of earlier centuries had not ended. Adams had narrowly escaped assassination during January 1971. He had been checking fishing nets on the Nisqually River in Washington when two men drove by him in a car. They cursed his advocacy of Indian fishing rights and shot him in the side. The bullet missed Adams's vital organs, and he recovered.[3] Mills had been drafted into the army and set to Vietnam, where his body was riddled with shrapnel. After returning to the United States, he was reunited with his heritage through Indian activists at Fort Lewis, near Franks Landing. Mills then walked out of the army to help uphold treaty rights he had not even known of before he went to Vietnam, facing the guns and clubs of county, state, and federal police, who were trying to deny western Washington Indians their treaty rights to fish, rights later upheld by Federal Judge George Boldt (chapter 8).

The death of Oakes had galvanized Indians heretofore involved in regional struggles in the North and West into forming a national movement, which would undertake a grueling journey to Washington, D.C., in late October 1972. Caravans from Seattle and San Francisco stopped in Minneapolis, where other activists joined them to draft a twenty-point petition of grievances for President Nixon's administration. The eulogy for Oakes would be the birth of a national movement, which during the following years would reawaken many Americans, Indians included, to the reality of a war of five hundred years, which had never ended, and to the brutality still being used to sweep aside those who would not idly assent to the *Wasi'chu* usurpation of their lands, resources, and lives.

Oakes had been active in a wave of Indian occupations during the late 1960s, one of which involved Alcatraz Island, based on Indians' legal right to first claim on federal land declared surplus. These occupations—others occurred at Ellis Island, New York City, and Fort Lawton in Seattle,[4] were among the first signs of militance in the new American Indian resolution to resist further decimation. In commemorating Oakes, Adams told the television cameras:

> Richard Oakes's presence beyond Alcatraz and his influence upon many Indian people shall continue to live within the body and soul of Indian experience. Born to the American soil and responding strongly to his peoples' struggle and suffering upon it, the living spirit of Richard Oakes could not now die or cease to be remembered upon the American land.

Oakes had died while walking, unarmed, along a dirt road near a YMCA camp outside Santa Rosa, California. On September 20, 1972, Michael Oliver Morgan, a caretaker at the camp, put a bullet through Oakes' heart.

That Morgan had shot Oakes was not disputed in court. What was disputed were Morgan's motives. Morgan asserted that Oakes, who was unarmed, had attacked him; attorneys for the prosecution pictured Morgan as trigger-happy and disturbed by Oakes's advocacy of Indian treaty rights—especially hunting rights.

Morgan testified in court that Oakes had jumped him from behind and threatened to kill him; prosecution witnesses told the jury that analysis of the scene of the shooting indicated Morgan had shot Oakes from a prone position some distance from where Oakes fell. At the trial Frank Greer, a visitor to the YMCA camp, testified that Morgan had told him, "It's open season on coons, foxes and Indians."[5] Despite such evidence, a state court jury, on March 16, 1973, acquitted Morgan of manslaughter charges.[6]

Antagonism between Morgan and Oakes had surfaced September 14, 1972, six days before the shooting. During late evening of that day Oakes had set out with his daughter, Little Fawn, who was two years old, and Billy Lazore, fifteen, from Oakes's home. They were looking for Oakes's eleven-year-old son, who was late for dinner. After leaving the Kashia reservation, where Oakes lived, Oakes dropped Lazore near the YMCA camp so that the boy could search on foot. A short time later Oakes drove into the parking lot of the camp. He saw Lazore facing another young man, Robert Myers. Myers, an employee of the camp, was holding a rifle. The two had been arguing about Indian hunting rights. Morgan then appeared near the door of his home, next to the parking lot, and joined the argument on Myers's side. Taking the rifle that Myers had been holding, Morgan cocked it and fired over Oakes's head. Billy then pulled a knife and told Morgan that if he shot Oakes, he would have to kill both of them. Oakes took the knife from Lazore, and after more heated words the confrontation dissolved.

Less than a week later Morgan shot Oakes to death not far from the parking lot.

The death of Oakes, a well-known and admired leader, was the catalyst which brought together fishing-rights activists in the Northwest, members of the relatively new American Indian Movement on the Great Plains, and other individuals and groups which had been pursuing disconnected, isolated treaty claims. Leaders from the Northwest fishing struggle, such as

Adams and Mills, had had a hand in the formation of AIM, which began in Minneapolis-St. Paul during 1968, a century after most of the Plains tribes had signed their last treaties with the United States. During its early years AIM was an urban-Indian group, which concentrated on such projects as a street patrol in Minneapolis to reduce police harrassment of Indian people. AIM also assisted Indians in difficulties with the welfare bureaucracy and slumlords. During this early period AIM members studied their history and culture—much of it being learned in prison or the universities—and realized that they had been indoctrinated with ideas that alienated them both from their spiritual heritage and their relationship to the land. Gradually they returned to reservations, primarily those of the Lakota, from which many residents of the Minneapolis Indian community had moved under federal relocation programs. About the same time Oakes was killed, AIM was invited to the Pine Ridge Reservation by the Oglala Sioux Civil Rights Organization to aid in its fight against the corrupt tribal government.

The new unity of purpose was displayed in the Trail of Broken Treaties, an automobile caravan across the United States, which began shortly after Oakes was killed. The caravan itself did not get much official attention, nor did the Indians. When they arrived in Washington, D.C., President Nixon, involved in his campaign against George McGovern, ignored the Indian visitors. The lack of media attention ended when the group occupied the head office of the Bureau of Indian Affairs, in order to get a hearing for the twenty-point bill of particulars they had brought.

The occupation was not intended; the Indians had first approached the BIA looking for a place to stay, which would replace a rat-infested church where they were housed while seeking appointments with government officials. A group of Indians entered the BIA headquarters asking to meet with officials. Police, who had surrounded the building, panicked and called the entry an occupation. The Indians, in turn, broke off a few table legs to defend themselves. And so the "occupation" began.

The media, as usual, emphasized the "violence" of the occupation and ignored the issues which had caused it. The government did the same; the Nixon White House set up the beginnings of the extensive program of physical subjugation outlined previously. The Indians' bill of grievances called for a renewal of treaty-making, relief from past treaty-rights violations, a Congressional investigation into the Bureau of Indian Affairs and related components of the colonial system, abrogation of multinationals' leases for Indian land and resources, repeal of termination acts carried out during the 1950s, repeal of Public Law 53-280,[7] establishment of an Indian grand jury at the national level, recognition of Indian jurisdiction over non-Indians on treaty land, improved treatment of prisoners, and financial aid to get Indians started on a path toward economic self-determination.[8]

Their demands unanswered, many of the Indians involved in the BIA occupation reassembled at Wounded Knee four months later, on the site where more than three hundred Lakota men, women, and children had been massacred by the United States Army in 1890. Many of the grievances were raised again. Again, the government responded with a deaf ear and a strong arm; after the seventy-one-day occupation, the physical repression of Indian resistance intensified.

In 1891, months after the massacre, Red Cloud, a Lakota chief, said of the army and the infrastructure supporting it,

> We felt mocked in our misery. We had no newspapers and no one to speak for us. We had no redress. Our rations were reduced again. You who eat three times a day and see your children well and happy around you cannot understand how starving Indians feel.[9]

In 1973, as in 1890, the *Wasi'chu* saw an "Indian problem" where there was, in actuality, a "*Wasi'chu* problem." And so, instead of addressing the fundamental causes of disorder, the response was one of armed force. During the seventy-one-day occupation, two people at Wounded Knee were killed in a government exercise in encirclement, which was later revealed to have been a test of a nationwide military plan, known as "Operation Cablesplicer," for suppressing civilian disorders.

What enraged the *Wasi'chu* even more than the occupation

was the fact that inside the rings of federal armor, despite day-to-day bombardment, the three hundred or so people inside Wounded Knee were forming their own government, separate from that of the United States, calling it the Independent Oglala Nation. These people, who had resisted or thrown off the more subtle and systematic forms of cultural and personal repression which make up the "Indian system," were in effect renouncing the tribal government of Dick Wilson. It was not just Wilson they renounced, but the entire system, which had been imposed by the United States on Indian nations as part of the Indian Reorganization Act of 1934. Having set up the tribal governmental system, the United States funded it and destroyed Indians' traditional means of economic survival, such as the buffalo and agriculture. The occupation of Wounded Knee was asking that the 1868 Fort Laramie Treaty be honored; the government's answer was the dispatching of the FBI, the twentieth-century Seventh Cavalry.

While the FBI spent millions of tax dollars to tie up as many Indian movement leaders in court and jail as possible (chapter 4), the movement to assert treaty rights continued to grow; the gross abuse of the judicial system on the part of the government helped to sharpen the contradiction between the myth of trust responsibility and the historical reality that the BIA and other government agencies were actually administering colonies within the United States. In 1976, as pledged by the Trail of Broken Treaties, another caravan crossed the country, shadowing the commercialized Bicentennial Wagon Train. This time, a Chicano-Mexican position paper accompanied the Trail of Self-Determination proposal. The Chicanos also had treaty violations to address: the trampling of the terms of the 1848 Treaty of Guadalupe Hidalgo had thrown many Chicanos off their land, forcing them into near-serfdom as migrant workers, a mobile nation, who followed the ripening crops north, then south through the West and Great Plains each year. The migrant stream became one of the largest "Indian reservations" in the country, and the only one on wheels.

The Trail of Self-Determination arrived in Washington, D.C., for the Bicentennial Weekend, and its participants pointed to the fact that they would have nothing to celebrate until the country that was celebrating its own freedom from colonization stopped colonizing the peoples within its own borders.

By the bicentennial year, American Indian self-determination and sovereignty had become a coherent doctrine behind scores of treaty-rights' assertions around the country. The legal value of the treaties was being realized—from Washington to Maine—as an outgrowth of the militancy of the early 1970s. The legal offensive had as its primary aim the ambition to end the spiritual and economic poverty which had marked almost two centuries of federal government "protection" of Indian interests.

In the state of Washington, for example, the Yakima Nation, which includes some of the richest farmland in the state, in 1977 served notice on non-Indian farmers that they would have to obtain permits from the tribal government for irrigation water. Most of the state's twenty-two tribes with land bases had, or were developing, tax codes. During 1977 two tribes enacted retail sales taxes—the Quileute and the Muckleshoot. The Muckleshoot, a small tribe southeast of Seattle, implemented a 2.5 percent sales tax which excluded prescription drugs and food purchased with food stamps. The same tribe also implemented a 0.4 percent business-and-occupation tax on gross sales. The taxes were aimed at a ready source of income: a suburban shopping center on reservation land serving the area between Seattle and Tacoma, which had been rapidly subdivided.

The Oglala Nation in South Dakota by 1977 was levying taxes on land sales, land use, grazing permits, occupation permits, cigarettes, and retail sales and services. In 1975 the Oglala raised 92 percent of their tribal budget—$660,000 of $720,000—from tribal taxes.[10] The reservation's residents were planning four small shopping centers which would be tribally owned, as well as two arrow factories and a prefabricated housing plant. Community gardens also were being planned.[11]

The Navajo have for years operated tribal businesses which competed with the expensive, non-Indian-owned trading posts.

The tribe also designed a sophisticated tax code aimed at corporations which exploit the reservation's rich stores of coal, uranium, and other natural resources. The value-added tax, intended to extract money from wealthy corporations rather than poor Navajo (as a sales tax would), was drawn up by Frank Ryan, a Blackfeet, who specializes in tax codes for developing nations from his post at Harvard. Ryan's objective is to break down a colonial relationship which draws wealth away from Indian nations in a manner similar to that which plagues many third-world countries. [12]

Given the sweep of treaty-based assertions by the late 1970s, only a few of which have been examined in this book, it was inevitable that economic interests which had benefited for so long from their violation of the treaties would strike back. As the treaty-rights movement spread, so did the "backlash" movement, made up of non-Indians whose economic interests stood to be impaired by Indian rights. In the state of Washington, for example, where both treaty assertion and backlash to it got an early start, opposition to Indian rights spread from non-Indian commercial and sports fishermen to reservation landowners and merchants to farmers and ranchers who chafed at asking the Yakima for irrigation permits. The political and economic opposition to the treaties included state governments in Washington and elsewhere. Political office seekers sought to mollify angry white constituents, and economically the states' saw themselves losing tax revenues on such ventures as Indians' sale of tax-free cigarettes.

In 1975 Howard Gray, a Seattle resident, traveled to Montana to speak to an antitreaty group calling itself Montanans Opposed to Discrimination. Out of that meeting grew a new organization, the Interstate Congress for Equal Rights and Responsibilities (ICERR). The group held its first convention in 1976 in Salt Lake City, with ten state chapters represented. By the end of 1977 ICERR had chapters in at least twenty states and affiliations with groups with different names but similar purposes in at least six others. [13]

The Interstate Congress was in many ways a historical product of the Allotment Act of 1887; it was that act which broke up the Indian land base, held communally since antiquity, in many areas and allowed non-Indians to buy into reservation lands on a broad scale. By the 1970s many reservations contained more non-Indians than Indians, and these non-Indians began to work against the legal powers that the tribes needed to assert self-determination.

For example, on the Suquamish Reservation, across Puget Sound west of Seattle, the tribe in 1977 proposed an eighteen-month building moratorium, which caused intense conflict with local developers who had been putting up tract homes on reservation land to accommodate several thousand workers from the Navy's new Trident nuclear submarine base at Bangor, less than ten miles away. Non-Indians already had acquired more than five thousand of the reservation's eight thousand acres.

It was on the Suquamish Reservation that another issue of tribal sovereignty was raised that had national implications. In 1978 the U.S. Supreme Court ruled that Indian police had no jurisdiction in criminal matters over non-Indians on reservation land. The case was brought by Patrick Oliphant, who, actively supported by ICERR, said that tribal police could not arrest him for a traffic violation on the reservation. Because the Supreme Court agreed with him, many reservations have been left without adequate law enforcement.

The ICERR during the late 1970s became a well-organized pressure group, operating in the manner of its larger ideological counterpart, the National Rifle Association. Robert Bogensberger, a Mt. Vernon, Washington, chicken farmer, quickly raised $100,000 during 1977 in an attempt to impeach Judge George Boldt, whose federal court ruling had said treaty fishermen had a right to half the western Washington salmon and steelhead catch; during August 1977 Washington State Attorney General Slade Gorton hosted a meeting of western states' attorneys general. The main pupose of the meeting was to discuss, and organize against, assertion of Indian treaty rights. State tax assessors of the region met at about the same time, for the same reason.

A month later the Western Conference of the Council of State Governments called for an end to Indian sovereignty. It advocated giving the states authority over reservation zoning and land use and prohibiting the Indians' governments from taxing reservation businesses owned by non-Indians; conversely, the council recommended that states be allowed to tax Indian-owned businesses on reservations, as well as Indian land itself. The council also advocated nearly total state authority over Indian police and judicial functions. The proposals were advanced on the fictitious belief that "the United States has always been a country of equals...with no individual or group subjected to subordinate or special rights."[14]

Gorton had used the same argument at a hearing of the United States Commission on Civil Rights in October 1977, when he coined the word "supercitizen" to refer to an Indian with treaty rights. Mel Tonasket, a Colville who has been president of the National Congress of American Indians, replied somewhat tartly by asking Gorton if he would be willing "to trade places with any of the supercitizens on my reservation and make less than $2,000 a year and have your children taken away by members of another race." He also asked Gorton whether he believed that certain non-Indian Americans, such as Nelson Rockefeller, might be enjoying "supercitizenship" status.

The Washington Congressional delegation rapidly caught the fever of antitreaty jingoism, beginning with the election from Seattle's South End of Jack Cunningham, a rabidly right-wing Republican, to Congress in a 1977 special election.[15] The day after he was elected, Cunningham pledged to seek abrogation of Indian treaties; he was so zealous in keeping his promise that he introduced a bill to abolish the treaties even before he had hired his staff. He borrowed other Congressional staff members to draft the bill, which he called the "Native American Equal Opportunity Act." For the record, he said that his plan for assimilation on a grand scale was a favor to the Indians, hastening their entry into mainstream American culture. This "favor" was bestowed against the wishes of every Indian organization in the country, from the conservative National

Tribal Chairmen's Organization to the American Indian Movement.

Cunningham's bill contained a clause designed to evade the constitutional requirement that compensation be granted for land and resources taken by governmental action. Referring to existing treaties, the bill said that Congress "shall provide that there be no taking without compensation of any property right [except that] specifically created for a particular individual by such treaty." The wording excludes compensation for land held in common in the traditional manner. Despite the pressures of allotment, more than half the land of most reservations is still held in common by the tribes; in Cunningham's home state the figure is 75 percent.

Another representative from Washington, Lloyd Meeds, at the same time introduced bills which were less spectacular, but regarded as more dangerous by many Indians, than those of Cunningham. Meeds' proposals to restrict Indian water rights and legal jurisdictions were in many respects similar to those of the Western Council of the Conference of State Governments. Meeds had often spoken of himself as a "friend of the Indian" until 1976, when a Republican running on an antitreaty platform came within a few hundred votes of defeating him for the district which includes a section of the state between Seattle and the Canadian border. Even as he appeased the antitreaty lobby, Meeds accommodated his own liberal self-image to his actions. As vice-chairman of the American Indian Policy Review Commission (AIPRC), Meeds submitted a 102-page dissent to the commission report, which, as a whole advocated increased Indian self-determination. He wrote, "The quickest and most certain way to destroy that uniqueness [of Indian nations] is to immediately implement all the recommendations of this report. . . the backlash of the dominant culture would be swift and sure." Picking up a strain from Southeast Asian history, Meeds indicated that Indian nations must be destroyed to be "saved."

Meeds also echoed another liberal "friend of the Indian," who almost one hundred fifty years earlier had laid the legislative groundwork for the Trail of Tears (chapter 1). In 1829 President

Andrew Jackson enlisted Thomas McKenney, former superintendent of Indian trade, to "sell" Congress on the need to remove the Cherokee and other Indian nations from the Southeast to "Indian Territory." McKenney established the New York Board for the Emigration, Preservation and Improvement of the Aborigines of America. He touted removal as a "humane" policy, which would allow the Cherokee and other Indian nations to preserve their identity in a new land. They must "remove—or perish," McKenney said. They were removed, and at least a quarter of them perished.

Fifty years later another burst of paternalistic liberalism produced allotment, which sowed the seeds for the antitreaty backlash of today, which, in turn, is being ridden by a new generation of self-styled "friends of the Indian," such as Meeds, who must reconcile their own humane self-image with the economic and political interests which sustain their power. Another Trojan horse, full of smiling diplomats, was being drawn up to the reservation gates, and the Indians—now, as a century ago—were not taking the offer so hypocritically proferred.

The decision in Indian country was not whether to accept or reject the proposals of Cunningham, Meeds, and politicians from other states. They had been rejected. The consensus was reached that the *Wasi'chu*—under cover of a domestic "energy crisis"—were reaching for the "final solution" of the "Indian problem," which would allow them the remaining fifty million acres, under which lay more than half the uranium, 10 to 15 percent of the coal, and 2 to 5 percent of the oil and gas under U.S. jurisdiction. The positions in the debate in Indian country ranged between advocacy of an increased measure of self-determination (the AIPRC position) and international recognition of Indian nations as sovereign entities with treaty relations to another nation, the United States. In the minds of sovereignty advocates was the persistent "catch 22" of American law: the courts have upheld the treaties in many cases, basing judgments on precedent, but Congress has asserted the right to unilaterally change the treaties. And Congress, despite the statements of the likes of Meeds that they are acting in the Indians' interest, has more often been the main agent of colonial control and exploitation.

Historically the Congress has moved in to reinforce its colonial control whenever Indian nations have begun to assert the type of self-determination which federal courts have occasionally upheld. The Cherokee had established farms, schools, their own government, a written language, and even a newspaper before they were forcibly removed in the 1830s; in recent times the Indian nations which have been terminated against their wills were beginning to develop the kind of economic base the AIPRC supports. [16]

So if true implementation of the Indian sovereignty and self-determination recognized by history and the courts is to become more than a paper promise, the structure of present-day Indian policy, which has promoted a colonial relationship, must be changed. The AIPRC supports such change, but its proposals do not go as far as those of Indian activists and students of history who recognize that in the past "reforms" in Indian policy have been promises to Indian nations of future well-being but in fact have resulted in further strengthening of the colonial relationship. For at least a century the reformers have imposed their ideas on the Indian nations—often over their protests. Allocation was announced in 1887 as "help" for Indians, as relocation had been earlier. In modern times "termination" was foisted on Indians to "help" them; today energy developers carry the same hypocritical message.

For those who have felt the bulldozer tracks of "Manifest Destiny" across their backs for so long, new "reforms" justifiably evoke suspicion. "Termination" has worn many faces—some benign: the "education" of missionaries, the exhortations of "moneyholics" to Indians that they trade their resources for greenbacks. With a growing knowledge of history, the realization has spread across Indian Country in the 1970s that the only survival plan for Indians ought to be developed *by* Indians.

Indian survival depends on ending the colonial relationship maintained by self-interested industries with government assistance; in its place must come development of resources by Indian labor, for Indian benefit in a manner congruent with the respect for the earth which is imbedded in Indian religion.

The logical process for terminating the colonial relationship which has kept Indians in poverty and bondage would seem to be destruction of the Bureau of Indian Affairs. The reality, however, is not so simple; the colonial relationship must be abolished only in a way which will ultimately complement the goals of self-determination.

History offers two warnings to those who would simply and unilaterally abolish the BIA. First, such an act might provide the *Wasi'chu* with a rationale for abrogating treaty rights and federal responsibility for Indian nations before all these nations had achieved sufficient land bases, political power, and cultural awareness to fulfill the promise of independence. Severing of federal responsibility without reciprocal plans for economic, political, and cultural self-determination—and the money to carry them out—could have the same effect as allocation did almost a century ago. It would intensify poverty and force reliance on the same extractive industries which already had done so much damage to Indian lands and communities. It would also mean displacement of even more Indians to the bleak skid rows of America's cities.

During the first half of 1978 Indians walked across the entire United States—from Alcatraz Island to Washington, D.C.—to tell the politicians the lessons of history. Arriving in the nations' capital in mid-July, more than a thousand Indian people from at least fifty nations and tribes found President Carter out of town. Ironically, the president was in Europe, lecturing the Soviet Union on the human rights of its dissidents. To the Indians, Carter was engaged in a policy of what newspaper workers call "Afghanistanism"—riveting people's attention on problems overseas in order to conceal abuses at home. Carter had just upbraided his envoy to the United Nations, Andrew Young, for telling a French newspaper that "hundreds, maybe thousands" of political prisoners were incarcerated in the United States. The Indians were telling Carter to clean his own house before he criticized others'.

Abolishing the present structure without a land base and the political power which would guarantee self-determination would only be another form of termination. One without the other could replicate the situation of the 1880s, during which reformers' well wishes were legislated into disaster. Indeed, in 1976 an internal memorandum from the Office of Management and Budget (OMB) urged gradual withdrawal of federal trust responsibilities and funding for Indian tribes. The memo by Harold S. Borgstrom of OMB's Interior Branch, did not complement this withdrawal with plans to establish the resource base, political and cultural awareness, and technical expertise which are necessary for self-determination.

In 1978, Washington state's two powerful senators, Henry Jackson and Warren Magnuson, asked Attorney General Griffin Bell to "reexamine" the trust responsibility. Bell agreed, at least in principle, to do so.

History offers a second warning to the abolition of the BIA: the agency has at least twice in the past used threats to its bureaucratic existence to fatten itself. Russel Barsh, formerly a consultant to the Crow Nation and the policy review commission, noted that both the 1887 Allotment Act and the termination programs of the 1950s were supposed to force the Indians' assimilation into the dominant culture and render the BIA useless. Both times the BIA requested and was given a "temporary" increase in funding to take care of anticipated paperwork, which was expected to take ten to fifteen years. In each case, however, federal policy had changed within that time, and the BIA was back in business—at about twice its previous funding level.

In late 1976, anticipating the policy review commission's recommendation that it be abolished, the BIA prepared a report advising that Indian affairs be transferred to a new agency —exactly what the ˙commission was considering. Could the BIA be preparing to weather yet another threat to its existence—by requesting a ten- to fifteen-year "transition period" to take care of paperwork?

With these cautions in mind Indians may proceed along the easy to define, but hard to travel, road to a sovereignty which will divorce them from the present colonial relationship. The policy review commission recommends that Indian nations' governments be upgraded from their present "wardship" status to one that gives them the powers that states and local governments possess—within the framework of United States law.[17] Specific proposals include increasing the scope of Indian nations' judicial powers over their lands—and over non-Indians who reside on them—ceding them the power to manage land and resource use without requiring consent of the BIA and Interior Departments, and giving them the power to levy taxes and issue business licenses.[18]

The AIPRC acknowledges that the federal government would still be supreme to the Indian nations and that Congress would retain the power to abrogate treaties.[19] This power could be fatal to Indians' hopes for true future sovereignty, for, under the pressures of a future "energy crisis" trumped up by multinational corporations, "state powers" could become useless and colonization imposed again. Just how limited the conception of self-determination embraced by the AIPRC could be was revealed in a report by the commission's Task Force on Federal, State and Tribal Jurisdiction, which stated, "It presumably still would be Constitutionally 'legal' to remove by legislation all Indian tribes from Georgia to Oklahoma."[20]

The limitations of a system which would still allow a *Wasi'chu*-controlled federal government to abrogate treaties have prompted many Indian groups to advocate a legal redefinition which would place Indian nations outside the national control of the United States, at least in matters of law. The International Indian Treaty Council, which now has observer status in the United Nations, advocates complete national sovereignty, as do the Iroquois Confederacy, the Trail of Self-Determination, the Longest Walk, and others.

Such a plan may help make an end to the colonial relationship now existing—but such an end is not guaranteed. For at a time when primary political influence in the United States is exercised by multinational corporations, political boundaries often do not completely guarantee economic and cultural integrity. Presidents of the United States have intervened in Indochina without the approval of Congress—a clear violation of the Constitution; a United States-backed coup deposed and killed the democratically elected president of Chile, Salvador Allende, when his programs threatened the interests of multinational copper companies—some of the same companies which are now strip-mining coal on the Navajo Nation, and would like to mine the Cheyenne and Crow. The international police force of the *Wasi'chu*, the Central Intelligence Agency, performs many of the functions that the FBI filled during the 1970s against the domestic Indian resistance. The list of controls which cross national boundaries is endless.

Because of the fragility of political boundaries in a world in which *Wasi'chu* have found so many ways to contravene them, complete Indian sovereignty rests upon more than the self-determination efforts of Indian people alone. It rests upon the efforts of all people who value the human spirit over the religion of profit. Herein lies the problem with Indian organizations such as the Council of Energy Resource Tribes, formed in 1977 at the behest of Navajo Tribal Chairman Peter McDonald. McDonald's position has been that Indian nations should allow their resources to feed the multinationals' resource extraction machine—if the price is right. The danger with such an approach is that even if the price is right, many Indian nations will lose their traditional economies—and, thus, economic bases—through energy development. Another danger is that Indian nations (such as the Navajo) with abundant energy reserves will require larger and larger amounts of money from resource-extraction royalties to maintain their tribal budgets. The Navajos already depend on mineral-related income for 65 percent of their tribal budget and are in danger of getting into a position where they must allow the land to be sacrificed, or starve. McDonald advocates a path which would provoke assimilation in the end, by making the tribes appendages of the energy companies. Such dependency has been called "an evolutionary form of colonialism."[21]

As long as Indian nations appeal for justice inside the United States political and economic system, as presently constituted, they are likely to be fitted into the needs of a predatory capitalism, in which "the functional role of the state...reflects the needs of the dominant sector of the economy."[22] The U.S. Supreme Court, for example, has upheld the power of Congress to abrogate treaties "with a clear indication of Congressional intent" in such cases as *Lone Wolf* v. *Hitchcock* (1903) and *Menominee Tribe* v. *U.S.* (1968).[23] It is that "clear intent" to eliminate treaties which is being sought by the non-Indian economic interests which are lobbying Congress.

Knowing this, much American Indian legal thought now is directed toward international law, which demands that a treaty be modified only after mutual agreement or an act of war. The International Indian Treaty Council has taken part in a United Nations-sponsored conference on Indians in the Americas during September 1977. Indians have more often been placing their case before such international bodies, making common cause with more than a few former colonies which are drawing parallels between the Indian peoples' present situation and their own past, parallels which will grow as contradictions heighten.

The problem is not at root the BIA. The problem, according to Richard Lundstrom, a Jesuit who worked with Indian people on the Great Plains, is profit:

> The line of attack is clear. It must go against profit. The profits demanded by this political/economic system come from satisfying the natural or artificially created desires of human beings reduced to consumers. Convince a consumer he wants something, get him used to "enjoying" it, manipulate him to the point where he demands it, and he will tolerate, encourage, even insist on, any tactic the supplier must resort to in order to supply the demand. Let the supply be acquired by normal production or trade where possible, by economic extortion or military intervention where necessary.
>
> And so...[the *Wasi'chu*] loot the land and impoverish or destroy the peoples of Southeast Asia, Asia, Latin America, Africa...and so are the native American lands and their people [treated]...[24]

10
The Final Indian War

In his presidential address to the Royal Geographic Society, President Strachey, assuming that the last barrier excluding us from unknown regions would soon be broken through, named the establishment of modern civilization and progress over Africa as the next geographical problem. That continent presents wholly different conditions from any other land that has been brought under civilization, and will call for different methods of management. It cannot be directly colonized, as were North America and Australia, or administered as India is; and amalgamation between European settlers and the indigenous races is wholly out of the question. The operation will necessarily be a long and in some respects, a painful one.

—Popular Science Monthly, 1882[1]

The reality is a continuum which connects Indian flesh sizzling over Puritan fires and Vietnamese flesh roasting under American napalm. The reality is the compulsion of a sick society to rid itself of men like Nat Turner and Crazy Horse, George Jackson and Richard Oakes, whose defiance uncovers the hypocrisy of a declaration affirming everyone's right to liberty and life. The reality is an overwhelming greed which begins with the theft of a continent and continues with the merciless looting of every country on the face of the earth which lacks the strength to defend itself.

—Richard H. Lundstrom[2]

Yanamo Indians along the Northern Perimeter Highway, Territory of Roraima, Brazil. Photo by Claude Dumenil, reprinted with the permission of the Anthropology Resource Center, Cambridge, Mass.

It would be enormously naive of us to end our story with the designs of a gaggle of conservative congressmen who are seeking to end more than two hundred years of American government policy toward Indian people by driving the last coffin nail in a policy of genocide. The reaction to the 372 treaties negotiated by the United States with indigenous peoples inside its borders is not an isolated struggle that just happens to be taking place at this time. This final "Indian war" is occurring within a nationwide, even a worldwide, context, within which many peoples are struggling against an economic system which rewards the domination of one over another. We could have arrived at the same destination by writing about Appalachian coal miners or Chicano farmworkers or black ghetto residents or many other peoples who live within that large (and often invisible) gap between American myth and reality. We have devoted most of this book to the lives of Indian people because it is they who have felt most deeply the tank treads of Manifest Destiny within the present-day political boundaries of the United States, the nation within which we live.

Within the borders of that nation and around the world there are many more "Indians" if the meaning of the word is broadened beyond that of genealogy to include a shared experience with the *Wasi'chu*. From the days when large trading companies such as Hudson's Bay implanted a mercenary order on North and South America (as well as on the African and Asian continents), large corporations, aided by national governments, have been the agents of the *Wasi'chu* in many parts of the world. Indians have many brothers and sisters under the skin in the United States and elsewhere.

The present campaign to abrogate United States government treaties with American Indian nations, tribes, and bands occurs as many third-world peoples are taking their lives and resources into their own hands; the predatory corporations which in the past have acted as the secular missionaries of the *Wasi'chu* economy are finding it necessary to retreat to land and resources inside the borders of the nations in which they are based. At the same time workers' and national minorities' assertions have contributed to demands against the *Wasi'chu* at home. Insistence that the treaties be enforced has been strengthened during the 1970s by the growing demands of Indians with non-Indian support. As these demands have achieved some victories, demands that the treaties be abrogated have also intensified.

Indian people have been historically regarded as place holders, "allowed" in the *Wasi'chu* mind to occupy land guaranteed them by treaty until it is "needed" for some other purpose, such as mineral exploitation. What was true of the Black Hills a century ago is true today; the purpose of efforts at treaty abrogation is centuries old: to clear the land of obstacles to full-scale colonization.

Waiting to move onto the last enclaves held by America's native peoples are giant corporations such as AMAX (American Metals Climax), frustrated in its attempts to mine coal on the Crow Nation in Montana. As AMAX leases on Crow land were being suspended in 1978, the same company was seeking leases elsewhere in Indian country, including the coal-rich Northern Cheyenne Nation, next to the Crow. The company is experienced at operating on colonized land. For example, it operates the Tsumeb copper mine in Namibia, one of the world's largest, in the area that South Africa calls South-West Africa, which is, in essence, that nation's largest "African reservation."

Like many American Indian reservations, Namibia is rich in minerals. It is also dominated by foreign mining interests, AMAX included. AMAX's 1957 *Annual Report* described a plan by which the company hoped to use profits extracted from its African operations to finance expansion in North America.[3] To maximize these profits, workers in the Namibian mines were treated brutally under a system known as "contract labor," whereby contracts are negotiated between the companies and the occupying South African regime. The native people in Namibia live on "homelands," as do most of South Africa's blacks, and are compelled by law to carry passes. Those who refuse to sign up for enlistment in the mines under contract labor face the threat of imprisonment, fines, or forced labor.

AMAX's Tsumeb mine is the largest single employer in Namibia, employing some 40 percent of all contract laborers recruited by the South African regime.[4] In 1972 black workers at the mine were paid an average of $29.64 a month; white workers averaged $550.00.[5] After strikes organized by the Southwest African Peoples' Organization (SWAPO), blacks' wages rose within two years to $64 a month. White wages, however, were raised to $750.

While working in the mines, black contract laborers are kept in compounds surrounded by walls topped by barbed wire. Except to work twelve-hour shifts in the mines, the laborers are not allowed to leave the compounds without passes. To leave the job itself is a criminal offense.

The criminal treatment of Namibian people in its mines is one reason AMAX has encountered extreme difficulty in getting the Crow and Northern Cheyenne to cooperate with the company's plan to expand its corporate empire by investing the blood of Namibia in Indian coal land. On the record, AMAX asserts that its mine is good for the people of Namibia, that it brings them money and jobs. The same promises have been made to the Crow and Northern Cheyenne.

Another reason for the reluctance of many Indians to invite in the multinationals is that they—like no other group of people in the United States—understand the purpose of the multinational corporation. It is, purely and simply, to maximize profits to satisfy investors and raise capital for expansion in the future. If the welfare of indigenous people contradicts the requisites of the bottom line, that welfare is sacrificed. The only compromise comes when workers demand it, through strikes such as those organized in Namibia by SWAPO or when the legal title holders of resources refuse to yield them, as have the Crow and Northern Cheyenne in dealings with AMAX.

Although many multinational corporations cannot choose the welfare of indigenous people over that of bottom-line profitability, their proposals often are swathed in promises. The Ralston Purina Company, for example, approached the people of Colombia in the early 1950s with a promise to provide protein (chicken in this case) to a hungry nation. Chickens eat grain, and that is Purina's business. In 1957 the company established its first Colombian factory at Cartagena, on the Caribbean coast.[6] Purina's sales and profits rose steadily; by 1973 the company was selling $12 million of chicken feed a year, about 40 percent of Colombia's feed production.[7]

A local chicken-and-egg industry grew up to consume the feed, and between 1966 and 1971 broiler production doubled from eleven million to twenty-two million chickens. Between 1970 and 1973 egg production increased from 1.1 billion to 2 billion.[8]

What did this increase mean for the majority of Colombia's people? Hunger. Why? Because chicken and eggs were too expensive for all except upper-class Colombians. The rest obtained their protein from beans—thousands of acres of which had been plowed under to grow the soybeans and sorghum which make up the chicken feed. In 1958 about 51,000 acres were planted in beans in the fertile Cauca Valley; in the early 1970s the average was less than 7,200.[9] During the same period the number of acres planted in sorghum rose from none to 61,446; for soybeans, from 15,000 to about 141,700.[10] Three-quarters of Colombia's population lived on an average of $75 a year in 1969. In 1970 chicken cost an average of eighty-four cents a kilogram (2.2 pounds) in Colombia; grade B eggs cost forty cents a dozen.[11] To take advantage of Purina's bounty, three-quarters of Colombia's people would have to spend a week's earnings for a dozen eggs and a kilogram of chicken! As a result of Ralston Purina's proposal, the gap between the amount of protein produced in Colombia and the amount required by its population tripled between 1960 and 1975.[12]

The corporate Trojan Horse came to Mexico about the same time it did to Colombia, dispossessing peasants of their land, which had sustained them for centuries, in order to grow fruits and vegetables for the lucrative United States winter market. By the late 1970s the corporate economy was enabling North Americans who could afford it to buy watermelons and cantaloupes in January, imported from the area which had once grown the dietary staples of northern Mexico. The former owners of the land were migrating to Mexico City, whose population, twelve million in 1978, was expected to top twenty million by 1985. Others crossed the United States border looking for work. They were derided as "illegal aliens," taking work from Americans, when in actuality the corporations had forced much of the migration. Once in the migrant stream, the Mexicans joined many American citizens of Mexican heritage, whose forefathers had been ousted from their land in what is now the Southwestern United States after that land was ceded by Mexico following the Mexican-American War.

As Colombians and Mexicans (among many other peoples) nibbled broken corporate promises, so did many American consumers. Studies by Barry Commoner, an environmental scientist, showed that the *Wasi'chu* followed the bottom line over the public good even when such behavior created products damaging to the environment:

> While production for the most basic needs—food, clothing, housing—had just about kept up with the 40 to 50 percent increase in population (United States, 1946-76), the kinds of goods produced to meet those needs have changed drastically...Soap powder has been replaced by synthetic detergents; natural fibers (cotton and wool)...by synthetic ones; steel and lumber have been displaced by aluminum, plastics and concrete; railroad freight has been replaced by truck freight; returnable bottles have been replaced by non-returnable ones. On the road, the low-powered automobile engines of the 1920s and 1930s have been displaced by high-powered ones. On the farm, while per capita production has remained about constant, the amount of harvested acreage has decreased; in effect, fertilizer has replaced land. Older methods of insect control have been replaced by synthetic insecticides, such as DDT ...Range feeding of livestock has been replaced by feed lots.[13]

What emerges from Commoner's study is that while the material standard of living for most Americans has not improved since 1946, changes in productive technology have vastly increased energy consumption—and pollution. In each case, Commoner found, industries changed production technology because the energy-consuming, polluting alternative also increased profits.

In the case of the change from soaps to detergents Commoner found that in 1947, when industry produced "essentially no" detergents, profit was 30 percent of sales. In 1967, when production was about one-third soap and two-thirds detergents, the profit margin was 42 percent—and for detergents alone, it was 52 percent.[14] The pattern followed wherever Commoner looked: "Displacement of technologies with relatively weak environmental impacts by technologies with more intensive impacts is accompanied by a significant increase in profitability."[15]

It was no accident, Commoner observed, that the energy-intensive, polluting technologies were promoted widely by advertising; consumers were to be persuaded—in the timeless fashion of the *Wasi'chu*—that products with higher profit margins were being sold "for the good of the public," when in actuality the only winner was the manufacturer. The consumer, manipulated by the higher expenditures on advertising, not only paid a dearer price in many cases but also suffered from the pollution that the change in productive technologies caused.[16]

Such technological changes, predicated on maximization of profit, also create the rationale for further corporate expansion into newly developed resource colonies—the fate being marked out for many resource-rich Indian nations in corporate boardrooms and among those members of Congress who seek to abrogate treaties. In a resource colony land and people are exploited under a system which facilitates the profitable extraction of the resources of the land and the labor of the people for the corporation. As we have shown, this expansion benefits only the company, despite the masquerades about human welfare or national interest that may be used, in the timeless fashion of Cotton Mather and generations of *Wasi'chu* rationalizers, to justify the usurpation.

The status of Indian nations under U.S. law makes them ideal targets for the mineral and human extraction which then takes place. The United States Department of Interior holds substantial power over leasing arrangements and development plans on Indian reservations, a device that is absent in many third-world countries which may be used by the multinationals.

Robert Engler commented in *The Brotherhood of Oil*:

> To a disturbing extent, Interior's performance has been most consistently shaped over the years by the assumption that it is holding public lands (up to one-third of the United States) for disposal to private claimants... Interior's working perspective has thus kept it a partner in development, responsive primarily to the private government which controls energy. It is an ineffective guardian of the public domain and insensitive to the long-run public interest in the development, use and conservation of energy resources.[17]

The government of the United States, through the Interior Department, tailors its policies to keep prices up and profits secure.[18]

Between 1968 and 1972 seven multinational energy companies—Exxon, Texaco, Mobil, Standard of California, Gulf, Standard of Indiana, and Shell—used a number of tax advantages to pay only about 5 percent of their total net profits in federal income taxes. The "creative" use of bookkeeping allowed these—and other—oil companies to accumulate capital, with which they absorbed other companies, many of them coal concerns.

In the 1960s Gulf bought Pittsburgh and Midway Coal; Continental Oil acquired Consolidation Coal; and Occidental Oil took over Island Creek Coal. Consolidation and Island Creek had been the United States's largest and third-largest independent coal companies. By 1976 Exxon had become one of the largest holders of coal reserves. Also by 1976 seven of the United States's largest fifteen coal companies were controlled by oil companies; oil controlled at least 25 percent of coal production and 30 percent of coal reserves.[19] The oil companies knew that supplies of crude would not last more than a few decades, so they diversified—becoming "total energy" companies.

The Interior Department aided the rush to the West, where a quarter of the known coal reserves of the world lie, not only by selling leases for much less than they were worth but also by advocating the use of strip-mining technology.[20] The government has also been helping energy companies in coal-gasification research since at least 1971; during that year the Interior Department entered into a cooperative research program which provided $20 million in tax money for gasification research. The American Gas Association (AGA), the partner, put up $10 million. By that time the AGA had located 176 sites where profitable coal-gasification plants could be located—including the ground around the Navajo Irrigation Project in New Mexico.[21]

Interior Department officials who had trouble making private profit seem patriotic were fired. For example, John F. O'Leary insisted that the coal industry "support the public interest rather than that of industry alone," and he insisted that mine-safety rules be strictly enforced. He was fired in 1970. The action led one observer to remark that O'Leary had been the first man to direct the Bureau of Mines who did not think it was "just the Washington Office of the coal industry."[22] Such sentiments were strangely unwelcome in the department charged with a trust responsibility for the resources of Indians—and all of the American people.

For more docile federal administrators the energy companies supplied ample rewards. A 1974 study by the General Accounting Office reported that 22 percent of the staff of the United States Geological Survey (USGS) held stock or drew pensions from private companies which held leases on land surveyed by the USGS.[23]

Many of the highest-ranking staff of the Interior Department's Oil and Gas Office had been weaned in the large energy companies. Recent heads of the office came from Continental Oil and Aramco (Arab-American Oil Company). Another former head of the Oil and Gas Office became a lobbyist for Sinclair Oil, and another for Lone Star Gas. Still another moved to the American Petroleum Institute.[24]

In the White House and the Congress, where the Interior Department's supervisors work, copious amounts of energy-company money fueled political campaigns, while the actions of underlings assured a profitable return on investment. A complete listing of these contributions, which is outside the scope of this book, has been provided in many sources.[25]

The reach of the *Wasi'chu* extended far beyond the shores of the United States, as corporate representatives bought influence in several other countries and sought a bountiful return from energy development on their investment. The pattern is pervasive, and not restricted to energy companies, as recent disclosures regarding pay-offs by defense contractors, such as Lockheed and Boeing, revealed. *Wasi'chu* complaints that their companies were being persecuted for accepted and customary business practices only underscored how pervasive the tactic has become.

The involvement of the United States government as an accomplice in the exploitation of native peoples the world over in protection of *Wasi'chu* interests has also been pervasive. Since the end of World War II the United States has carried out 215 "shows of force" around the world, many of them to protect multinational companies from assertions of national economic and political liberation.[26] From Guatamala in 1954, to the Dominican Republic in 1965, to Vietnam, the "shows of force" have been justified "in the public interest"—just as the rape of the Black Mesa has been pardoned as "in the national interest." It is but another example of making private profit patriotic.

The wars of the *Wasi'chu* are often waged covertly, both within and without the United States. Economic "destabilization" was used to create economic turmoil in Chile and weaken the regime of Salvador Allende, while U.S. aid financed the armed forces, which eventually deposed and killed him. A major reason for the covert aid was copper, and a major copper miner in Chile is Kennecott, which owned Peabody Coal, which is stripping the Black Mesa.

The State Department acts as an "understanding and reliable ally" to the *Wasi'chu* overseas—just as the Interior Department does at home.[27] President Lyndon Johnson held back food shipments from India until that country abandoned plans for its own fertilizer plants and accepted those of Standard of Indiana.[28]

The worldwide reach of the *Wasi'chu* produces cultural destruction and enforced political and economic dependence—as well as the loss of life and the rape of land—around the world. To visit the Black Mesa, to travel the strip mines with Emma Yazzie is to visit Puerto Rico, Chile, South Africa, Brazil, the "paleface reservations" of Appalachia, or any of many other places where land and resource hunger prevails over human life.

In all of these places, in a fashion similar to that practiced on Indian nations within the United States, the corporations, aided by the United States government's melding of patriotism with private profit, attempt to extend their reach. Not only do the companies want the resources which lie under the land, they also want the cheap labor of the people who live on it. This is, again, a convenient arrangement for the corporations, which promise employment, as they do in Namibia. Those who do not want to wed themselves as laborers to the companies' interests can starve, in the companies' view, since many extractive industries, especially those which involve strip mining and power-plant construction, destroy the traditional livelihoods of native people, such as hunting, ranching, and farming.

On the Navajo Nation during 1969 the Fairchild Corporation, a multinational electronics firm, opened a plant, which employed about twelve hundred Navajo.[29] Fairchild hired mainly women, who the management assumed (erroneously, it turned out) would be more docile than men. During 1974 a thousand employees at the Navajo plant received a total payroll of about $1 million—or less than $1,000 each. In contrast, the top twenty-three officers and directors of the corporation drew checks for $1,588,792.[30] As bad as wages were at the Shiprock Navajo plant, in other places they were lower. In Indonesia, for example, workers at a Fairchild plant were paid twelve cents an hour.[31]

In an area where more than half the Navajo people were unemployed at the time, Fairchild apparently thought the workers would remain docile. They did not; by 1974 workers were trying to organize a union. During the organizing efforts several hundred Navajo were laid off, an action which precipitated an occupation of the plant by workers and community people. During the occupation workers discovered memos that revealed the company's plans to close the plant and transfer its operations to its other plants in Singapore, South Korea, Hong Kong, Japan, Mexico, Brazil, or Indonesia, where presumably the workers would be paid less and remain more docile than had the Navajo. The message was clear: workers who demand anything closer to the actual value of their labor have no place in Fairchild plants. Fairchild, like other multinationals, is more interested in maximizing the profits which enable the corporation to expand than in workers' welfare. Thus, the surplus value of the workers' production must, by the law of the bottom line, remain with the company.

Although Fairchild moved out of the Navajo Nation, other extractive industries did not, for they were seeking immobile natural resources, not labor. As the fingers of extractive industry crept into the sacred Black Mesa, multinationals also were penetrating one of the last refuges of free Indians in the Americas—the Amazon Valley. Aided by a dictatorial military regime which models its Indian policy on that of the United States a century ago, the *Wasi'chu* were expanding their global reach. They were perfecting technology to reach the earth's last untapped storehouses of mineral wealth. During the 1960s oil companies, such as Gulf, Texaco, and Mobil, began prospecting in the Amazon Basin. They were joined by mining concerns, such as United States Steel, Alcan Aluminum, and Rio Tinto Zinc. The whole operation carried with it a cruel echo of the land booms in the American West a century ago, after the discovery of minerals and the technology of dry-land farming made formerly "worthless" land valuable in the eyes of the *Wasi'chu*.

The tone of press coverage has not changed; the *Los Angeles Times* headlines, "Brazilian Indians Murder Another White Man"; the *New York Times* proclaims, "Indians From the Amazon Kill Three in Raid." The savage of myth is dusted off again to justify the taking, which is portrayed as the necessary cost of civilization: "The 100,000 Indians of Brazil are becoming extinct in the whirlwind of progress and modernization sweeping this South American country," as one Associated Press story put it.[32]

Hidden in these news reports are the full dimensions of people's struggle for survival against a military onslaught: 1.2 million native people lived in the Amazon Basin in 1960; 100,000 remained by 1976.[33]

As it had to the north, the subjugation of native peoples included plans to make them dependent on the *Wasi'chu* by depriving them of their land base and economies:

> And so the familiar pattern seen in the Northwest Territories [of Canada] or Navajo Nation is the same as in the Amazon. Self-sufficient communities which co-operate in any way are integrated into the regional labor force and made dependent on foreign supplies of goods. By the middle of the 1970s, the welfare of these peoples had become dependent on the national and international economies.[34]

As it had been in the United States, a welfare economy was set up in Brazil for surviving Indians, and legal protection was promised to them. Six Indian "parks" and seventeen "reserves" were established by Brazil in 1968.[35]

On one of the parks, the Cintas-Largaas were settled. This group had been reduced from ten thousand to four hundred since 1949; several hundred had been massacred in 1963. In 1971 Brazil's press carried reports that an "Indian uprising" had taken place in Aripuana Park, the homeland of the Cintas-Largaas. What was left unsaid at the time was that the Brazilian Ministry of the Interior had authorized mineral prospecting and colonization of the park; more than fifteen hundred non-Indians had rushed in to stake their claims. In March 1972 Apoena Meirelles, director of the park, wrote a formal letter to the Brazilian National Indian Foundation describing how the settlers had provoked fights with the natives and spread fatal diseases among them. Meirelles told the foundation that "I would rather die fighting alongside the Indians in defense of their lands and right to live than to see them tomorrow reduced to beggars on their own land."[36]

Aripuana Park contains one of the world's largest, richest known deposits of tin; the illegal seizure of Cintas-Largaas land was a replay of the Georgians' seizure of the Cherokee Reservation in the 1830s or the invasion of the Black Hills in the 1870s.

To complete the parallel, the Brazilian government announced a new Indian policy after the Aripuana Park incidents and promised to "protect" Indian rights. The fine print of the new plans, however, said that in cases of "national development interests," Indian peoples could be rounded up and *relocated.*

Many of the Indians who have survived the murders and diseases have been put to work picking coffee and rubber for their nonresident master. The coffee sometimes ends up in cups in the United States, and the rubber goes into special tires for racing cars and passenger jets. The slaves, called *boas frias*, are paid ten cents a day for fourteen hours' labor seven days a week. They are guarded around the clock; those who attempt to escape are tortured or killed. [37]

In return for the coffee, rubber, and other products, the United States exports finished products to Brazil—such as used cowboy-and-Indian movies, which aid in the justification of subjugation.

The colonization of Brazil's last frontier evoked statements very similar to those of some United States politicians in the nineteenth century (see chapter 1). For example, when a large uranium deposit was found on the lands of the Yanomamo people in February 1975, General Fernando Ramos Pereira, governor of the Territory of Roraima, said, "I am of the opinion that in an area as rich as this—with gold, diamonds and uranium—we cannot afford the luxury of conserving half a dozen Indian tribes who are holding back the development of Brazil." [38]

Brazil's official Indian policy is similar to that of the United States a century ago: the surviving Indians are to be "integrated" into the dominant economy and "educated" to value private property. The fruits of this policy have also been similar: death, dispossession, and disintegration of native cultures. Brazil's military government has welcomed the "assistance" of the multinationals in development. The faces and technology and location may have changed, but the practices are those of the Hudson's Bay Company. The grotesque behavior of such corporations is not limited to third world nations, or to Indian reservations inside the United States. Anyone who believes that all Americans benefit from such corporate behavior should visit the areas in Appalachia which Henry Caudill has called "white reservations."

Not too many years ago the rolling hills of eastern Kentucky were lush and green and populated by farmers. Then the miners of coal came, offering jobs and money. By the early 1960s the converging trends of technology and profitability were forcing the mining companies out of the deep shafts and onto the ground. The land was being stripped. In October 1963 Homar Bigart of the *New York Times* described the effects of the rape of the land and the reduction in employment. Children were so hungry that they ate the dried mud which held their houses together. Seventy percent of the ten thousand people in the eastern Kentucky hills were unemployed; per capita income was $300 a year. Twenty of the nation's thirty-four poorest counties were clustered in the area. The land, which had once sustained the people, lay bare in many places, bleeding mud, useless for farming. The coal companies had used up the land—and used up the people—and cast both aside for the thick, rich coal seams of the West.[39]

The Navajo, the Northern Cheyenne, and the Crow could look into the eyes of these dispirited white people and find brothers and sisters under colonialism. In thirty-five years, under the plans of the *Wasi'chu*, they, too, would be sitting on ashes. Even while employed, the Kentucky miners had been exploited, and often killed, in their occupation. They died in the mines at ten to twenty times the rate that coal miners were killed in Europe, while supervisors of the Bureau of Mines who dared enforce safety standards were fired because, the coal industry said, they were making much ado about nothing.[40]

The people of eastern Kentucky had been left with little useful land, reduced to a life of enforced idleness; Caudill called their settlements "Appalachia's paleface reservations."

The central Appalachians—and eastern Kentucky in particular—
are probably the only colonial territories in the world where
elected officials gain and hold public office by blatantly upholding
the antisocial and exploitative prerogatives of nonresident
masters.[41]

Caudill apparently had not looked a thousand miles to the
west, where Dick Wilson and Peter McDonald were inviting the
same energy companies and other *Wasi'chu* interests which had
ruined, and then cast aside, the land and the people of his
beloved Appalachia.

One need not be a coal miner to lose one's life to the bottom-
line consciousness of the *Wasi'chu* economic system. Thanks to
the many chemicals and drugs that the advertisements tell us
are for our benefit, it is becoming increasingly easy to become a
social statistic while doing little more than occupying a comfortable, nondescript nook in the middle class. In the early
1950s, for example, a new "wonder drug" came onto the
market. The drug, sold at a hefty markup, was touted as
helping pregnant women avoid miscarriages and premature
births. That it did. It also did other things, such as cause
uterine cancer in the female offspring of the mothers who took
the substance. The effects produced by the drug, which goes by
the chemical shorthand DES, had a latency period of about
twenty years. The companies that marketed the drug had, of
course, failed to pretest it. The victims were the guinea pigs.
They, too, were Indians to the *Wasi'chu*.

Such an example of the victimization of even the middle and
upper-middle classes by the *Wasi'chu* may be only a harbinger
of things to come, according to Donald Kennedy, administrator
of the U.S. Food and Drug Administration. "We're just experi-
encing the first frontal edge of human experience with the new
chemical environment," Kennedy said. He predicted that the
number of environmentally caused cancers—most of them from
chemicals in air, water, and food—would rise dramatically as
persons born after World War II reach age forty, "prime time"
for development of many forms of cancer.[42] The accelerated use
of environmental chemicals, as noted by Barry Commoner earlier in this chapter, began shortly after World War II.

Once everyone who is afflicted by the *Wasi'chu's* relentless pursuit of profit understands that he or she has a common bond with the Navajo, the Cheyenne, the Lakota, the Namibians, the Mexicans, the Colombians, and many other peoples, it beomes easier to shed the assumption, programmed into us since childhood, that what is good for our employers is also automatically good for us. In actuality, the malignant behavior of the *Wasi'chu* is not in the "national interest," as is so often asserted, nor in the interest of anyone except the *Wasi'chu* themselves. Most of us, in our own way, are Indians in this "final Indian War."

Indians by blood, the original victims, sensed the lines of ultimate conflict long before many other people. Chief Sea'lth,[43] for example, told President Franklin Pierce in 1855, "Continue to contaminate your own bed, and you will suffocate in your own wastes." He also said:

> We know that the white man does not understand our ways. One portion of the land is the same to him as the next, for he is a stranger who comes in the night and takes whatever he needs. The earth is not his brother, but his enemy, and when he has conquered it, he moves on. He leaves his fathers' graves and his childrens' birthright is forgotten. The sight of your cities pains the eyes of the red man.
>
> There is no quiet place in the white man's cities...no place to hear the leaves of spring or the rustle of the insect's wings...The air is sacred to the red man, for all things share the same breath. The white man does not seem to notice the air he breathes. Like a man dead for many days, he is numb to the stench.
>
> Whatever befalls the earth befalls the sons of the earth...the [*Wasi'chu*] too shall pass, perhaps sooner than the other tribes.

Even so conservative a historian as Arnold Toynbee, who had lived through half of the industrial revolution, was seeing the same vision 120 years after Sea'lth:

> It looks as if [Western] man will not be able to save himself from the nemesis of his demonic material power and greed unless he allows himself...to abandon his present objective and espouse a contrary ideal.[44]

Toynbee referred to Genesis 1:28 for the "present objective": Be fruitful, and multiply, and replenish the earth, and subdue it; and have dominion over the fish of the sea, and over the fowl of the air, and over every living thing that moveth upon the earth.

Since the advent of the industrial revolution, the *Wasi'chu* have carried this commandment to excess through the vehicle of monopoly capitalism. They have been fruitful. They have multiplied. And they have, with careful application of technology to the arts of industry and war, subdued the earth. In the process many animals, fish, fowl—and human beings—have been released from the *Wasi'chu*'s dominion only in death. This commandment carries the assumption that anyone with the material power to do so has the natural right to dominate another. In two thousand years this assumption has given us the environmental destruction which comes from attempts to subdue (exploit) the earth without concern for its needs. It has given us weapons which threaten to destroy all of us in minutes. The point at which the *Wasi'chu* gained the power to destroy everything is little more than thirty years in the past. Within those thirty years, the engines of abused technology and the relentless pursuit of profit have joined to provide us a military-industrial complex which perpetuates itself by designing new weapons systems to replace those it has just deployed. The arms race is lubricated by the artificial paranoia of a powerful enemy so necessary to the *Wasi'chu*.

A society which did not assume that one must dominate another or be dominated—in other words, a society not predicated upon class relationships—does not need nucelar weapons to protect itself against its "potential adversaries." It would be able to turn its engines of technology toward more fruitful ends. A society which did not reward excessive profit-making would discourage such squandering of resources, and such creations of threat to all life. A system not based on profit would not be compelled to rape the earth for fossil fuels to fill artificially created appetites for energy and power. Such a society would be able to conserve its resources and replace fossil fuels with those which are renewable. The technology is at hand to provide solar, wind, and other renewable forms of energy. Technology may be manipulated to fill a demand—just as the *Wasi'chu* created the six-gun so that Indians could be shot from horseback without stopping to reload.

Given the threats of the *Wasi'chu* to all of us—and keeping in mind our long progression from an economy based on slavery—it is the duty, and in the self-interest, of all people to insist that the *Wasi'chu* no longer be allowed to subvert our basic rights to life, liberty, and the pursuit of a creative livelihood. It is no longer possible to ignore the path down which the "present objective" of the *Wasi'chu* leads.

If survival is in the national interest, it also is in the national interest to resist the actions and plans of the *Wasi'chu*. It is in the national interest to realize that the *Wasi'chu*—eager to retain a position of privilege—have never accepted equality willingly. Unless we force them to, we all will remain in line for sacrifice on the altar of profit.

Resistance—not debilitating guilt over past atrocities or cynicism because of their continuance—is called for now. Everyone with a common bond of affliction must see the needs of other brothers and sisters if we are to build a livable, humane world for our children. Most of America's institutions are in a stage of decay as a majority of the world's population painfully builds new societies. Against the *Wasi'chu*, in favor of a system which puts human need above profit, we must stand in unity so that generations unborn may walk in beauty.

How to Get More Information

The preceding chapters contain several hundred footnotes, each keyed to a particular fact or quotation. We have used the footnotes to enable readers and researchers to more easily follow the printed trail on the subject of their choosing. During our more than two years of research, we may have missed books, reports, or other studies which individual readers may believe are worth examining. We will be indebted to anyone who opens our eyes to material which, from lack of citation, it seems we may not have seen. Our present addresses are available from Monthly Review Press or the Seattle telephone directory.

This brief section contains tactical advice for those who wish to pursue specific items we have surveyed. If the material desired is not available in ordinary libraries (much of our primary research was not), an interested reader may obtain it from us. Much of the material in chapter 4, for example, is not widely available; we can copy it from our own archives at ten cents a page, to cover costs.

For printed material which is available in library systems or from the federal, state, or local governments which have issued it, keep the following in mind:

1. While much government information is theoretically open to the public, getting it can be a major problem. Many of the agencies with which we dealt were understandably reluctant to go out of their way to send us data not usually released to the public. This is especially true of the Bureau of Indian Affairs. Unless you have a willing contact within the agency from which you need a report or other information, you stand a better chance of getting it from the member of Congress who represents your area. These people have a direct interest in meeting your requests and employ assistants to supply information to constituents. Do not write to a member of Congress (or the Senate for that matter) who does not represent the area in which you live. Such letters will probably be ignored.

2. Court transcripts and other records are also, in theory, open to public scrutiny. However, you must usually travel to the court in which a case was tried to obtain complete records

237

(including transcripts) for most cases. Once you have found the clerk of the court's office, you will usually have to examine the records (sometimes thousands of pages) in cramped quarters, during office hours. Such records may not be checked out by ordinary people and if you want photocopies, the charge for them may be fifty cents to a dollar a page. Copies of federal appeal and Supreme Court rulings usually may be examined in the law libraries of many universities and bar associations. A friendly attorney in a large law firm may be of help in such matters, too. For court records of all types, as well as interpretation of the often complex maze of legalia, defense attorneys for specific cases may be helpful.

3. Large libraries can be used to great advantage; most major universities have nearly complete collections of the historical works cited in the text of our book. If such a library does not have a specific book, chances are they can get it through an interlibrary loan program. The same goes for microfilmed newspapers and copies of magazines and academic journals. Many of these libraries also have government document centers, where at least some of the material discussed under point 1 may be obtained. The holdings of public libraries tend to be more limited than those of universities, but access to university libraries is limited. If you are not a student or an academic by profession but have an academic degree from a large school, you may be able to get a borrower's card through the alumni association. If not, you may have friends who will check out source materials for you. If you can find no way to borrow the materials, the libraries close to you almost certainly will let you browse in the stacks.

4. Involvement in day-to-day struggles also can be educational. Native American organizations, and those committed to Indian issues with predominantly non-Indian memberships, are constantly in need of money and personal energy. Almost any city in the United States of more than a half-million inhabitants has an Indian center—a good place to get local contacts in your own area. If you are interested in a specific group (American Indian Movement, National Coalition to Support Indian Trea-

ties, Native American Solidarity Committee, etc.) and can not find a contact in your area, write to the authors, and we will refer you to one. Knowledge is vital to the struggle, but knowledge without struggle is useless.

—BJ and RM

Notes

1. The Past Is Prologue

1. Cited in William Meyer, *Native Americans: The New Indian Resistance* (New York: International Publishers, 1971), p. 15.
2. "Long Hair," the Lakota name for General George Armstrong Custer, who led an army expedition into the Black Hills, holy land of the Lakota, in 1874 and who prompted a settlers' invasion by finding gold there.
3. Black Elk, *Black Elk Speaks*, as told to John G. Neihardt (New York: William Morrow and Co., 1932), p. 79.
4. *North American Review* 99 (1863):449-64.
5. For examples of Indian influence on European thought and art, see Charles L. Sanford, *The Quest for Paradise: Europe and the American Moral Imagination* (Urbana, Ill.: University of Illinois Press, 1961).
6. For a discussion of the European image of Indians, see Robert F. Berkhofer, Jr., *The White Man's Indian: Images of the American Indian from Columbus to the Present* (New York: Alfred A. Knopf, 1978).
7. Alphonso Pinkney, *The American Way of Violence* (New York: Random House, 1972), p. 95.
8. Wilbur R. Jacobs, "The Indian and the Frontier in American History—A Need for Revision," *Western Historical Quarterly* 4 (January 1973):45. See also Calvin Martin, "Wildlife Diseases as a Factor in the Depopulation of the North American Indian," *Western Historical Quarterly* 7 (1976):47-62.
9. Later, this low resistance to smallpox was considered a military tactic. Historians Francis Parkman and Howard Peckham have described plans made in 1763 by General Jeffery Amherst and Colonel Henry Boquet of the British Army to present smallpox-infested blankets to Senacas and Cayugas along the western frontiers of Pennsylvania, Maryland, and Virginia. See also Pinkney, *American Way of Violence*, p. 102.
10. Robert Burnette and John Koster, *The Road to Wounded Knee* (New York: Bantam Books, 1974), p. 3.
11. Meyer, *Native Americans*, p. 17.
12. Reginald Horsman, "Scientific Racism and the American Indian in the Mid-nineteenth Century," *American Quarterly* 27 (May 1975):153.
13. *Democratic Review* 18 (June 1846):43.
14. Horsman, "Scientific Racism," p. 165.

15. *Weekly Arizonian* (Tubac), April 21, 1859, and January 28, 1871. It is interesting to note that some of the frontier newspapers which muted their calls for Indians' extermination realized that for their readers' economic fortunes Indians were better alive than dead. For example, the Yankton (Dakota Territory) *Daily Press and Dakotian* called in its issue of July 6, 1876 for extermination after the Custer battle, but recanted that opinion in its October 7, 1878 issue. "It [removal or extermination] would be disastrous to our commercial interests," the newspaper wrote. Local merchants made money from provisions sold to the army; they also profited by selling the government food and clothing for reservation-bound Indians. Howard Roberts Lamar comments that "feeding and clothing 25,000 Sioux (on reservations) as well as the military troops maintained in the Dakota territory for protection purposes had turned Yankton and other Missouri River towns into quarter-master depots." See *Dakota Territory 1861-1889: A Study in Frontier Politics* (New Haven: Yale University Press, 1956), p. 182. Journalism historian Elmo Scott Watson observed that frontier newspapers often manufactured Indian "threats" to get the army into town so that local merchants could provision the troops: "Much of the so-called 'news' was nothing more than propaganda to influence the federal government to send more troops to the 'threatened' areas, thus giving local tradesmen an opportunity to sell more goods to the troops." See "The Indian Wars and the Press 1866-67," *Journalism Quarterly* 17: 301.

16. U.S., Congress, Senate, *Congressional Globe*, 27th Cong., 3rd sess., 1846, Appendix, p. 74.

17. U.S., Congress, Senate, *Congressional Record*, 46th Cong. 2nd sess., 1880, p. 2462.

18. Josiah Strong (Congregationalist minister), *Our Country: Its Possible Future and Present Crisis* (New York, 1885), p. 176.

19. *To the Point International* (Brussels), October 4, 1976, p. 52. See also John Toland, *Adolf Hitler* (Garden City, N.Y.: Doubleday & Co., 1976).

20. For an extensive treatment of the role played by land speculators in the removal of Indian nations from the Southeast, see Mary Elizabeth Young, *Redskins, Ruffleshirts and Rednecks: Indian Allotments in Alabama and Mississippi 1830-1860* (Norman, Okla.: University of Oklahoma Press, 1961).

21. Pinkney, *American Way of Violence*, p. 106.

22. Sam G. Riley, "The *Cherokee Phoenix*: The Short and Unhappy Life of the First American Indian Newspaper," *Journalism Quarterly* 53 (Winter 1976):670-71.
23. Pinkney, *American Way of Violence,* p. 106; Meyer, *Native Americans*, p. 23.
24. The Black Hills never were signed away by treaty. As we shall see in chapter 5, the mineral wealth of the Black Hills remains an explosive treaty issue today.
25. Meyer, *Native Americans*, p. 34.
26. Ibid., p. 23.
27. U.S., Congress, American Indian Policy Review Commission, "Tentative Final Report," xerox., 1977, section 7, pp. 21-22.
28. For more extensive documentation than this brief survey of historical Indian land losses, see Brophy and Aberle, *America's Unfinished Business* (Norman, Okla.: University of Oklahoma Press, 1966); Kickingbird and Ducheneaux, *One Hundred Million Acres* (New York: Macmillan Co., 1973); U.S., Congress, Senate, *Indian Education: A National Tragedy—A National Challenge*, 91st Cong., 2nd sess., 1969 S. Rpt. 501; U.S., National Resources Board, *Report on Land Planning,* part 10, *Indian Land Tenure, Economic Status and Population Trends* (Washington, D.C.: Government Printing Office, 1935).
29. Meyer, *Native Americans,* p. 86.
30. American Indian Policy Review Commission, "Tentative Final Report," sect. 7, p. 3.
31. Ibid., sect 7, p. 24.
32. U.S., Bureau of Indian Affairs, *Report on the Purchase of Indian Land* (Washington, D.C.: BIA, 1976), Appendix B.
33. American Indian Policy Review Commission, "Tentative Final Report," sect. 7, p. 29.
34. Ibid., sect. 10, p. 3.
35. Ibid., sect. 10, p. 9.
36. Arthur C. Parker, *Parker on the Iroquois: The Constitution of the Five Nations* (reprinted, Syracuse, N.Y.: Syracuse University Press, 1968), p. 60. The exact date of the establishment of the Great Law of Peace is not known; the Iroquois, of course, did not count time before and after Christ. Parker determined the date of 1390 by using genealogical histories.
37. The Great Law of Peace was not committed to writing until about 1900, after several of the wampum belts had been destroyed. See Parker, *The Constitution of the Five Nations*.

38. Ibid., pp. 60-75.
39. Cadwallander Coldern, *The History of the Five Indian Nations Depending on the Province of New York in America*, 2 vols. (1727, 1747, reprint ed., Ithaca, N.Y.: Cornell University Press, 1954), p. xx.
40. Parker, *The Constitution of the Five Nations*, p. 38.
41. Alfred Owen Aldridge, *Benjamin Franklin, Philosopher and Man* (New York and Philadelphia: J. B. Lippincott, 1965), p. 112.
42. There is evidence that Franklin was using the term "ignorant savages" not out of disdain, but to satirically twit colonists who did not value Indian thought as he did. Franklin wrote a fascinating essay entitled "Remarks Concerning the Savages of North America," in which he expressed admiration for the Indians' absence of "artificial wants" and placed great value on the sharing and hospitality practiced by the Indians he knew.
43. Carol Van Doren, ed., *Ben Franklin: Writings* (New York: Viking Press, 1938), p. 209.
44. J. E. Chamberlin, *The Harrowing of Eden* (New York: Seabury Press, 1975), p. 136.
45. John R. Brodhead, ed., *Documents Relative to the Colonial History of New York* (Albany, N.Y.: Weed, Parsons and Co., 1855) 6: 828-910.
46. Benjamin Franklin, *The Papers of Benjamin Franklin*, ed. Leonard W. Labaree (New Haven: Yale University Press, 1962), vol. 5, *July 1, 1753- March 31, 1755.*
47. Emmanuel Terray, *Marxism and "Primitive" Societies* (New York: Monthly Review Press, 1972), p. 21.
48. David McLellan, *Karl Marx, His Life and Thought* (New York: Harper & Row, 1973), p. 424.
49. W. O. Henderson, *The Life of Friedrich Engels*, 2 vols. (London: Frank Cass & Co., 1976), p. 605.
50. Carl Resek, *Lewis Henry Morgan: American Scholar* (Chicago: University of Chicago Press, 1960), p. 126.
51. Terray, *Marxism and "Primitive" Societies*, pp. 21-22.
52. Karl Marx and Friedrich Engels, *Selected Works* (New York: New World Paperbacks, 1968), p. 527.
53. Ibid., p. 528.
54. Ibid.

2. The Making of a Savage: The FBI's Creative Writers' School

1. Earl Shorris, *The Death of the Great Spirit* (New York: New

American Library, 1971), pp. 64-65.

2. For a historical description of the uses of savage-Indian stereotypes, see Robert F. Berkhofer, *The White Man's Indian* (New York: Alfred A. Knopf, 1978).

3. A copy of the memo was leaked to the Colville Indian Agency in eastern Washington, home of Mel Tonasket, president of the National Congress of American Indians. From there, the copy was sent to South Dakota Senator James Abourezk, who notified Rene Howell.

4. "Dog Soldiers" was one of many names given to traditional northern plains warrior societies. The societies did more than wage war; in times of peace they acted as tribunals, tribal police, and social organizations.

5. This location was misplaced by some two hundred miles. Porcupine is on the Pine Ridge Reservation. Charlie Abourezk's home is also misplaced by seventy miles.

6. No such street exists in Pine Ridge.

7. Wounded Knee Legal Defense/Offense Committee, "How South Dakota's Dual System of Justice Works," mimeographed (Rapid City, S. D., 1975).

8. *Washington Star*, June 26, 1976, p. 1.

9. Ibid.

10. The memo did not describe how a group with only two vans was to kill "a cop a day in each state." Vernon Bellecourt, AIM founder, compared such tactics with terrorism used by officials a century ago, when one band of renegade Indians might be blamed for "six raids in six days—on horseback." (See *Open Road* [Vancouver, B.C.], early summer 1976, p. 21.)

11. U.S., Senate, Committee on the Judiciary, Subcommittee on Internal Security, *Revolutionary Activities Within the United States: The American Indian Movement,* April 6, 1976 (Washington, D.C.: Government Printing Office, 1976), p. 61. Note that the FBI compiled more than one thousand files for each member of the occupation.

12. *New York Times*, August 1, 1976.

13. South Dakota's "liberal" senator, George McGovern, perhaps recognizing his constituents' possible reaction to such appeals to fear, advocated violent removal of the occupants of Wounded Knee in 1973.

14. The Internal Security Subcommittee was disbanded in early 1977, shortly after it named AIM as one of six groups dangerous to U.S. "national security."

15. Senate, Subcomm. on Internal Security, *Revolutionary Activities*, p. 10.
16. Ibid., p. 6.
17. The account does not appear in Indians' oral or written histories of the Wounded Knee occupation either. According to his testimony, Durham was at Wounded Knee for only about five hours on March 20, 1973, and he did not witness the "crucifixion."
18. Senate, Subcomm. on Internal Security, *Revolutionary Activities*, p. 2.
19. Senate, Subcomm. on Internal Security, *Revolutionary Activities*, p. 29.
20. Ibid., p. 36.
21. Ibid., p. 67; emphasis added.
22. Ibid., p. 68.
23. U.S. Senate, Select Committee on Federal Intelligence, *Supplementary Detailed Staff Reports on Intelligence Activities and the Rights of Americans* (Washington, D.C.: Government Printing Office, 1976). See especially pp. 3-70 (Cointelpro) and pp. 185-223 (Black Panther Party).
24. *New York Times*, September 27, 1974.
25. *New York Times*, October 18, 1977; October 30, 1977.
26. Undated mailgram from Jeanne Baum, reacting to appeals court decision, January 7, 1978.

3. Hearts and Minds

1. Edgar Cahn, *Our Brother's Keeper* (New York: World Publishing Company, 1969), p. 10. Cahn is dean of the Antioch Law School, Washington, D.C.
2. Chapter houses are Navajo local governmental units. The Navajo Nation contains 102 of them.
3. Dart held the chief of police job for the BIA on the Navajo Nation until late 1976.
4. On August 30, 1976, in magistrate's court in Aztec assault charges were dismissed against Jean Lange and Thomas D. Perry, both of nearby towns. Charles C. Merriam and Herbert L. Miller were convicted of battery and fined $25 each plus $10 in court costs.
5. *Sun News* (Las Cruces, N.M.), June 30, 1972.
6. Unexplained Indian deaths have occurred with alarming frequency throughout the country in recent years. The many mur-

ders on the Pine Ridge Reservation (discussed in detail in chapter 4) are examples as is the case of Clayton Hurst, a young Indian of Cut Bank, Montana, who was arrested and charged with criminal mischief in late February 1976. He died March 7, and jail officials said that he had "hung himself," purportedly with his belt. Hurst was hurriedly buried before hs parents were notified. The parents demanded the body be exhumed for a second autopsy. A San Francisco pathologist, Dr. Robert Wright, who examined the exhumed body concluded that the cause of death had been electrocution—not hanging (*New York Times*, August 10, 1976).

7. *Navajo Times*, May 19, 1974.

8. *Akwesasne Notes*, late spring 1974, p. 20.

9. Cahn, *Our Brother's Keeper*, p. 10.

10. *Seattle Times*, April 4, 1977.

11. Cahn, *Our Brother's Keeper*, p. 13.

12. Ibid., p. 2.

13. Ibid., p. viii.

14. Amilcar Cabral, *Return to the Source: Selected Speeches of Amilcar Cabral* (New York and London: Monthly Review Press, 1973), p. 40.

15. Ibid., p. 43.

16. For a more complete discussion of this topic, see William Meyer, *Native Americans: The New Indian Resistance* (New York: International Publishers, 1971), pp. 42-43.

17. *Navajo Times*, June 27, 1974.

18. U.S. Civil Rights Commission, *The Farmington Report* (Washington, D.C.: U.S. Commission on Civil Rights, 1975), p. 19.

19. U.S. Civil Rights Commission, *The Farmington Report*, pp. 73-74.

20. *Farmington Times*, August 30, 1976.

21. U.S. Civil Rights Commission, *The Farmington Report*, pp. 51-52.

22. Native American Solidarity Committee, *The Spirit of the People* (St. Paul, Minn.: Native American Solidarity Committee, May 1976), p. 8.

23. U.S. Civil Rights Commission, *The Farmington Report*, pp. 62-63.

24. Ibid., pp. 60-61.

25. William Byler, "Removing Children: The Destruction of Native American Families," *Civil Rights Digest* (Summer 1977), p. 25.

26. *New York Times*, September 18, 1975.
27. U.S. Civil Rights Commission, *The Navajo Nation*, p. 107.
28. Ibid., p. 108.
29. Ibid., p. 110.
30. Ibid., p. 108.
31. The Indian Health Service is a division of the Public Health Service, Department of Health, Education, and Welfare.
32. *Washington Post*, June 11, 1975. This story was first developed by Clark Mollenhoff in the *Des Moines Register*.
33. March 23, 1977, p. 8.
34. U.S., Congress, General Accounting Office, *Report on Sterilizations at Indian Health Service Hospitals*, xerox., November 5, 1976, p. 1. The report was compiled at the request of Senator James Abourezk.
35. Ibid., pp. 3, 4, 23.
36. *The Guardian*, March 23, 1977, p. 8.
37. *Akwesasne Notes*, early spring 1977, p. 5.
38. Byler, "Removing Children," p. 19.
39. Ibid.
40. Ibid., p. 20.
41. Ibid.
42. Ibid., p. 23.
43. Ibid., p. 24.
44. Cahn, *Our Brother's Keeper*, p. 28.
45. Rupert Costo before U.S. Senate Indian Education Subcommittee, 90th Cong., 1st and 2nd sess., part 1, (January 4, 1968), p. 243.
46. Cahn, *Our Brother's Keeper*, p. 40.
47. Ibid., p. 45.
48. Cabral, *Return to the Source*, p. 45.

4. The Colonial Police Force

1. David Weir and Lowell Bergman, "The Killing of Anna Mae Aquash," *Rolling Stone*, April 7, 1977, p. 55.
2. *New York Times*, April 22, 1975.
3. Cheryl McCall, "Life at Pine Ridge Bleak," *Colorado Daily*, May 16, 1975.
4. Ibid.
5. Ibid.
6. The Black Hills, on which Mt. Rushmore stands, have never been ceded by treaty. The significance of the cloud on this title will be

discussed in the next chapter, as will the relation between the land signed away June 26, 1975, and the repression of AIM.

7. U.S., Congress, Joint Economic Committee, *Toward Economic Development for Native American Communities* (Washington, D.C.: Government Printing Office, 1969), p. 357.

8. U.S., Congress, American Indian Policy Review Commission, "Tentative Final Report," 1977, xerox, section 7, p. 31.

9. William Meyer, *Native Americans: The New Indian Resistance* (New York: International Publishers, 1971), p. 78.

10. Al Trimble, "Land Use Patterns on the Pine Ridge Reservation," mimeographed (Pine Ridge: Bureau of Indian Affairs, October 1974), p. 8.

11. Ibid., p. 9.

12. Ibid., p. 8.

13. Ibid., p. 11.

14. *F.B.I. Uniform Crime Reports* (Washington, D.C.: Government Printing Office, 1975).

15. Ibid.

16. *New York Times*, January 24, 1974.

17. U.S. Commission on Civil Rights, "Report of Investigation: Oglala Sioux Tribe, General Election, 1974," mimeographed (Washington, D.C.: Civil Rights Commission, October 1974).

18. Ibid., p. 17.

19. Ibid., p. 18.

20. Federal authorities have jurisdiction over major crimes (including most violent crimes) on Indian Reservations.

21. Wounded Knee Legal Defense-Offense Committee, "Chronology of Violence," p. 3.

22. Wounded Knee Legal Defense-Offense Committee, "How South Dakota's Dual System of Justice Works," mimeographed (Rapid City: WKLD-OC, 1975).

23. WKLD-OC, "Chronology of Violence," p. 3; see also Jack Anderson, *Albuquerque Journal*, May 8, 1975.

24. *New York Times*, April 22, 1975.

25. John Trudell, speech at University of Washington, Seattle, March 11, 1977.

26. U.S., Senate, Committee on the Judiciary, Subcommittee on Internal Security, *Revolutionary Activities Within the United States: The American Indian Movement* (Washington, D.C.: Government Printing Office, August 1976), p. 61.

27. Wounded Knee Legal Defense-Offense Committee, "Letter to Contributors," mimeographed, February 1976, p. 1.

28. Short summaries of the Rockefeller and Church reports appear in *Congressional Quarterly,* September 27, 1975, p. 2090, and November 22, 1975, p. 2574; a more extensive summary is in *Akwesasne Notes,* late autumn 1976, pp. 4-7. The literature on the illegal programs of both the FBI and CIA is extensive.

29. *Congressional Quarterly,* September 27, 1975, p. 2090.

30. *Congressional Quarterly,* November 22, 1975, p. 2574.

31. *Akwesasne Notes,* late autumn 1976, p. 6; *New Times,* February 18, 1977, p. 20.

32. *New Times,* February 18, 1977, p. 20.

33. Sanford Unger, *FBI* (Boston: Atlantic, Little-Brown, 1975), p. 120.

34. Legal assault includes threatening gestures; the act of striking is defined as battery.

35. *New York Times,* September 17, 1974.

36. Ibid., September 26, 1974.

37. Ibid., September 18, 1976.

38. Ibid., March 13, 1975, p. 31.

39. Ibid.

40. Senate, Subcomm. on Internal Security, *Revolutionary Activities,* p. 61.

41. Ibid., p. 10.

42. Joel Weisman, "About that 'Ambush' at Wounded Knee," *Columbia Journalism Review,* September/October 1975, p. 29.

43. Ibid.

44. Ibid., p. 30.

45. Ibid., p. 29.

46. Ibid., p. 31.

47. South Dakota has no legal jurisdiction on the reservation.

48. Held had been one of the designers of the FBI's Cointelpro activities; he also cooperated with Chicago police in planning the raid which ended in the deaths of Black Panther leaders Fred Hampton and Mark Clark.

49. Wallace Little, Jr., was falsely implicated by the FBI in the "Dog Soldier memo" episode a year after the above incident.

50. *Minneapolis Tribune,* May 30, 1976.

51. Ibid.

52. The account of the automobile explosion and subsequent events in Kansas has been furnished by Bruce Ellison, a Rapid City, S.D., attorney, who has represented several Wounded Knee defendants.

53. Tom Bates, "The Government's Secret War on the Indian," *Oregon Times*, February-March 1976, p. 14.
54. Ibid.
55. Ibid., p. 15.
56. Ibid.
57. *New York Times*, February 7, 1973.
58. Bates, "The Government's Secret War," p. 17.
59. *Minneapolis Tribune*, May 30, 1976, p. 1.
60. Weir and Bergman, "The Killing of Anna Mae Aquash," p. 53.
61. *Minneapolis Tribune*, May 30, 1976.
62. Weir and Bergman, "The Killing of Anna Mae Aquash," p. 54.
63. Ibid.
64. Ibid. About the time of the "informer" controversy the Senate Intelligence Committee was releasing information which showed that the FBI, as part of its Cointelpro tactics, had spread false rumors that Black Panthers and other radical leaders were FBI informers in an attempt to discredit them and possibly provoke violence inside groups the FBI was attempting to suppress.
65. *Rapid City Journal*, March 11, 1976.
66. Ibid.
67. *Washington Star*, May 24, 1976.
68. Weir and Bergman, "The Killing of Anna Mae Aquash," p. 52.
69. Interview with Bruce Johansen in Rapid City, S.D., June 12, 1978.
70. *Akwesasne Notes*, early winter 1977, p. 7.
71. Bruce Johansen, "Peltier and the Posse," *The Nation*, October 1, 1977, p. 306.
72. Statement to author by Bruce Ellison in regard to Bob Robideau.
73. Ibid.
74. *Cedar Rapids Gazette*, July 14, 1976.
75. In addition to Kunstler, the defense team included Bruce Ellison; Lew Gurwitz of the Wounded Knee Legal Defense-Offense Committee; local attorneys Mike Fay and Fred Dumbaugh; Margie Ratner, who did research on motions; Karen Bagh, Carl Nadler, and Liz Raditz, legal assistants; Diane Wiley and Roz Klein, jury selection; Dr. Jay Schulman; and Andy Mosley.
76. Weir and Bergman, "The Killing of Anna Mae Aquash," p. 54.
77. *United States* v. *Butler and Robideau*, July 7, 1976, Appendix A, p. 3; emphasis added.
78. Ibid., p. 9.
79. Ibid., p. 19.

80. Ibid., pp. 37-40.
81. National Council of Churches, "Medicine Man in Prison," mimeographed (New York: Due Process of Law Fund, 1976), p. 3.
82. Charges against the third, Jimmy Eagle, were dropped immediately following the Butler-Robideau trial.
83. Johansen, "Peltier and the Posse," p. 306.
84. Ibid. The FBI used the same tactics against Poor Bear to extract testimony against another AIM member, Richard Marshall. Poor Bear in an affidavit filed June 3, 1977, recanted her coerced implication of Marshall in the trial at which he was convicted of murder April 9, 1976. Despite the recantation of the government's key witness, the South Dakota Supreme Court upheld Marshall's conviction.
85. This statement, as well as the description of the preceding incident, was made by Ellison during a forum on the trial of Peltier held at Daybreak Star Center, Seattle, June 24, 1977. See *University of Washington Daily*, June 30, 1977, p. 2.
86. *United States* v. *Leonard Peltier*, April 15, 1977, p. 5121.
87. Ibid., p. 5070.
88. *University of Washington Daily*, January 31, 1978, p. 7.
89. Ibid., April 14, 1978, p. 6.
90. Ibid., April 14, 1977, p. 24.
91. Native American Solidarity Committee, "Paul Skyhorse and Richard Mohawk" (Ventura, Calif: NASC), p. 2.
92. *Seattle Times*, May 25, 1978.
93. Ibid.
94. *Akwesasne Notes*, late spring 1978, page 22.
95. Ibid.
96. Statement to Canadian extradition hearing, May 13, 1976.

5. How to Steal a Continent, Continued

1. Cited in George Novak, *Genocide Against the Indians: Its Role in the Rise of United States Capitalism* (New York: Pathfinder Press 1970), p. 10.
2. The story of what Black Elk saw is contained in Black Elk, *Black Elk Speaks*, as told to John G. Neihardt (New York: William Morrow and Co., 1932).
3. Ibid., p. 66.
4. Ibid.
5. Ibid., p. 68.
6. Ibid., p. 78.

7. *Rapid City Journal*, April 24, 1977.

8. Ibid.

9. Ibid.

10. Ibid.

11. *Independent Nuclear Opinion* (St. Paul, Minn.), Spring 1978, p. 14.

12. *Akwesasne Notes*, late spring 1978, p. 5.

13. Lindquist's analysis is contained in a short report entitled "Summary of Key Elements of the Water Quality Project for Western South Dakota," published by the Six District Council, an organization which includes South Dakota's six westernmost county governments.

14. *Rapid City Journal*, September 24, 1977.

15. Interview by author Bruce Johansen with Bruce Ellison, Rapid City, S.D., June 12, 1978.

16. Ibid.

17. *Rapid City Journal*, June 6, 1978.

18. W.H. Raymond and R.U. King (U.S. Geological Survey) and J.P. Gries (U.S. Bureau of Mines), "Status of Mineral Resource Information for the Pine Ridge Indian Reservation, South Dakota," typescript (Bureau of Indian Affairs, 1976), p. 72.

19. Ibid., p. 36.

20. *Akwesasne Notes*, late spring 1978, p. 5.

21. U.S., Bureau of Reclamation, "Draft Environmental Impact Statement: Water for Energy" (Washington, D.C.: Bureau of Reclamation, October 8, 1976).

22. The Sheep Mountain range: it is often called the "gunnery range" because it has been used for that purpose in the past by United States military units.

23. *Akwesasne Notes*, late spring 1978, p. 11.

24. The following incident was described by Wanrow in a communication to author Bruce Johansen, August 3, 1976.

25. Robert McLaughlin, "Giving It Back to the Indians," *Atlantic Monthly*, February 1977, p. 72.

26. Ibid.

27. Ibid., p. 73.

28. John Stevens et al. to Maine Governor James B. Longley, January 18, 1977.

29. Ibid.

30. Richard Ehlke, "Congressional Consent Under the Indian Non-Intercourse Act and the Maine Indians," Congressional Research Service (Washington, D.C.), February 8, 1977.

31. *New York Times*, June 1, 1977.
32. U.S., Department of the Interior, Office of the Solicitor, "Litigation Report in the Case of United States v. Maine," January 10, 1977.

6. The Navajo and National Sacrifice

1. The Navajo call themselves *Dine*, which means "the people." Navajo is a Spanish modification of the Dine-language word *Navahu*, meaning "where the *Dine* live." Navaho, in turn, is an anglicized version of the Spanish Navajo.
2. *Seattle Post-Intelligencer*, August 29, 1976, p. B-6.
3. *Akwesasne Notes*, late autumn 1976, p. 10.
4. Edward Abbey, *The Journey Home* (New York: Dutton, 1977), p. 183.
5. Box, Thadis, et al., National Academy of Sciences, *Rehabilitation Potential of Western Coal Lands* (Cambridge, Mass.: Ballinger Publishing Co., 1974).
6. Ibid., p. 2.
7. This characterization of gold is from Black Elk. See Chapter 5.
8. *Navajo Times*, March 31, 1977.
9. Speech of Fred Johnson to United States Civil Rights Commission; Archives, National Indian Youth Council, Albuquerque, N.M.
10. Box, Thadis, et al., *Western Coal Lands*, p. 85.
11. Ibid., p. 2.
12. James Cannon, *Leased and Lost: A Study of Public and Indian Coal Leasing in the West* (New York: Council on Economic Priorities, 1974), p. 17. Cannon's conclusions were confirmed in a follow-up report released by the Council in 1978.
13. Ibid.
14. Ibid., p. 18.
15. Ibid.
16. Ibid., p. 16. An acre-foot is the amount of water which will cover one acre a foot deep, or 326,000 gallons.
17. Ibid.
18. Ibid.
19. National Indian Youth Council, "What Is Coal Gasification." (Albuquerque, N.M.: NIYC, 1976), p. 4.
20. Ibid.
21. Western coals provide an average of 6,100 to 9,500 British Thermal Units per pound, compared with an average of 13,000 for Eastern coals.

22. *Capturing the Energy of the Sun*, proceedings from National Conference on Bioconversion as an Energy Resource, March 11-13, 1976, p. 249.
23. Ibid., p. 255.
24. *Albuquerque Journal*, October 6, 1976.
25. Ibid.
26. National Indian Youth Council, *Annual Report* (Albuquerque, N.M.: NIYC, 1976), p. 2.
27. Lucy Keeswood, Coalition for Navajo Liberation, cited in United States Commission on Civil Rights, *The Farmington Report* (Washington, D.C: Government Printing Office, July 1975), p. 128.
28. "Mother Earth, Father Sky and Indian Survival," *The Nation*, March 29, 1975, p. 359.
29. *New York Times*, October 9, 1977.
30. *The Wall Street Journal*, January 24, 1978.
31. *Navajo Times*, June 22, 1978.
32. Ibid., May 4, 1978, p. 21.
33. Ibid., September 1, 1977.
34. Ibid., June 29, 1978.
35. Ibid.
36. Ibid.
37. Tom Barry and Beth Wood, "Uranium on the Checkerboard: Crisis at Checkpoint," *American Indian Journal*, June 1978, p. 10.
38. *Navajo Times*, June 15, 1978.
39. Ibid.

7. Montana: Stopping the Strippers

1. James Cannon, *Leased and Lost: A Study of Public and Indian Coal Leasing in the West* (New York: Council on Economic Priorities, 1974), p. 35.
2. Ibid., p. 4.
3. Ibid., p. 6.
4. Ibid., p. 4.
5. Ibid., p. 7.
6. Ibid., p. 2.
7. Ibid. Note that the forty-two power plants planned for the northern plains do not include several dozen more planned for the Southwest, including the Navajo Nation.
8. "Moving Gary, Indiana, to the Great Plains," *Mother Jones*, July 1976, pp. 34-35.
9. Cannon, *Leased and Lost*, p. 1.

10. Ibid., p. 35.
11. *Navajo Times*, April 7, 1977.
12. *Akwesasne Notes*, early autumn 1975, p. 10.
13. Cannon, *Leased and Lost*, p. 31.
14. *Akwesasne Notes*, early autumn 1975, p. 10.
15. Friends of the Earth, *Not Man Apart* (San Francisco: Friends of the Earth, March 1977), p. 10.
16. *Akwesasne Notes*, early spring 1977, p. 9.
17. Ibid., p. 8.
18. Statement to Northern Cheyenne people, Lame Deer, Montana, July 30, 1976, p. 3.
19. Russel Barsh, "Corporations and Indians: Who's the Villain?" *MBA* 46 (June 1975):12.
20. *Akwesasne Notes*, early spring 1976, p. 24.
21. The "Winters doctrine," adjudicated by the U.S. Supreme Court in 1908 and affirmed several times since then, holds that Indian nations have first option on water which flows through or along their borders.

8. Usual and Accustomed Places

1. Anthony Netboy, *The Atlantic Salmon: A Vanishing Species* (Boston: Houghton Mifflin, 1968), pp. 23-26.
2. Ibid., p. 331.
3. Ibid., p. 387.
4. U.S. Department of Interior, Bureau of Reclamation, *Columbia River Comprehensive Report on Development* (Washington, D.C.: Government Printing Office, 1947), p. 353.
5. U.S., Congress, Senate, Committee on Interior and Insular Affairs, Subcommittee on Indian Affairs, *Indian Fishing Rights: Hearings on S.J.R. 170 and 171*, 88th Cong., 2nd sess., August 5-6, 1964; statement of Frank Wright, chairman of the Puyallup, p. 105.
6. Ibid.
7. American Friends Service Committee, comp., *Uncommon Controversy: A Report on the Fishing Rights of the Muckleshoot, Puyallup and Nisqually Indians* (Seattle and London: University of Washington Press, 1970), pp. 19-23.
8. Indians were not classified by the United States government as citizens until 1924.
9. American Friends Service Comm., *Uncommon Controversy*, p. 23.
10. Ibid., p. 27.

11. William Meyer, *Native Americans: The New Indian Resistance* (New York: International Publishers, 1971), p. 70.
12. Ibid.
13. Bruce Brown, "A Long Look at the Boldt Decision," *Argus* (Seattle), December 3, 1976, p. 4.
14. United States Federal Task Force on Washington State Fisheries, "Settlement Plan for Washington State Salmon and Steelhead Fisheries," mimeographed, June 1978, p. 232.
15. Russel L. Barsh. *The Washington Fishing Rights Controversy: An Economic Critique* (Seattle: University of Washington School of Business Administration, 1977).
16. Ibid., p. 21.
17. Brown, "The Boldt Decision," p. 5.
18. Fred Brack, "Fishing Rights: Who Is Entitled to Northwest Salmon," *Seattle Post-Intelligencer Northwest Magazine*, January 16, 1977, p. 6.
19. An excellent film called *As Long as the Rivers Run* was produced by the Survival of American Indians Association, which grew out of the fishing rights struggle, during 1968.
20. The Chicanos were recognizing their own Indian ancestry, as well as the fact that the United States had signed, and broken, the Treaty of Guadalupe Hidalgo after the conclusion of the Mexican-American War in 1848.
21. Brack, "Fishing Rights," p. 4.
22. Ibid., p. 7.
23. Ibid., p. 8.
24. *Wassaja* (newspaper of the American Indian Historical Society, San Francisco), May 1978, p. 1.

9. The Third World at Home

1. *Trail of Self-Determination Proposal*, delivered to the United States Congress by the Trail of Self-Determination Caravan, Washington, D.C., July 4, 1976.
2. Statement of Mary Elizabeth Young, author of studies on the role land speculation played during the erosion of Indian land bases, especially during the nineteenth century. Contained in U.S., Congress, American Indian Policy Review Commission, "Tentative Final Report" xerox (Washington, D.C., 1977), sect. 1, p. 1.
3. Despite the fact that Adams had been shot in the side, Tacoma, Washington, police demanded that he undergo tests to disprove their suspicion that he had shot himself.

4. Fort Lawton is named after the United States Army officer who had forced Geronimo to surrender a century before the Indian occupation of the fort named for him.

5. *Akwesasne Notes*, early summer 1973, p. 37.

6. Many Indian people who have been targets of shootings during recent years have seen their assailants charged with the less serious manslaughter, instead of murder, which is the usual charge when an Indian is charged with killing someone white. See chapter 4.

7. This law allows states to assume criminal and some civil jurisdiction over Indians from the federal government; where this jurisdiction has been assumed, Indians often have been told that they must give up treaty rights in exchange for social services guaranteed by the same treaties!

8. The proposals were drawn up October 22-29, 1972, in Minneapolis and circulated in mimeographed form. Details are available from the American Indian Movement, Minneapolis office.

9. James P. Boyd, *Recent Indian Wars Under the Lead of Sitting Bull and Other Chiefs* (New York: Publishers Union, 1891), p. 288.

10. Bruce Johansen, "The Reservation Offensive," *The Nation*, February 25, 1978, p. 205.

11. Interview with Bruce Ellison, Rapid City, S.D., June 12, 1978.

12. Johansen, "The Reservation Offensive," p. 205.

13. Ibid., p. 206.

14. Ibid., p. 206.

15. The special election was held to fill the seat of Rep. Brock Adams, who was appointed secretary of transportation by President Carter. Cunningham was defeated in a bid for reelection in 1978.

16. The establishment of the AIPRC was a condition for ending the 1973 occupation of Wounded Knee.

17. American Indian Policy Review Commission, "Tentative Final Report," sect. 5, p. 2.

18. Ibid.

19. Ibid., sect. 2, p. 24.

20. *Akwesasne Notes*, early spring 1977, p. 28.

21. Raymond B. Pratt, "Developing Nations or Internal Colonies? Tribal Sovereignty and the Problem of Resource Exploitation" (paper prepared for the 1978 annual meeting of the Western Political Science Association, Los Angeles, March 16-18, 1978), p. 24. Pratt is a professor at Montana State University.

22. Ibid., pp. 40-41.
23. Bruce Johansen, "The Indian Wars Have a Common Thread: Money," *Argus* (Seattle), September 30, 1977, p. 10.
24. Richard H. Lundstrom; "For If the Indian Peoples Die, Who Among Us Deserves to Live?" reprinted by *Akwesasne Notes*, 1974, p. 8.

10. The Final Indian War

1. *Popular Science Monthly*, 1882, p. 320.
2. Richard H. Lundstrom, "A Hard Look at Catholic Folklore," reprinted by *Akwesasne Notes*, 1974. Just how closely the realities of past and present are intertwined may be understood by studying history. See, for example, Stanley Vestal, *New Sources of Indian History* (Norman: University of Oklahoma Press, 1934), pp. 132-41, for a description of inflated "body counts" during the U.S. Army campaigns against the Lakota and Cheyenne between 1865 and 1876. Vestal discusses the internal pressures within the army which produced these counts. Readers may be reminded of similar occurrences during the Indochina war.
3. Peoples Grand Jury, "The AMAX War Against Humanity" (Washington, D.C.: September 19, 1977), p. 23.
4. Ibid.
5. Ibid., p. 25.
6. Ralston Purina Company, *Annual Report*, 1957.
7. Robert J. Ledogar, *Hungry for Profits: U.S. Food and Drug Multinationals in Latin America* (New York: International Documentation, 1975), p. 95.
8. Ibid., p. 96.
9. Ibid., p. 94.
10. Ibid.
11. Ibid., p. 96.
12. Ibid., p. 98.
13. Barry Commoner, *The Closing Circle* (New York: Bantam Books, 1972), p. 146.
14. Ibid., p. 258.
15. Ibid., p. 263.
16. Ibid., p. 155.
17. Robert Engler, *The Brotherhood of Oil* (Chicago: University of Chicago Press, 1977), p. 146.
18. Ibid., p. 84.
19. Ibid., pp. 40-41.

20. Ibid., p. 169.
21. *New York Times*, August 22, 1971.
22. Engler, *The Brotherhood of Oil*, p. 172.
23. *New York Times*, March 5, 1975.
24. Engler, *The Brotherhood of Oil*, p. 171.
25. For example, see ibid., pp. 57-83, 88-89, 102, 200-2, 203, 210, 251 on domestic contributions; pp. 19, 67, 68, 74, 110-13, 216 on overseas contributions. See also *New York Times,* March 13, 1976; United Nations, "Foreign Economic Interests and Decolonization," 1969, p. 27; U.S. *Congressional Record,* January 22, 1974, pp. E 86-89 and January 24, 1974, p. E 175; *New York Times* August 24 and September 30, 1974. The preceding is a small sample of the documentation concerning corporate contributions made to political figures to secure influence.
26. *Washington Spectator*, April 1, 1977.
27. Engler, *The Brotherhood of Oil*, p. 117.
28. Ibid., p. 106.
29. *Navajo Times*, January 12, 1978.
30. Ibid.
31. Ibid.
32. Cited in *Akwesasne Notes*, early spring 1977, p. 12.
33. Ibid.
34. Ibid.
35. Ibid.
36. Ibid.
37. Ibid., p. 13.
38. Ibid.
39. Harry M. Caudill, *The Watches of the Night* (Boston: Atlantic, Little-Brown, 1976), p. 5.
40. Ibid., p. 88.
41. Ibid., p. 242.
42. *Seattle Times*, June 26, 1978.
43. The city of Seattle was named for Sea'lth, over the chief's protests. The name was slightly changed to accommodate European tongues.
44. Arnold Toynbee, *Mankind and Mother Earth* (New York and London: Oxford University Press, 1976).

Index